HUMAN RELATIONSHIPS

An Introduction to Social Psychology

by
STEVE DUCK
University of Iowa

SAGE Publications
London • Beverly Hills • New Delhi

SAGE Publications Ltd
28 Banner Street
London EC1Y 8QE

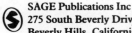 SAGE Publications Inc
275 South Beverly Drive
Beverly Hills, California 90212

SAGE Publications India Pvt Ltd
C-236 Defence Colony
New Delhi 110 024

British Library Cataloguing in Publication Data

Duck, Steve
    Human relationships: an introduction to social psychology.
    1. Interpersonal relations
    I. Title
    302   HM132

Library of Congress Catalog Card Number 86-060438

ISBN 0-8039-9755-8
ISBN 0-8039-9756-6 Pbk

Phototypeset by Sunrise Setting, Torquay, Devon
Printed in Great Britain by J.W. Arrowsmith Ltd., Bristol

Contents

Acknowledgements vi

Preface vii

Chapter 1 Social Emotions: Feelings about Relationships
and Other People 1

Chapter 2 Communication Skills and the Languages of
Interpersonal Relationships 35

Chapter 3 Interaction and Daily Life in Long-term
Relationships 72

Chapter 4 Relationships with Relations: Families
and Socialization 112

Chapter 5 Dealing with Strangers, Acquaintances, and
Friends 155

Chapter 6 Staying Healthy . . . with a Little Help from
Our Friends? 187

Afterword 230

Appendix: To Help You and Your Instructor 232

References 239

Author Index 263

Subject Index 269

Acknowledgements

I am grateful to many people for their help, both witting and unwitting, in preparing me for the writing of this book. These include: Jesse C. Stickler, Miss Jordan, Miss Burt, Robin Ovens, F.C.G. Langford, John Radford, Michael Booker, Lynda Cox, Mike Gardner, J.C.B. Glover, my father and mother, Carole Wade, Brian Little, Chris Spencer, George Kelly, Sanchez and John Davies, Pembroke College (Oxford), Sheri Meserow, Diane Lowenstein-Pattison, Sandra, Christina, and Jamie.

The following students read and commented on the first draft: Alistair Black, John Lahiff, Karin Gray, Cheryl Travers, and, particularly, Daryl Rayner and Catherine Thomasson, to whom I am very grateful.

Also, I thank those who helped and supported me during my guest professorship in the University of Connecticut, Storrs, when the second draft was prepared: Carol Masheter, Reuben Baron, Barbara Montgomery, Ross Buck, Bob Ryder, Jeff Fisher, Dave Kenny, Steve Anderson, and, above all, Linda Harris who fixed it all up.

I thank also Peter Collett, David Clarke, Jill Crosland, Robert McHenry, and Michael Argyle at Oxford University for their hospitality whilst I was a visiting scholar during the preparation of the book.

David Watson, Mark Leary, and Andrew Colman made extensive and careful comments about various drafts, which did more than anything to improve the final product. Robin Gilmour gave sustained discussion of some of the key ideas to the point where I sometimes find it hard to distinguish the thoughts which are mine and those which were originally his. Joanna Lawson read several drafts very thoughtfully and provided many excellent critiques and case examples. Sheila Whalley provided superhuman secretarial help. I am grateful to them all.

Preface

When I finish reading a social psychology textbook I always regret that I learned so little about much that is a familiar part of the real social life of myself and my students — liking and disliking, falling in and out of love, shyness, jealousy and embarrassment, loneliness, friendship and family, health, everyday concerns about the way that we appear to other people, and our problems and successes in relationships. Why should my students' learning be focussed on what the SS (Schutzstaffel) did during the Second World War, why madmen climb clocktowers in Texas and fire machine guns randomly at people, what attracts us to strangers we know that we'll never see again, how people sell us insurance or encyclopaedias, or what Charlie Brown said about attitude change? Whilst much of this is interesting, it is remote from my life and my students' personal experience.

For this reason, I often feel uncomfortable when I ask my students to rely solely on introductory social psychology textbooks even when they do, admittedly, an excellent job of presenting current research. What we read in them is interesting but stops short of being the social psychology with which we actually live because the research descriptions are, on their own, incomplete accounts of the living social psychology of our personal experiences and daily lives. Therefore, my aim is to supplement available introductory texts by covering some important elements of life which they do not.

I focus upon the essence and substructure of social behaviour: the long-term and the short-term relationships which we have with other people and which so strongly influence our thoughts and behaviour. Most of us realize that we find our major sorrows and joys in personal relationships, that we can achieve our goals more easily with the help of friends, and that our feelings about other people can influence the direction of our lives from time to time. But there is more to it than that — important though those facts are — and the influence of relationships runs deeper through the fabric of social behaviour and social psychology.

Relationships are not just attitudes or feelings about other people but affect our behaviour and the ways in which we spend our time. Equally, the groups, communities and societies which we talk about in the abstract are actually composed of real people and the personal and social relationships that bind them and bring them together. When we speak or write of 'students' or 'social psychologists' or 'society' we are actually referring to real human beings with real personal ties and real relationships with one another (Wellman, 1985). These relationships affect the ways in which information is transmitted. They exert pressures on individuals to act in certain ways (e.g., in their dress or even their responses to fashionable attitudes) in order to be accepted and liked. They influence the sorts of social behaviour that we choose from our repertoire on a given occasion, for instance, whether we treat someone in a special way because we know him or her or merely as 'yet another person in a hurry who thinks he or she deserves special treatment'.

I believe that everyday life and everyday relationships should be the starting points for the exploration of social psychology. Therefore, I begin the book with some commonplace emotions, going on to interpersonal communication, personal relationships, dealing with strangers, and social relationships in childhood. I look at the development of courtship, at sexual decision-making in dating, and at the family. I discuss problems in relationships and how to put them right, deal with gossip and persuasion, and apply research on relationships to the psychology of health.

Mainly for the instructor . . . a psychology of human concerns

My argument is that people spend a large part of their time involved in relationships which are underrepresented not only in the introductory textbooks but also in research. My intent is not a non-standard version of the familiar attack on laboratory research, to criticize the old for the sake of it, it is to point in some new directions. The status of laboratory research is prematurely attacked, since we cannot properly claim that it is 'artificial' until we know exactly what daily life is made up of (or unless one relies on intuitions about the value and representativeness of laboratory research that are truly the kind of assumption that laboratory research is itself designed to replace!).

That the typical present-day textbook on social psychology gives so little space to relationships is surprising, but I believe that it is a reflection of the broad assumptions of social psychologists that most average people are leading orderly interesting lives doing important things. We tend to write as if everyone spends each day on a jury, making life or death decisions or deriving complex scientomimetic attributions instead of shouting at his or her children or admonishing a spouse for leaving the top off the toothpaste tube.

We are 'nice' to people in all our other assumptions, too: we assume that everyone is good and we 'explain' the bad side. For instance, we assume altruism and spend years 'explaining' bystander apathy; we assume impartiality and 'explain' prejudice; we assume scientific rationality and 'explain' fundamental errors. Overall, our present model of social life is one where essentially nice, interchangeable, serious-minded, calculating laboratory technicians meet one another for brief periods of time to do significant, positive things in an environment void of context, where today is an exact replica of yesterday and no-one has any shopping to do or a summer holiday to plan or a disagreeable colleague.

By contrast, our own daily lives are more likely to consist of quite humdrum experiences with the same people we have known for years, whom we meet for insignificant social, emotional, or relational purposes, in a special context where we have plans about the future. Furthermore, some of these people will be colleagues with whom we have a long-standing relationship, be it friendship, formality, or feud. We often see people squabble and make stupid, irrational mistakes; we have meetings where no-one acts like a scientist; and we may deal with deans and tenure committees to whom none of our kindly textbook assumptions can possibly be applied. In short, our real social lives are based on complex but routine relationships which we do not emphasize in the textbooks, and we go around believing 'It's not what you know but who you know' and writing as if we didn't. Relationships run through the fabric of our lives, too, but are regarded as too unimportant or too obvious to write about.

My students were wiser than the textbooks and unashamedly reverted to this general human concern over relationships. After they had had one whole year of social psychology, I taught them advanced library skills. They were to pick a topic in social psychology and evaluate the important research on it in the last five years, using tools such as *Current Contents* and *SSCI* (see the exercises in the Appendix). I gave them a list of topics derived from the adopted text, but did not restrict them to that list.

Not one of them picked a 'pure' topic. Instead, all chose personally relevant research that, broadly, focussed on relationships. Admittedly shy people researched shyness; students from broken homes followed research on the effects of parental divorce on children; unattractive students wrote about self-fulfilling prophecies and Pygmalion effects. Moreover, the answers invariably were better than those for the usual class assignments and often were thoughtful and even exciting to read. I realized not only how much more effectively students learn from being personally involved but also the great potential of social psychology for illuminating their personal involvements.

I believe that, for all the preceding obvious and unobvious reasons, everyday relationships are significant subject matter for social psychology and consequently I have structured this book around the theme of personal relationships. They are simultaneously the most personally important part of most people's lives, a potentially cohesive force in social psychological theory, and a recently booming area of research. Not least of my reasons for taking that position, however, is the belief that social psychology lacks substance when it addresses only the large-scale societal issues of the day. Social psychology has a supplementary and equally significant role: to be informative about the familiar; to explain the everyday; and to understand life as it is lived by the individual relating to other people in the street.

CHAPTER 1

Social Emotions: Feelings about Relationships and Other People

Emotions are the stuff of which the peaks and troughs of life are made, as when, for example, we feel exhilarated, depressed, shy, lonely, jealous, or in love. Those emotions which cause us to focus on other people are particularly powerful, for example, love and jealousy — some countries accept these as legal defences against the charge of murder. Emotions are the starting point for this book, not only because of their power but because they are the bases for relationships with other people and have an intimate connection with less obvious parts of social life.

BOX 1.1 Points to think about

— *Why do we become embarrassed?*
— *What is jealousy and why do we feel it?*
— *Some 41% of people regard themselves as shy and about 26% of us have felt deeply lonely within the last few weeks. How can shyness be cured? What is loneliness and what can be done about it?*
— *Who feels lonely most often and why?*
— *Do men feel love as intensely and in the same ways as women?*

For example, we may think that we simply feel an emotion and express it, but a moment's reflection will show us lurking social constraints. First, there are relationship rules about communication and expression of the emotions that we actually feel. 'Politeness' often requires us to conceal negative feelings which we harbour towards someone else; 'pride' causes us to tone down strong emotions, as when we communicate coolness even when we feel infatuated. Conversely, we often exaggerate positive feelings, as when the boss makes a joke, and we even pretend them sometimes, as when we meet boring strangers or relatives on festive occasions. Apart from the obvious ways in which such relationship concerns affect our expression of emotion, why are they relevant in this book? First, the strong social imperatives about communication of emotion spoil some people's relationships; relationship problems, like shyness, often show up as unusual or inappropriate ways of communicating feelings.

Second, when we report or describe them, we frequently edit our accounts of social emotions so that they make sense to people. Usually, this means that we summarize them as enduring or continuous states rather than momentary feelings (Duck & Sants, 1983). For instance, we are more likely to report that 'I am in love with you' or 'I love you' or 'I am friends with you' rather than 'I felt a twinge of love for you during the moment when you looked at me' or 'I felt friendship for the moment when you shared the secret with me'.

Summarizing makes it hard to pinpoint the causes of enduring emotions or long-lasting relationships like love and friendship. Maybe we can explain it as love at first sight, but usually we prefer to look back over a whole range of experiences and events to explain love for someone. Our accounts usually state publicly that emotions and relationships are on more sound bases than momentary reactions or single causes. We would feel foolish saying that we love someone just because of the shape of his or her nose, and our culture prefers to believe that it takes time to fall in love, often challenging the belief that there is such a thing as love at first sight.

In more technical language, statements about social emotions use dispositional or continuous language to provide 'summary affect statements' about our partner and they are socially appropriate. They summarize our feelings about someone using culturally approved terminology and accepted explanations for relationships' causes. They are not simple descriptions of short-term emotional peaks or troughs; they emphasize the implicit continuity in the relationship.

Labelling our feelings

Assuming that we communicate our emotions by displaying and labelling them in a way that makes sense to other people in the culture, does it also make sense to say that our social surroundings can affect the definition of our emotions more than 'the feelings' themselves? To answer this we have to re-examine our thinking about emotions.

Many of us probably think that emotions are sorts of feelings which stem from some bodily change (e.g., we feel our heart speed up and we know that we are afraid, or we feel butterflies in the stomach and know that we are anxious). A theory along those lines was proposed by two psychologists working independently: James in the USA and Lange in Denmark. (It became known as the James-Lange theory.) There are, however, problems with it: if parts of the nervous system are surgically disconnected from parts of the body (e.g., the relevant nerves to the stomach are severed), we can still feel the emotion that was supposed to come from that part of the body (i.e., we can still feel anxious even when we cannot feel the butterflies in the stomach). The artificial induction of bodily changes (e.g., the injection of drugs that are like adrenalin) does not create specific emotions, but creates only a general feeling of arousal and expectancy that 'something' is about to happen. So the range of bodily changes that we experience is far more limited than the range of emotions that we feel (Cannon, 1929). There are too few distinct physical patterns to account for all the subtleties of emotions.

Social emotions involve not only physical events but our experience of the social environment, such that our personal history and social context help us to define the emotion that we are having (McDougall, 1921). For instance, we may remember that the last time we felt this way we had been frightened, so maybe that's what it is this time too. Some of the emotions, particularly complex ones like disappointment or regret, may have a social component to them on top of a physical one.

What could this social component be? In 1962, Schachter & Singer produced an answer. Their claim is that there is a basic physical cause for emotions but that it has to be accompanied by some cues that help us to label it in an appropriate way. In their classic studies, they show that subjects who had been artificially aroused, by an injection of a stimulant, subsequently define their emotion according to the situational cues available. Those who are placed with laughing companions experience happiness, whilst those who are placed with aggressive companions report feeling hostile.

The 'two factor theory' of emotion (Schachter & Singer, 1962) thus claims that to report an emotion we must experience physiological arousal *and* be able to provide a satisfactory label for the experience. Most often this label will be apparent from the situation or environment in which we find ourselves.

The theory is applied to love (Berscheid & Walster, 1974). According to this approach, we experience love when we are aroused and when the environmental cues tell us that love is the right thing to feel (e.g., the presence of an attractive partner, a romantic sunset, sweet music playing in the background). It may be one reason why people report falling in love at dances where they get aroused by the dancing and have a companion that they feel attracted to.

Love

Love is blamed for a lot of things from the Trojan War to various crimes of passion that appear in the tabloids. It is called 'a temporary insanity' (Bierce, *The Devil's Dictionary*. He went on to add that it is 'curable by marriage'). So what is it?

Are there different types of love?

'Love' may not be one emotion but several — or, at least, it may have several components: some good, some bad. You can decide for yourself if they are good or bad, but there are different types. One distinction is between passionate love and companionate love (Berscheid & Walster, 1974): passionate love is the steamy sort that Casanova and Don Juan specialized in, whilst companionate love is the kind that kin and long-term marriage partners may have. Companionate love is enhanced by an increased sense of commitment (Kelley, 1983) whilst passionate love derives primarily from physiological arousal and excitement.

Is love really just either madly passionate or boringly dispassionate? Is this passionate-companionate dichotomy too simple to account for all the feelings that we can have towards a lover? Another proposal suggests that there are *six* types of love (Lee, 1973) and that persons can mix the types together in various ways. The six types are: Eros, Ludus, Storge, Pragma, Mania and Agape. Each has a typical character and a brief explanation may assist in determining the nature of love.

Eros (Romantic love)

Eros, or romantic, love focusses upon beauty and physical attractiveness; it is a sensual love that expects to be returned. People who score highly on Eros typically believe in 'love at first sight' and are particularly sensitive to the physical blemishes of their partner, such as overweight, broken nose, smelly feet or misaligned teeth. They are attracted to partners on the basis of physical attraction, like to kiss and cuddle soon after meeting a new partner and report a definite genital response (lubrication, erection) to the first kiss.

Ludus (Game-playing love)

Ludus love is like a game and is seen as fun, not to be taken seriously. People scoring high on Ludus typically flirt a lot, keep partners guessing about their level of commitment to them and stop a relationship when it stops being fun. They get over love affairs easily and quickly, enjoy teasing their lovers and will often go out with someone even when they know they do not want to get involved.

Storge (Friendship love)

Storgic love is based on caring, not on passion. People scoring high on Storge typically believe that love grows from friendship, that lovers must share similar interests and enjoy the same activities. For Storgic lovers, love grows with respect and concern for the other person. They can put up with long separations without feeling that the relationship is threatened and are not looking for excitement in the relationship, as Ludic lovers are.

Pragma (Logical, shopping-list love)

Pragmatic love is practical and based on the belief that a relationship has to work. People scoring high on Pragma ask themselves whether their lover would make a good parent and they evaluate their partner's future career prospects. Pragmatic lovers take account of their partner's background and characteristics like attitudes, religion, politics and hobbies. Pragmatic lovers are realistic and unromantic.

Mania (Possessive, dependent love)

Manic love is essentially an uncertain and anxious type of love; it is obsessive and possessive and half expects to be thrown aside. Manic lovers get very jealous. People scoring high on Mania typically believe in becoming ill or doing stupid things to regain their partner's attention if ever the partner ignores them or takes them for granted. They also claim that when the relationship gets into trouble, they develop illnesses like stomach upsets.

Agape (All-giving, selfless love)

Agape is selfless and compassionate and generally loves other human beings in an unqualified way, as preached by Gandhi, Buddha, and Jesus. In their close relationships, Agapic lovers would claim that they use their strength to help their partner through difficult times and may say that if their partner had a baby with someone else, they would want to help to care for it as if it were their own. Lee (1973) reports that he did not encounter any persons who were perfect examples of Agapic lovers, although many people reported brief Agapic episodes.

If there are these types of love, then do men and women experience them to different extents? Yes. Men are Erotic and Ludic in their attitudes to love (Hendrick et al., 1984), whilst women are Pragmatic, Manic, and Storgic. In other words, men's love is typically passionate and uncommitted, with an element of game-playing coupled with romance. Women's love is typically practical and caring, with an element of possessiveness. This is not to say that women do not base their love on passion or that men do not care about their lovers. The sexes mix their experience of love in different blends.

Developing love?

So far, we have seen love as a state of feeling, but this can most definitely develop and change (Cunningham & Antill, 1981). One possibility is that falling in love is a transition between different blends of the types of love. For instance, initial attraction to a possible lover might begin as Erotic love, mixed perhaps with Mania (desire for possession) and Ludus (game-playing). As the relationship develops, the lovers might experience greater feelings of Storge (friendship) as they develop caring on top of passion. This may lead them on to question the working of the relationship in the long term, that is, to concern over the partner's potential as a long-term mate, co-parent of the children, and so on — in short, to an assessment of pragmatic concerns. If the partner seems to pass that test, then they might begin to feel Pragma love.

All of this would suggest that married couples would score more highly than other couples on Pragma love, whilst new dates might score more highly on Erotic love, that is, views about the 'right type' of love for different sorts of relationship will vary. As the relationship to our partner develops, so the type of love will alter also.

Another suggestion that follows from this idea is that women (who are generally more Pragmatic in love than men) get to the Pragma stage earlier than men do and will either fall in Pragma love sooner than men will or else decide to get out of the relationship because their partner fails the test. Women get out of relationships earlier than men do (see 'LIFOS' BOX 1.2). What remains to be seen is whether women pass through the love stages more quickly than men do, as suggested. What do you think? Different people may have different styles of loving, on top of the general differences between the sexes, so the picture would probably become more complicated, and indicates the need for further research.

The behaviour of lovers

Aside from the *feelings* of love which drive us into relationships, there are behavioural consequences also (Maxwell, 1985). Love is both an emotion *and* a behaviour through which we communicate to partners — and to the outside world — that we love them. Obviously, partners who are married often choose to wear wedding rings to communicate the fact; dates hold hands and may dress alike or share clothing; partners embrace or put their arms around one another in the street. These indications are slight but well known. They are called 'tie signs' (Goffman, 1959) in that they indicate that two people are 'tied' to one another. They show that emotions affect the tiny behaviours of everyday life. Furthermore, lovers sit closer to one another than do 'likers', and they gaze at one another more than do people who are just friends (Rubin, 1973). One part of love, then, is a display of the fact that we love our partner; it reassures the partner and it tells the outside world, too.

Loving behaviour develops as love attitudes themselves

BOX 1.2 Some facts about love

— *Men 'fall in love' at an earlier point in a relationship than women do, but women fall out of love sooner than men do (Walster & Walster, 1978). This has led to men being called 'FILOS' (First In, Last Out) and women 'LIFOS' (Last In, First Out). Research should look at the possibility that men are satisfied that they are 'in love' when they experience mere Ludus, while women wait until they reach the Pragma stage. If this notion is valid, then it 'explains' the difference reported here.*

— *Men and women report experiencing the same levels of intensity of love (Rubin, 1973) although their experience is made up of a different mix of love types (Hendrick et al., 1984; described in text here).*

— *Women say that they have been infatuated more often than men (on average, 5.6 times for women and 4.5 times for men), but both sexes report being in loving relationships about as often — around 1.25 times (Kephart, 1967).*

— *Contrary to popular myth, men are more romantic in their views of love than women are, and over two-thirds of the women surveyed say that they would marry a man whom they did not love — if everything else about the person was acceptable (Kephart, 1967). Again, this could be explained by men's tendency to be Erotic/Romantic and women's tendency to be Pragmatic.*

develop. For instance, we gradually pay more attention to our new lover and we spend less time with old friends; we start to share more activities and adjust our lifestyles as we let our new lover into our lives; we arrange to spend more time with our partner and less with other people (Milardo, 1982; Parks & Adelman, 1983). In short, part of falling in love is an increased binding together of the routines of daily life and a developing interdependence.

What happens when you fall in love?

Given that the routines of life are comfortable and important to us, then a break with ordinary routines — such as occurs when we fall in love with a new partner — could be a problem. Surely, it is a pleasant experience to be in love, but it means that we have to restructure our lives, accommodate to the routine lifestyle of someone else, adopt new routines, and bring our new partner into our own daily pattern of activities.

People who *fall in love frequently* report that it is highly disruptive and that they develop a high level of nervous disorders and skin problems (Kemper & Bologh, 1981). It is disruption to love that is more problematic; however, when love is going well, people report feeling good both in mind and body (Reis, 1984). People who have *never been in love* claim that they have a high number of minor bodily disorders like colds and flu, and people who have *recently broken up* suffer similar physical disorders too (Kemper & Bologh, 1981). Those who were 'broken off with' by their partner typically report sleep problems, headaches, and loss of control of emotions. Those who caused the break-up suffered less, except that females reported stomach upsets.

Love, then, can take several forms and exerts an influence on our lives by restructuring our routines. It also exposes us to the need to adjust our behaviour; for example, by restricting our romantic activities exclusively to our lovers. When that does not happen and lovers stray, the partner probably experiences another emotion: jealousy.

Jealousy in Love

Love makes us feel valued by someone else, and we feel jealous when we fear that he or she does not value us. Positive emotions are often reported in a way that suggests they make us feel competent whilst negative ones are explained in terms of inadequacy (Davitz, 1964) — inadequate relative to other people and their feelings for us. The negative emotions in relationships (like jealousy) are often unpleasant precisely because they affect our self-esteem or our sense of competence as a social performer or partner (White, 1981).

According to research, men feel jealous when they feel inadequate. Women feel jealous when they feel dependent on the relationship and believe that it is better than any other relationship possibilities presently open to them. Men are more likely to react to jealousy with anger and women with depression (Shettel-Neuber et al., 1978).

Obviously, it is a powerful emotion, but what exactly is jealousy? Buunk & Bringle (1986) define it broadly as 'an aversive emotional reaction caused by an extra-dyadic [i.e., extramarital] relationship of one's current or former intimate partner — a relationship that is real, imagined, likely to occur, or has occurred in the past'. In other words, it is a negative feeling that we get when our partner 'steps out' of the relationship — or when we 'think' he or she might.

This definition is broad and allows for considerable personal differences in jealous reactions. Look, for instance, at the phrase 'likely to occur'. People will differ in beliefs about the likelihood of a partner getting into an 'extra-dyadic relationship'. These judgements will depend on a whole mix of possible influences (e.g., our feelings about the partner's attractiveness, past knowledge of the partner's behaviour, age and availability of alternative partners, partner's trustworthiness — even our own personality, possessiveness and ability to trust others).

Note also that the definition focusses on extramarital relationships. Buunk & Bringle's (1986) work is based on sexual affairs; although most of us have felt jealous when we see partners just showing an interest in other people (or having an interest shown in them by others). In some cases, people also report feeling jealous not about a real partner but about a desired one. One sign of increased desire for involvement with someone is precisely when we start to get upset that he or she is going out with someone else.

Since we can feel jealous about different sorts of relationships and since the different relationships have varying levels of importance to us, it is possible that they are afflicted by different sorts of jealousy. What we need to understand is what exactly makes us feel one sort rather than another. Is it entirely personal, or are we influenced by social rules about how we 'should' experience jealousy? Let us look first at types of jealousy and then at the point about rules.

Types of jealousy

Maybe, like love, there are different types of jealousy. Mazur (1977) distinguished five types: possessive, exclusive, competitive, egotistical, and fearful.

Possessive

A jealousy in response to perceived violation of 'property rights' is referred to as possessive. We feel this type of jealousy about things or status or even other people if we think that they belong to us or are our property. For instance, we sometimes feel possessive jealousy if our partner acts in an independent way.

Exclusive

A jealousy in response to occasions when we are omitted from a loved one's important experiences or when we are not allowed to share a loved one's private world is exclusive. For instance, if our partner wants to go camping in the mountains to commune with nature and specifically forbids us to accompany him or her, then we might feel a twinge of exclusive jealousy.

Competitive

A competitive jealousy with our partner is our reaction to a feeling of inadequacy and an attempt to restore the balance. In this case, we may feel competitive jealousy if our partner is actually better than we are at something that we want to be The Best at.

Egotistical

The feeling that our way is the only way and an inability to expand our ego awareness and role flexibility is called egotistical jealousy. It consists of difficulty in altering our perspective or accepting the need to change ourselves or our routine ways of behaving and a desire to stay as we are, being uninfluenced to adapt to other people's wishes or needs.

Fearful

A fearful jealousy is a reaction to the threat of loneliness or rejection. This type is felt when we are rejected and left alone by our partner, whether or not that partner runs off with someone else.

The blend of feelings experienced

Is jealousy identified with any particular visible display of behaviours? No, but different instances of jealousy do all seem to have one underlying theme, namely loss of control (or believed loss of control) over our partner's feelings for us. This results in a general sense of hurt or anger (Ellis & Weinstein, 1986), but this sense is 'blended' in different ways by different persons on different occasions.

We might feel hurt and angry on some occasions, whereas in other circumstances we would feel only mildly aroused. For instance, we may feel a mild type of excitement if we know that our partner is just teasing us with the prospect of entering another relationship (indeed, we may now recognise it as Ludus love), but we would probably feel both hurt and angry if we found out that the partner really had another relationship going.

Our blend of feelings is provided partly by the context and by the particular interpretations or symbolic meanings that we give to the acts that 'cause' jealousy on a given occasion. These will probably direct a person's attention to specific parts of the whole jealousy-evoking event (e.g., to a sense of feeling helpless or to angry words). Contexts vary as a result of the degree of 'attachment' or relationship or intimacy between the relevant parties (Ellis & Weinstein, 1986). They vary according to: the 'valued resources' that flow through and are controlled by that attachment (i.e., whether the relationship runs through our life fabric or is marginal and peripheral to it); and the perceived degree of 'intrusion' into that attachment by the third person (whether he or she really threatens it or just slightly unsettles it). This latter is important because no-one expects a relationship to someone else to exclude all outsiders in all respects all of the time. We recognize that our partner will need and want other friends too: we cannot have him or her all to ourselves. Rather, we feel jealous when a third party threatens an area that is seen as central to our attachment to someone else (e.g., we would feel jealous if someone else looked like becoming our best friend's best friend).

In our society, we usually have labels, 'friendship', 'marriage' and 'engagement', that help us to mark out our relationships and warn outsiders that our partner is central to our attachment in this way. The labels indicate where the limits of the attachment lie, and the community helps in various ways to enforce the relationship. Thus, to announce an engagement or a marriage is to use a tie sign to tell the community to act as an extra guardian against intrusion or trespass on the relationship by outsiders.

Rules about jealousy

We feel specific emotions partly as a result of social context and partly as a result of general social rules about the appropriateness of expressing certain emotions about relationships (Jellison, 1984). We may feel outrage as well as jealousy if someone infringes cultural rules, for example, committing adultery with our spouse; in Victorian times, husbands were often encouraged to go and shoot their wife's lovers. However, if the relationship between sexual partners has not been formally agreed by society (e.g., if we are living together but are not married) then no rules govern the expression of feelings about the same sexual transgression. We may feel jealous but get no social support for feeling outraged.

Further, our personal experience of our partner — the ways our lives are intertwined by routines — provides a basis for interpreting the meaning of certain behaviours that may affect our reactions. For instance, if we both agree that flirting with other people is an acceptable behaviour then we should not feel jealous when we catch a partner doing it.

In open marriages people feel jealous of their partner only when his or her behaviour violates the agreed rules about sexual behaviour in the relationship and not just because the behaviour has occurred (Buunk, 1980). For instance, they sometimes agree that it is acceptable for their partner to have sex with another person so long as he or she does not 'get emotionally involved'. They would not feel jealous because the partner had extramarital sex — they would feel jealous only if the partner did 'get involved'.

Such rules stabilize the relationship and act as guides for feelings about the partner's behaviour in it (Hochschild, 1979). They can even specify whom a society expects to be jealous of whom and in what circumstances (Davis, 1936). For example, Trobriand Islandsmen used to be expected to 'offer' their wives to a visitor and were specifically forbidden to feel jealous if the visitor accepted (Malinowski, 1929). In our own ways, we often attempt to suppress and control jealousy, partly because it may be socially disapproved, partly because we may feel that it reveals too much of a dependency on the relationship, and partly because it creates an unpleasant degree of restrictive possessiveness of the partner.

An emotion like jealousy can be experienced in everyday life, then, in a social context that defines the appropriateness even of strong emotions. With jealousy, it seems that loss of control or of social 'face' is one important element in the emotion. Jealousy is an appropriate emotion to feel when our social status, self-esteem, or control over a relationship is threatened.

To put it slightly differently, but only slightly, jealousy is a response to an imagined loss of influence over a routine part of life, namely over the feelings of another person towards ourselves. When we imagine that we have lost influence over another person's feelings for us or when we are given evidence that they do not care, then we experience jealousy. The more we took those feelings for granted and the more extensively they are threatened, the more jealousy we feel — unless, of course, we were in Manic love and experienced a strong sense of threat and dependency.

A rather similar idea, but one that does not employ the notion of loss of control, is offered by Berscheid (1983) who suggests that jealousy is an interruption to our usual patterns of behaviour and feeling, caused by factors outside the relationship and by partners' perceptions of the relationship. So, we are brought back to the idea of interruption to the routine and taken-for-granted aspects of life as a 'cause' of emotions in relationships.

Embarrassment and Shyness

Embarrassment

Interruption to something that is a taken-for-granted part of the present social encounter can also cause embarrassment, to which I now turn. To understand more fully, let us imagine the following scene. You are talking to your favourite professor about a great idea you had concerning the class and as you get excited about the idea you spill coffee all down your leg. Do you think that you would feel Good or Bad about it? Would you be more likely to laugh or not? If it happened to your enemy, when you were watching, would the emotion be the same? If you observed this in a comedy on television or in a clown's act in a circus, what emotions if any do you think that you would feel?

Loss of face or centre of attention?

One obvious element in the preceding scenario is that you look awkward, incompetent, and clumsy, which is opposite to how you were trying to look. Embarrassment follows from the discrepancy between the self-image a person wants to project (i.e., how you want to appear) and the self-image that gets projected in the event (i.e., how you actually appear).

In one definition, embarrassment is the unexpected and unqualified discrediting of a central assumption in an interaction (Gross & Stone, 1964). Thus, in the example, if you were trying to seem intelligent, cool, competent and commanding, you undermined the assumption of competence quite thoroughly by spilling the coffee, and you would feel embarrassed since you have 'lost face' by acting inconsistently with your image. The loss of face, however, has to be 'undesired'. If you had been play-acting the whole scene and trying to be a good actor or get sympathy, then you would not feel embarrassed at all. In that case, you would not have acted inconsistently with the image you wanted to project and the 'discrediting' would not be undesired. This definition, then, emphasizes a kind of personal diminishment as the cause of embarrassment.

A different approach to embarrassment suggests that it comes from being made the unwanted centre of attention rather than from a feeling of personal diminishment (Semin & Manstead, 1982). According to this view, a person's self-image is unaffected by the incident and the embarrassment comes, instead, from the heightened sense of self-attention, that is, from being 'thrown unexpectedly into the spotlight'.

Social anxiety is another component of embarrassment (and also of shyness). Social anxiety depends on evaluation ('anxiety resulting from the prospect or presence of personal evaluation in real or imagined social situations', Schlenker & Leary, 1982, p. 642). When the evaluation comes as a result of unintentional and undesired social predicaments or transgressions, as in spilling the coffee, then it is embarrassing. It is still important, however, that the person is concerned with the 'public image and reactions from real or imagined others to inappropriate behaviour' (Edelmann, 1985, p. 196). The idea implicit in Schlenker & Leary's definition is that the evaluation of self is either negative or undesirable, and Edelmann makes that explicit.

Embarrassment is not a simple, single event but a sequence of events and Edelmann (1985) uses 'self theory' to explain how it works and why it is so painful to us. Self theories tell us that we have a *private self* (those aspects of our self that cannot be seen or observed directly by other people, such as our private thoughts) and a *public self* (the extremely visible and observable aspects, such as physical appearance and the ways we behave).

An undesired discrepancy between our behaviour and our internal standard for that behaviour leads to the focus of attention falling onto the public self. The embarrassed person quickly becomes concerned about public identity and feels negative. This negative feeling sets off a chain of expressive or communicative behaviours (like blushing, looking down at the floor, becoming agitated) that get labelled and felt as embarrassment. Both the person involved and, usually, the others present also then begin a series of behaviours to distract everyone and cover the embarrassment.

There is a range of strategies, for example, minimizing the importance of the incident or the failure to carry it out success-fully ('Don't worry, it doesn't matter; the coffee is less important than your contribution to my course'); referring to mitigating circumstances ('It's difficult to balance a coffee cup on the arm of that wobbly chair'); or referring to one's own experience of similar predicaments ('Oh! don't feel bad about that; I've done things like that myself when I get excited by an idea!'). Other tactics for restoring the status quo are for the person to apologize (usually countered by the other person saying that there's no need to since it doesn't really matter anyway) and 'jokework', that is, the use of humour and laughter in an attempt to minimize the incident. All these methods go some way to restoring the transgressor's public image or indicating that negative evaluations have not really been made.

The key feature of embarrassment, then, seems to be anxiety about our self-image caused by heightened self-attention. Here, 'self-image' means not only 'what I think about myself' but 'what I think other people think about myself'. If I feel that their estimation of me is lowered then I feel anxious about my worth and value to other people. This threat can be minimized by the onlookers stressing that their response to the person and their long-term relationship with him or her are not spoiled by the embarrassing transgression. The sooner that routine can be restored, the more quickly the embarrassment goes away.

Shyness

Shyness is rather similar to embarrassment in some ways but is an affective-behavioural syndrome consisting of social anxiety and inhibition. Everyone feels shy from time to time, but some people are likely to feel more shy than others will (Buss, 1980; Cheek & Busch, 1981). Shyness is caused by an anticipation of a discrepancy between a person's desired self-image and his or her way of projecting the self-image so that the actual projection is expected to fall short of the desired one. Shyness is embarrassment in advance, created by the belief that our real self will not be able to match up to the image we want to project.

Some 41 percent of people believe that they are shy and up to 24 percent think that it is a serious enough problem for them to do something about it (Pilkonis, 1977). If you are not shy yourself, then two out of the next four people you meet will be and one of them will feel that it requires seeking professional help.

There is one key feature to shyness and it revolves around problems with interpersonal communication (Kelly, 1982). A central problem for many shy people is their unwillingness to communicate (i.e., 'reticence'), characterized by avoidance of and ineptitude at social interaction and performance in public or at the centre of attention in a social encounter. Is the cause: deficient communication skills; anxiety about communication (so-called 'communication apprehension'); or simple avoidance of communication? In other words, is it because: the person generally dislikes communication; becomes paralysingly anxious about it; or just cannot do it well behaviourally? In practical terms there are few differences among the results of these three possible causes (Kelly, 1982), although the first two seem to be attitudinal or cognitive causes whilst the last is a behavioural or communicative problem. Programmes that improve (behavioural) performance actually reduce anxiety also, so we cannot distinguish the behavioural and the attitudinal components readily. What is readily distinguishable is that part of shyness is the experience of communicative difficulties and that part of it is the communicative difficulties themselves.

The remaining problem for shy people is that the reticence is evaluated by outsiders as showing that they feel negative towards people rather than being shy about them (Burgoon & Koper, 1984). When strangers are asked to assess videotapes of reticent persons talking to other people, the strangers rate the reticents quite negatively. They see reticents as expressing too little intimacy/similarity, being detached and uninvolved in the interaction, and showing too much submissiveness and emotional negativity. They also rated reticents as not credible or somewhat 'shifty'. When the shy persons' friends saw the same videotapes, however, they usually rated the behaviour as more positive. In other words, shy persons' behaviour appears negative to strangers, but their friends become used to it. Once shy people get friends they are seen positively; the problem is that their behaviour is such that strangers probably would not want to become their friends in the first place.

Leary & Dobbins (1983) show that there are quite severe relational consequences of shyness, in that surveyed persons who were highly shy had had fewer sexual experiences, less sexual intercourse, and a smaller number of sexual partners than people who were not very shy. Dating, a usual preliminary to sexual encounters, is a situation that gets rated as highly anxiety-provoking by between 37 percent and 50 percent of men and 21 percent to 50 percent of women, in any case. Presumably, the very shy are at a considerable disadvantage in dating; their shyness effectively cuts them off from normal social life.

What would help depends on the precise nature of the problem. There are different elements to shyness; some stem from anxiety about communication ('communication apprehension') and some from reticence or lack of skill in performing communication adequately, because of a speech impediment or a belief that we have nothing to say that would interest people or an awkwardness and inability to converse easily (Kelly, 1982). The end result is the same — the person does not communicate — but the reasons are different.

The anxious person may be a perfectly competent communicator if the anxiety could be overcome and many such people are perfectly good communicators when they are relaxed in the company of friends, but the unskilled person would perform badly even when not anxious. The anxious, or 'privately shy' person typically focusses on the subjective discomfort and fear of negative evaluation whilst the 'publicly shy' person thinks of the behavioural inadequacies as the main problem.

If the problem is identified as anxiety then a cognitive therapy would help, and if it is lack of skill that causes the shyness, a social skills training programme might be the solution.

Cognitive therapy

Cognitive therapy (Beck, 1976) is based on changing a person's beliefs. If someone believes that he or she is unattractive or awkward (even when no-one else agrees) then that will influence his or her attitudes towards encounters with other people. If such persons are challenged to provide evidence of their beliefs about themselves and to give instances of their own awkwardness it often becomes clear that they have double standards for their own and for other people's behaviour. Usually, they are highly critical of themselves and their own performance, but overlook examples of other people being and performing the same. By confronting them with their misperceptions, cognitive therapy reshapes their false beliefs and so reduces their anxieties.

Social skills training

Social skills training programmes are effective in alleviating shyness that results from communicative inadequacies (Kelly,

1984). The bases, usually, are that shy people lack conversational skills, do not ask the right questions, cannot offer social invitations effectively, or do not talk openly and easily about themselves. By training such people through direct instruction, through modelling or example, through coaching, and through feedback of videotaped conversations with new partners, it is possible to increase their conversational effectiveness and help them to overcome the skill deficits that led to their reticence (Kelly, 1984).

Shyness is shown to relate to loneliness in new situations (Cheek & Busch, 1981). Shy students entering college are significantly more lonely than non-shy students, although both groups become less lonely in time. Shy students improve their situation more dramatically than do the non-shy ones — but, obviously, they have more room to do so (Cheek & Busch, 1981). Unfortunately, even after such improvements, the shy students are still much more lonely than the non-shy ones.

It does seem as if something about shyness affects the system of social communication with other people and as if that serves unintentionally to keep others away. Communication problems contribute to the difficulties of the shy person and help to ensure that they stay lonely, although it may work the other way around such that social isolation contributes to communication difficulties, for instance, through lack of practice (Zakahi & Duran, 1982). One particularly important problem is that shy or communicatively incompetent persons become used to not being intimate or open with others. They thus 'learn' to give out signals in their routine social behaviour that are interpreted as meaning that they are not interested in relationships with other people (Zakahi & Duran, 1985). Clearly, a state like shyness is built into a person's routine ways of handling life, other people, and new situations and is the habitual style of behaviour in such new situations. Thus, shy persons contribute to their own social rejection by other people and hence to their future loneliness.

Loneliness

Loneliness is more common than we may believe, is not confined to a group of odd or abnormal people, is associated with both unhappiness and illness, and can be cured. People who are lonely do not necessarily have fewer relationships or daily interactions than other people have, but they are often less satisfied with the ones they do have (Larson et al., 1982; Reis et al., 1983). Satisfactory interactions — especially sexual interactions — are associated, on the other hand, with better feelings about health (Wheeler et al., 1983).

Who becomes lonely?

Who becomes lonely? We all do. Roughly 26 percent of a large sample reported feeling 'very lonely within the past few weeks' (Bradburn, 1969), and almost everyone experiences intense loneliness at some time or another (Peplau & Perlman, 1982). We often think of loneliness as more rampant in elderly rather than younger populations, but research casts doubt on this. What is important is the presence or absence of a feeling of control over interactions with others (Shulz, 1976). Also important is the availability of a close confidant (Peplau et al., 1982) and whether the person has been used to being single through life (Shanas et al., 1968). In one study, contrary to popular myth, only 15 percent of old people report that they feel lonely quite often (Tunstall, 1967).

There are some situations where everyone becomes lonely, and we can distinguish *trait loneliness* (a stable and persistent pattern of feeling lonely — definitely a feature of the person; he or she takes the feeling with him or her into new situations) and *state loneliness* (a transient, temporary feeling of loneliness — probably resulting from the situation or a move to a new environment rather than to the specific person; everyone might feel lonely in the same circumstances).

What is loneliness?

Clearly, loneliness is not necessarily the same as being alone (Perlman & Peplau, 1981). We can be lonely in a crowd and can be perfectly happy on our own sometimes in the 'bliss of solitude'. The crucial feature of loneliness, according to Perlman & Peplau (1981), is a discrepancy between what we're doing and what we expect or hope to do; or, to put it more precisely, 'a discrepancy between one's desired and achieved levels of social relations.' (Perlman & Peplau, 1981, p. 32). If we desire a *small* number of friends and that is what we have, then we will be happy and not lonely. If, on the other hand, we desire 126 friends and have only 120, then we shall feel lonely.

To assess loneliness, we must look at the person's desired or needed levels of social contact rather than at just the levels of social contact that he or she actually achieves. Our expectations, desires, and needs can fluctuate from time to time independently of our actual levels of social contact. For example, when we are under some sort of stress we might want company, but when we are working on a difficult task we would rather be alone and would find company annoying. Also, the Perlman-Peplau model is perfectly comfortable with the finding that our experience of loneliness can vary according to internal factors like feelings or beliefs when our number of friends or social contacts stays the same. In other words, even when our contacts stay the same and our number of friends is constant, we could still feel lonely on some days and not others or in some circumstances and not others, depending on our present desire for company or solitude. For example, people feel more lonely just after they have been beaten at racquet ball (Perlman & Serbin, 1984), whilst teenagers experience more loneliness at weekends (Larson et al., 1982) not because they have fewer contacts then but because they expect to have more.

Our expectations about relationships and about loneliness will be influenced by our personality, our beliefs about our attractiveness, and whether we tend to take credit for our social successes in meeting new people or blame for our failures to make friends.

We learned in the preceding section that shy people habitually fear making new friends and may be anxious in ways that could affect their adequacy in carrying out new encounters. Those who usually assume that social failures are their own fault ('because of the person I am and the problems I always have') are likely to overlook other factors that could account for loneliness — such as 'circumstances' or 'moving to a new neighbourhood'. They will probably blame their isolation in the new circumstances on their habitual and personal difficulties. Accordingly, they are much more likely than everyone else to feel negative about themselves and personally hopeless. Trait lonely people (i.e., the long-term lonely) are found to have exactly the characteristics that make it more likely that they will blame themselves in this way. They have a low opinion of themselves, see themselves in negative terms, dislike talking about their feelings, and are low in intimate behaviours (Jones et al., 1981; Solano et al., 1982).

What do lonely people do?

Lonely people do habitually report quite consistent feelings that go with loneliness (Rubenstein & Shaver, 1982). These are: *desperation* (being panicked and feeling helpless); *depression* (feeling sad and worthless); *impatient boredom* (restlessness and boredom simultaneously); *self-deprecation* ('What's wrong with me?' and 'Why am I so useless?'). Chronically lonely males have characteristic sets of beliefs about themselves and other people that lead them to act in an aggressive and hostile way (Check et al., 1985). Lonely males are more punitive than nonlonely males are, particularly towards female partners who make errors on a learning task that the male is 'supervising'. Many violent males, particularly rapists, are found to score highly on loneliness scales and to have been socially isolated well before they committed their violent assaults (Howells, 1981).

Lonely persons are self-absorbed, nonresponsive, negativistic, and ineffective in their interactions with strangers (Jones et al., 1985). They spend more time alone, particularly at weekends, and are less involved with voluntary organizations, dating, relatives, and neighbours or social activities generally (Jones et al., 1985). They sometimes show 'sad passivity', which involves overeating, oversleeping, watching television, crying, drinking alcohol, or taking tranquillizers (Rubenstein & Shaver, 1982).

Other typical styles of coping with loneliness are to engage in 'busy-busy' activity, solitary hobbies, jogging alone, or taking vigorous exercise. Other people react to loneliness by self-indulgent actions, particularly buying themselves 'toys' like microcomputers and stereo systems, or just generally running riot with their credit cards. When we get lonely we often turn into 'big spenders' in an effort to make ourselves feel better about ourselves. More useful are coping strategies that involve visiting other people, writing to friends, calling them (briefly!) on the phone, or just attempting to increase social contact.

The key feature is the beliefs that we hold about the causes of our loneliness and about our ability to control it. If we believe that it will go away if we take positive action, we are more likely to attempt to socialize. If we believe that it is somehow 'our fault' — and a permanent feature or, at least, a stable feature of our lives at that — then we are more likely to become depressed. Several studies show that it is possible to reduce loneliness by giving the person a sense of control over it. Thus, for instance, Shulz (1976) found that old persons who were allowed to schedule visits from volunteers workers felt less lonely than those whose schedule was fixed for them by someone else even though the total number and length of the visits was *the same* for both sets of people.

When you are forced to be alone

The sense of control is probably one reason why not all 'being alone' is loneliness, as the Perlman-Peplau model makes clear. If our desired level of social contact is low for some deliberately controlled reason (e.g., if we are feeling creative and want to write a novel) then low levels of social contact will be highly enjoyable and high levels may be unattractive to us.

The problems arise when someone is forced to be alone willy-nilly. For instance, students typically report feeling lonely soon after they arrive in their new university at the start of their freshman year. *Friends* rather than dates or lovers are the best buffer against loneliness in those circumstances (Cutrona, 1982).

What happens, then, when new students go to college? Shaver et al. (1985) look at ways of predicting which students would stay lonely and which would develop fuller networks in the new environment and so cope with loneliness. Their results show that the transition to college was particularly stressful for males, whose loneliness increased four times more than females'. Also males' dating frequency declined more than females'. The latter may have resulted from freshman males having a smaller pool of dates available to them since there is a cultural norm that encourages females (but not males) to date older as well as same-aged members of the opposite sex and to decline requests for dates from younger males.

Old relationships back home decline both in number and perceived quality, whereas new ones do not reach the satisfaction levels of pre-college ones. The transition to college causes the end of almost half (46 percent) the pre-college romantic relationships and also produces strain in the other 54 percent, which were rated much less positively after the transition than before it.

On the more positive side, the students were quick to establish new groups of casual acquaintances, but experienced considerable uncertainty about them. Their feelings about family and kin became more positive, and they experienced less conflict with parents even though they did not see them as often — or perhaps because of it. Seemingly, though, this was a subjective change rather than a real or objective one, since there obviously was little interaction going on with the family that could improve; the students just felt better about their family.

Curing chronic loneliness

Loneliness causes loneliness, that is, people who are presently lonely may, like shy persons, behave in such a way that other people do not feel inclined to relate to them or just disregard them and find them unattractive (Jones et al., 1985). Whole programmes of research are now geared up to identifying the interpersonal skills (or rather the lack of skills) of the chronically lonely person in an attempt to understand the most effective ways of helping them (Jones et al., 1985).

The basic argument here is that lonely people, like shy people, lack certain skills in communication and social behaviour, such as assertiveness, or else they are higher in shyness and self-consciousness (Jones et al., 1981) and experience inhibited sociability (e.g., difficulty making friends). Lonely people in a laboratory setting select less effective power strategies and are generally less effective in meeting new people (Perlman et al., 1978). Lonely students are below average at sharing their opinions on personal topics (Hansson & Jones, 1981). Jones et al. (1984, p. 146) conclude provocatively that 'the interpersonal behaviours often associated with loneliness may actually reduce the likelihood that the lonely person will be able, without intervention, to restore mutually satisfying relationships with others'.

A number of successful programmes for treating chronic loneliness have been developed recently to help people to cope with loneliness, prevent the more serious consequences like depression and suicide, and help them to create broader and more satisfying networks — as well as preventing people from becoming lonely in the first place (Rook, 1984). In essence there are four approaches:

1 Cognitive treatment, aimed at changing lonely people's expectations that they will be rejected in social encounters (similar to the one used on shy people in the preceding section);

2 Social skills training, aimed at improving people's ability to be effective in encounters with other people;

3 Group therapy, aimed at increasing sensitivity to other people;

4 Community-based approaches, aimed at increasing people's opportunities for interaction.

The community-based approaches are not much use to people with underlying social skill deficits since 'Go out and meet more people' really just amounts to 'Go out and be rejected by more people' unless the underlying problem is solved first (Duck, 1983).

In one social skills training programme, Jones et al. (1982) trained some very lonely males to increase their attention to their partner in a conversation (e.g., by asking questions about the partner, continuing, rather than changing, the topic of conversation, showing interest in partner's views). Training involved exposure to audiotapes of 'good' and 'bad' conversations in which the instructor pointed out places where attention to the partner would have been particularly appropriate. In a similar programme, Gallup (1980) trained lonely people in other interactional skills (e.g., paraphrasing partner's comments; summarizing their statements; giving positive evaluations). In both programmes, lonely people became more skilful in conversation and reported subsequent increases in sociability, reductions in loneliness, and reduced feelings of shyness.

Cognitive treatments, on the other hand, aim to restructure the way in which the lonely people think about themselves and the interpersonal events in which they participate. Individuals who are lonely usually are high in social anxiety, just as shy people are, and they feel that they are being judged or ridiculed by other people. Treatments such as Young's (1982) cognitive therapy are intended to change these attitudes and to encourage the person to engage in activities with other people, including open disclosure of his or her feelings and emotions.

One method of effecting such change is to challenge the person to produce evidence that other people are ridiculing or judging him or her. Examples of other people making errors are then discussed and comparisons made of the subject's reactions to them. Often, it can be shown that the lonely person has a higher standard for his or her own behaviour than for other people's. Another means of changing the unhelpful beliefs is to videotape lonely persons in an interaction. Frequently, they are surprised to see how relaxed they look from the outside even when they feel anxious inside.

It is encouraging that such therapies are being developed. Loneliness is something that we all experience from time to time and that we all try to avoid or correct. It is thus a common human concern for which social psychology can by systematic study provide some answers and correctives. It is a good instance of the fact that relational problems affect our lives fundamentally by getting incorporated into our routine ways of interacting. We should also note that since relational problems lead to pronounced loss of concentration, one of the most dangerous people in the world is a lonely air traffic controller.

Looking at Emotions: Some Thoughts and a Summary

A theory of emotions

Emotions are explained as the result of interruptions in routines (Mandler, 1975). Mandler argues that emotions are based in physiology, particularly in the autonomic nervous system (i.e., the system or rather the systems largely concerned with bodily functions over which we have little direct control, such as muscles of the heart, blood vessels, and digestive system). This is a rather slow-acting system (e.g., our heart rate may not increase until one or two seconds after we have been shocked by a loud noise). However, Mandler argues that since this is tied up with attentional processes, it ensures that we will attend to those cues that trigger it to operate. This will prepare us to act upon them vigorously if necessary (e.g., by running away).

We, therefore, attempt a 'meaning analysis' on anything that triggers the system, and we will continue to analyse it until we are happy that it is no longer necessary to do so. This analysis is made easier because we have experience of past events or routines stored in our memory, and we often have organized routines for dealing with them stored there too (organized action sequences, OAS). No matter how long or complicated an OAS may be, it is often completed automatically or unthinkingly, once it has begun. Often, we cannot stop it happening, but, when it is somehow stopped or interrupted, we notice it. That is where this becomes a theory of emotions.

Mandler argues that interruption of an OAS is enough to set up a feeling or emotion. So, an OAS is interrupted, the autonomic nervous system fires, attention is focussed on the stimulus causing the interruption, and, if the sequence cannot be resumed and completed, the meaning of the stimulus is analysed and we feel an appropriate emotion. This can be applied to emotions in relationships (Berscheid, 1983).

Two persons in a relationship are interdependent in various ways in that their thoughts and actions interconnect. For Berscheid, 'emotion in relationship' refers to an emotional event in one or other partner's chain of thought or actions that is caused by a thought or action of the other person. In other words, something that one person does or thinks or says interrupts the flow of thought or speech or action of the other person and so prevents him or her from carrying out an organized action sequence. Then, he or she feels an emotion in relationship.

However, if we focus only on the interruptions to routines that result in feelings of irritation then we miss the important point that most feelings about other people in the course of everyday life are long-lasting ones. Friendship, marriages, and courtships are not momentary states but enduring or developing relationships built into the fabric of our daily life. The consistency of our transitory feelings towards a partner is important and makes it seem that the emotion *lasts*.

A couple of hypotheses occur to me: the duller and more routine the relationship is, the more its disruption should upset and disturb us; the more the lives of the partners are built around the same routines, the more emotion they will feel about, for example, moving to a new house; the less time I spend thinking about a close relationship (or the more I take it for granted), the more emotionally disturbing it will be to be forced to think about it.

I do not know how these speculations would turn out if they were studied, but they seem to follow from what has been said. Further, while two partners are building a relationship (i.e., while they are restructuring their lives to build the new relationship into their routines), their emotions about one another should be less predictable in direction but more intense. The same is true concerning the phase just before separation (i.e., when at least one partner is considering restructuring the routines of life by getting out of an established relationship); emotions should be frequent but also ambivalent and contradictory. There is ample evidence to support the latter claim (Baxter, 1979; Duck, 1982b), but less to bring to bear on the former (Bochner, 1983). One side thought on this is that *any* change to routine should be disruptive to the person, not just a negative change. We have seen that the positive change that we call 'falling in love' can be disruptive and any parent will tell you that the birth of a child, whilst positive, is also disruptive not only to routines but also to emotional life.

From what we have considered so far, it is clear that feelings about other people consist of: many different parts and components; a set of behaviours through which we communicate our feelings; and a set of routines that either bind us to our partner (in love and jealousy) or keep us from other people (in shyness, loneliness and jealousy). Jealousy, you will note, both binds us to and keeps us from partners. Feelings about other people impact on the rest of our life and take part of their meaning from the ways in which they affect our interpersonal communication and social behaviour.

A final notable point about the material here is the extent to which enduring emotions and feelings about relationships involve minute expressive and communicative details, like conversational skills of topic management or the number of questions that a person asks of a stranger. It would be interesting to know how our communications change as we fall in and out of love. What do we talk about and how does it differ from the things that we talk about at other times? It would also be interesting to know more about the systems of communication upon which social behaviour is based. In chapter 2, therefore, let us consider the communication systems that are the basis for our relationships with one another.

Summary

The four emotions that we have looked at here (love, jealousy, embarrassment/shyness and loneliness) have a number of features:

1 They occur in relationship to other people, involve expressive and communicative behaviour, and are closely connected to the notion of worth and competence in relationships. Each in its own way is a feeling that states our assumed value and worth to other people.

2 Emotions do not need specific external events to spark them off but can all be rekindled just by thought and by fantasy or imagination about social encounters, past, present, or future. They can be experienced in the absence of other people but are still 'about' them.

3 They are rarely experienced as just hot surges of emotion, but are more often enduring emotional states reported in dispositional language (I am in love; I am a shy person). They can become ways of social life, enshrined in ways of communicating and expressing ourselves through behaviour.

4 They are structured into or impact upon social routines and everyday behaviours. That we feel jealous or shy or lonely or in love influences the way we behave towards other people *in the long term*, as well as in the short term. It can affect how we look at them, how we speak to them, and how we deal with them, as well as how we choose to relate to them.

5 The isolating ones (shyness, loneliness) can be treated by training programmes that affect the person's behaviour, other people's responses and hence the lonely or shy person's feelings about their own worth.

Further reading

Berscheid, E. (1983) 'Emotion'. In H.H. Kelley et al. (eds.) *Close Relationships*. Freeman: New York.

Buunk, A. & Bringle, R. (1986) 'Jealousy'. In D. Perlman & S.W. Duck (eds.) *Intimate Relationships*. Sage: Beverly Hills.

Daly, J.A. & McCroskey, J.C., (eds.) (1984) *Avoiding Communication*. Sage: Beverly Hills.

Leary, M. (1984) *Understanding Social Anxiety*. Sage: Beverly Hills.

Peplau, L.A. & Perlman, D. (1982) *Loneliness: A Sourcebook of Current Theory, Research and Therapy*. Wiley-Interscience: New York.

CHAPTER 2

Communication Skills and the Languages of Interpersonal Relationships

Bodies talk. Whenever we sit, stand, walk, or look at someone else, we give off messages — some of which we may not have intended to make public. Equally, we can learn that someone dislikes us when they have not even said a word, that he or she is deliberately lying to us, or that a person finds us sexually attractive — and we can do all this by understanding the hidden languages of social behaviour. These languages are essential in relationships, and they help us to express our emotions more effectively than we can by speech alone.

Our social relationships with one another are based not on one language but on two. Whilst spoken language is the one that we recognize more easily, there is an unspoken language, too: the language of nonverbal communication. Nonverbal communication is made up of, for instance, the spacing between people when we interact, the gestures, eye movements and facial expressions that accompany or supplement our speech, and a range of other cues. We hardly ever speak without adding to the message by intimate body language, by frowning or smiling or looking interested, impressed, or bored. These messages are more powerful than speech itself. If someone spoke to you saying that he or she was interested in you but looked bored, which would you believe, the verbal or the nonverbal message?

So, if we were asked, for example, to teach the deaf to be fully social members of the community, we would need a complete system of communication that could represent the inflections and tones of voice that speaking normally conveys. If we decide to teach the deaf to use signs that occupy the hands or face to convey the actual grammatical language (called 'Langue' by

---

BOX 2.1 Points to think about

— *What are the social skills of interpersonal communication and how do our verbal messages combine with the silent, nonverbal messages, like facial expressions?*
— *Is social behaviour a skill, like riding a bicycle?*
— *What kinds of people are best at interpersonal communication and how can the less skilled person be trained to improve? In chapter 1, we learned that the lonely, the depressed, the embarrassed, and the shy often behave inappropriately or show a lack of 'social skills': they often fail to make their behaviour 'fit' with a partner's behaviour or they appear to be too sullen and aggressive. Precisely what are they doing wrong? How can we train such people to communicate more effectively?*
— *Where and how do children learn to combine their speech with other social behaviours and skills? How is such learning related to learning of the self concept?*
— *If there are two languages of interpersonal relationships (verbal and nonverbal) then should we teach the deaf how to 'speak' or how to 'communicate'?*

---

linguists), then how are we to communicate the other parts of social messages (called 'parole' by sociolinguists), like accent, humorous sarcasm and the twinklings, winks, significant stares, gestures, and loudness/softness that are the embroidery on the cloth of common speech? We would also need a way to represent formality and informality in messages, such as the way we can show we like or dislike someone, the way we create status differences and all the usual messages about who is in charge. When we can do at least these things we will have found ways to deal with the *social* handicap of deafness as well as a means of skirting the purely physical deficiencies.

Silent Language: Nonverbal Communication

Have you ever wondered why we do not keep bumping into people in the street? If, as I, you have not, consider how it points to some complicated signalling that we all understand quite well. Children who are still learning this unspoken signalling system actually *do* bump into people quite often, not because they do not look where they are going but because they do not realise where the *other* people are going. They cannot interpret the signals about use of space. What signals? How do we communicate intentions about where we will walk, who will talk, when to stop, whose turn is next, and the like?

Are there social rules about space?

Actually, there are social rules governing the use of space in social situations and movements through space. These work *nonverbally*, by means of bodily cues to do with posture, gesture, orientation (i.e., the way our body is facing) and various other subtleties like eye movements (Argyle, 1983). Unfortunately, the very discussion of it is something that is embarrassing and hard to do. We hardly ever refer directly to someone's nonverbal behaviour and to do so is usually rude or aggressive ('Wipe that smile off your face', 'Look at me when I'm talking to you', 'Don't stand so close to me').

What would the existence of a rule system mean? If there is a nonverbal rule system then:

1 the use of nonverbal cues must be identifiable and recognizable;

2 the operation of nonverbal cues must be systematic;

3 we all must be able to translate our feelings and intentions into nonverbal messages (i.e., we must be able to '*encode*');

4 observers must be able to interpret (or '*decode*') it;

5 whether or not we intend it, observers may decode our behaviour systematically, even attending to signals that we thought we had successfully concealed.

Territories in space

One familiar observation is that animals have 'territories' so maybe human animals do too. Some birds fight other birds that come into their 'patch', baboons control space and attack invaders, dogs mark out their territorial boundaries with body products. Are there echoes of this style of behaviour amongst humans, too? Yes. We use space in a systematic way that has territorial overtones (i.e., we use space as if it is invisibly 'attached' to us or under our control). This occurs both in fixed settings, like offices, and in dynamic settings, during conversations.

The study of human spatial behaviour is known as 'proxemics' (Hall, 1966). Space can be differentiated into *intimate* (i.e., from direct contact to around 18 inches [46cm]

BOX 2.2 Dividing space

Desmond Morris (1971) points out that families on a beach fill up the available space systematically and when the beach is empty, people space themselves wide apart. As the beach fills up, so the newcomers divide up the space more or less equally. The same thing happens elsewhere, too.

Try it in the library or a cafeteria. If you are faced with an empty table of 6 chairs (3 each side), you are most likely to take a middle seat. The next person who arrives (assuming he or she is unknown to you) is most likely to sit on the opposite side of the table in an end seat; the next one in the remaining end seat on that side, and so on. My prediction is that the last seat to be taken (assuming that all persons are unknown to one another) will be the one directly opposite the one you first occupied.

See what happens and see what difference it makes if you start off in another position or if people arrive in pairs or if they know one of the occupants of the table.

---

away from another person — obviously used with someone we know and like); *personal* (from around 18 inches [46cm] to about 4 feet [1.4m] apart — usually used when talking to casual friends or acquaintances); *social* (from around 4 feet [1.4m] to around 12 feet [4.2m] apart — usually used for business transactions and impersonal encounters), or *public* (from around 12 feet [4.2m] or more apart — e.g., when a speaker at public events and formal encounters stands away from the rest of the group or audience).

In different settings we are comfortable with different distances; imagine talking to friends, to a teacher, and going to a lecture. Another thing to notice is that as we get to know someone better so we indicate this by holding conversations standing at smaller distances (Argyle, 1969). The more intimate we become emotionally, the more intimate we get spatially; we get closer in *two* senses.

As long as we can breathe comfortably then sociocultural rules for distribution of space will be the ones we follow. These rules have several interesting features: space claims are information about status, ownership, and the social or personal relationship between participants; and, position and relative distance during conversation are important. Just think for a moment about the rich array of metaphorical statements about power and position that are made in spatial terminology. For example, space can be used to provide metaphors about relationships, which can be close or distant. Furthermore, we talk of people being 'high and mighty', they can be 'head and shoulders above the rest', 'big wheels', 'way above the competition', 'the greatest'. Good experiences are 'highs' or 'highpoints'. We have *high* moral principles and are *above* doing anything mean such as showing *low* cunning.

Spatial metaphors are also used to refer to 'inferiority' (which is derived from the Latin word *inferus*, meaning 'lower'): people are of low status, lowly, lowdown no-goods, beneath (rather than above, beyond, outside) contempt. A bad experience is a 'downer', and we feel low. In doing something bad, we may be accused of stooping low, and the like. When we assert ourselves, on the other hand, we stand up for ourselves or stand up to someone powerful: we 'walk tall, walk straight and look the whole world in the eye'.

In some clinical contexts, these metaphors take on a real meaning. For instance, in 'hysterical conversion', a client's emotional problems can take a physical form, as when a person with pathologically low self-esteem walks stooping over very low and may change posture as moods vary. In an extreme case that I am familiar with, a fourteen-year-old boy who is six-feet (183cm) tall used to stoop right over and walk along bent almost double, so that his highest point was usually some three-and-a-half feet (106cm) off the ground. As his mood altered, so he would straighten up, actually unbending to four feet (122cm) on a good day.

Claiming space is claiming power

Human beings decorate their rooms, houses and, to some extent, their cars and themselves. For instance, furniture in offices is arranged in ways that indicate who owns what, who is superior to whom, and how much of the space is public. Desks and tables can be arranged in such a way that they show *power differences* between people, in addition to any reasons to do with lighting or ease of communication (Davitz, 1964). For example, Hitler's office was enormous, and visitors had to walk a considerable distance from the entrance to reach the desk (from which, of course, as part of the power ploy, he did not move). Bank managers usually make you sit across the desk from them as a distancing device to indicate their power, whilst counsellors may have low tables, instead of desks, to remove or reduce physical and psychological barriers and to increase informality.

Furniture can also act as a barrier (itself an implicit statement of a social rule indicating who is in charge and how far you can go); for example, receptionists' desks stop you entering beyond them. It is physically possible to break the rules, but is a social offence (e.g., moving your chair round the barrier so that you sit next to the bank manager, moving round to the other side of the table, opening a door marked Private, or sitting on a receptionist's desk, all violate a social rule and would most probably lead to comment or discomfort or possibly to the other person becoming angry).

Symbolic decoration

Symbolic decoration also indicates ownership of space and so it too affirms control and power. The most obvious example is clothing: I could put my hand in your pocket, but . . . Furthermore, if, in a library or refectory, we observe an empty seat with a coat hanging over the back, we know it is a symbol: the coat owner is indicating that he or she will return and use the chair. If we see sets of books arranged on library tables in such a way that someone could read them, when no-one is in fact doing so, then we would probably go somewhere else to seat ourselves and look for another chair with no implicit territorial claim upon it.

A further way of claiming space is achieved through *self-extension*. Placing our feet on a coffee table or desk, sprawling across an otherwise empty sofa or airplane seat, and leaning across a doorway are all ways of claiming control over the space. Claiming space is claiming power, ownership, and, above all, status. The first-class seats on airlines are broader and have more foot room in front of them rather than merely being more comfortably made. As people are promoted in an organization, so this is symbolically recognized by the award of larger offices, longer desks, broader areas of carpet, taller chairs, and wider blotter pads. Space is status.

Most often, a spatial claim is horizontal and concerns the amount of floor space allocated to a person. Status claims, however, are often related to vertical space too, as in 'higher' or 'lower' status (Argyle, 1964). Kings, queens, judges, and professors sit on raised platforms. Popes are carried round at shoulder height when they are elected. Equally, temporary changes in status can be acknowledged by height changes as when a scoring footballer jumps up in the air or is lifted up in triumph by teammates. More subtly, persons sometimes bow or curtsy (thus reducing their height) when they are introduced to someone of much higher status, and in Ancient China persons introduced to the emperor had to reduce their height to the extent of hurling themselves to the floor and banging their foreheads on the ground. Nowadays, only assistant professors seeking tenure do this.

Space and conversation

Space matters not only in the fixed ways mentioned but in the dynamic flux of conversations and social encounters (Argyle, 1975). Space claims therein often claim not only the space but the person in it (i.e., to dominate that person). To lean across someone's desk more than about half way is to threaten them personally; to lean beside someone with your hand on the wall next to his or her shoulder at a party is to claim and threaten the person so enclosed. The other person in these circumstances can obviously escape by brushing past, but to do so would violate a social rule about the 'meaning' of space. It would be rude; it would be hostile; it would be aggressive, too.

Systems of meaning

What, then, is the meaning of proximity in social encounters? Broadly speaking, proximity (or physical closeness) often indicates intimacy, or emotional closeness. We tend to sit next to people that we like and to sit closer to those we like more. Closeness, however, can also indicate invasion of territory and thus be taken as a threat. When someone stands close to us we can experience intense threat, irritation, or fear. Blood pressure will sometimes rise if we are touched against our will (Clore, 1977).

The same kinds of meaning are attached to eye movements as well as to proximity. Gazing at a person's eyes is often, but not always, an indication of intense liking; we look at a person more often if we like them. Eye contact (i.e., when two people look one another in the eye) indicates interest, liking, and acceptance (Argyle & Cook, 1976). Pupil size marginally increases when we see someone or something that we like, and we prefer faces where the pupils are dilated — presumably because it signals that the face likes us.

As with proximity, however, staring and gazing can carry threatening messages also. An intense stare can be used as a threatening cue both in animals and in humans (Morris, 1971). Furthermore, the stare is a stimulus to flight, and persons who are stared at when they stop at traffic lights will move away faster from the junction when the lights go green (Ellsworth et al., 1972). How do people decide which reaction is the right one when bodily invasion or a stare can be seen as either highly pleasurable or else intensely threatening?

The answer is that the nonverbal communication system is a system, and the parts work together to help us to work out meanings intended in particular cases. For one thing, the individual cues, like proximity, hardly ever happen on their own in isolation. A complex interrelationship exists between space and other nonverbal cues, such as eye movements.

The way in which we can learn the full message is by attending to the system of cues, not to just one in isolation. We work out meaning from eye contact plus context or from proximity plus words. When someone stares and smiles, then we know that he or she likes us; if someone stares and frowns, then he or she is a threat.

Does eye contact plus closeness take the intimacy level beyond what people can bear? Argyle & Dean (1965) propose an equilibrium model, namely, that the intimacy level of an interaction is held steady by a balancing of proximity and eye contact. As proximity increases so eye contact will decrease; that way, the total level of signalling for intimacy will stay about right. If proximity decreases then eye contact should increase to maintain the equilibrium of the encounter. This works with other signals for intimacy, too. For example, as an interviewer's questions become more personal, so the interviewee reduces eye contact when giving answers (Carr & Dabbs, 1974; Schulz & Barefoot, 1974).

BOX 2.3 Some research findings about space usage

We find it more appropriate to sit opposite people with whom we will have an argument and to sit next to people with whom we agree (Sommer, 1969; Cook, 1968). Conversely, it is 'harder' to disagree with someone sitting next to us.

There are cultural differences in tolerance for closeness in conversation. Watson & Graves (1966) observe that Arabs habitually stand close to partners and touch them during conversations whilst Americans stand further apart. Legend reports that if you put an Arab and an Englishman in a room to converse you get exciting results. The comfortable distance for the Arab is too close for the Englishman, who will therefore edge back. This makes things uncomfortably distant for the Arab, who edges forward. But, for the Englishman, this is now too close. The two gradually edge all the way round the room.

Violent prisoners in Glaswegian prisons react negatively to spatial invasion (Kane, 1971), particularly to someone entering the 'body buffer zone' that they perceive around themselves. Such body buffer zones are the area that we regard as 'ours' immediately around our body. Since these Glaswegian body buffer zones were larger than those for normal nonviolent subjects, they were more easily violated. That is, normal people had smaller body buffer zones so other people could get closer to them without upsetting them. For the violent prisoners, the body buffer zone was larger, and so they more easily and frequently became upset when other people got close. A negative reaction was particularly likely for invasion from behind. 'Don't crowd me, man' can be a fatal reaction in Glasgow.

It could be noted also that young children are not very aware of other people's space and often crawl all over adults without much thought about 'the rules', since they have not yet learned them.

The importance of nonverbal communication

Nonverbal communication serves to indicate the intimacy of an encounter, and does so by means of apparently trivial and unimportant but specific cues in social settings, ranging from the use of space to eye movement. These cues are essentially affiliative, that is, they indicate relationships, they concern liking and approval, although they can also indicate disliking and disapproval. They interact as a system in powerful ways that influence our social relationships with one another.

Nonverbal signals as interaction regulators

Nonverbal communication serves another important function besides acting as an indicator of liking. The second function is to smooth out and 'regulate' social behaviour. Interactions have rules about who speaks when, for instance, and interactions do not run smoothly if one or both partners violate(s) the rule. Most people have a good understanding of these rules, but some do not. There is, nevertheless, a wide variation in people's skills at using such rules and almost everyone would have great difficulty in saying what the rules are even though we all use them familiarly. It is rather like riding a bicycle; we might know *how* to do it without understanding the logic, the physics, or the mathematics of our balancing movements. Can *you* state what the rules of social behaviour are? Yet such skilful regulation of social behaviour is essential to the conduct of interpersonal communication. The behaviours that enable it are termed 'social skills' and teaching of such behaviours is called 'social skills training'.

Interactions have to be started, sustained, and ended in appropriate ways, and this is usually managed by nonverbal means. Two nonverbal signals are generally used to start typical interactions: one is eye contact (or, in this case, 'catching someone's eye'); the other is orientation (i.e., we need to face the right way and have our body oriented openly towards the other person). It is inappropriate, rude, and extremely difficult to open up a conversation without looking at the person and having them look back. It is also hard to continue an interaction when one is wrongly oriented; for instance, try sitting back-to-back with a friend and have a cosy chat. Curiously, however, even when we do not look at or face the other person he or she can still hear what we say, so what we are considering here in these examples is a social rather than a physical constraint on interaction.

A person can refuse to engage in a conversation merely by refusing to establish eye contact or orientation. However, eye contact conjoins with many other cues to serve a regulatory function in interactions also (Argyle & Cook, 1976). Eye contact, gaze, looking, and eye movements are associated with 'floor-sharing' (i.e., turn-taking in conversation) and with power and dominance of interactions. Speakers look at listeners less than listeners look at speakers, but speakers start to signal that they have come to the end of their 'speech' by looking at the listener and establishing eye contact; this lets the listener 'take over the floor', if desired (Kendon, 1967). High power, on the other hand, is associated with high levels of looking at a listener whilst you are talking (Exline, 1971).

Our conversations are regulated also by other factors. Specifically, we alter our speech patterns and conversational turns as a result of the 'reinforcements' that we receive. Reinforcements are nonverbal cues that reinforce, encourage or lead us to an increase in whatever behaviours they positively reinforce or seemingly approve. Several forms of reinforcement for speaking are available (Argyle, 1967). Smiling, nodding, and gazing at other persons in an interaction, for instance, will induce them to continue talking. This can be generalized: the same nonverbal cues will encourage and reinforce quite subtle parts of behaviour. This can include the production of plural nouns, use of abstract concepts, or particular kinds of topic, each of which can be reinforced and increased by nonverbal encouragements from a listener.

Without such reinforcements, speakers will often stop, under the impression that the listener is bored or, perhaps, wants to intervene (Argyle, 1967). One way of 'taking the floor' (or getting a word in edgeways) is to stop being reinforcing and to signal one's disinterest. The speaker gets the message that says 'It's my turn now'.

Does nonverbal communication show how we really feel?

A final role of nonverbal communication is to convey attitudes (Argyle, 1969). These may be attitudes: about self (e.g., conceited, diffident, mousey, shy, humble); towards the other person (e.g., dominant, submissive, attracted, disliking, hostile, aggressive); or about the interaction (e.g., affability, comfortableness, relaxation, intimacy, nervousness).

Some findings in Functions of Gaze (Box 2.4) indicate that we tend to assume nervousness and anxiety just by detecting the presence or absence of certain particular nonverbal behaviours. Several studies find that such cues are the ones used by police and customs officers in detecting criminality or smuggling (Stiff & Miller, 1984). However, there are many reasons for nervousness apart from criminality (e.g., embarrassment, low self-esteem, shyness). Let us consider the issue of whether such nonverbal cues actually indicate anxiety, deceit, and the like, or whether people just continue to believe that they do. In a provocative paper, Stiff & Miller (1984) look at: the behaviours that people show when they lie; and, the behaviours that people use to determine when someone else is lying to them. They point out that in many studies of this issue, subjects are asked to pretend to lie whilst their behaviour is filmed, recorded, and rated. By and large, the studies show that such 'liars' are accurately detected by observers as a result of their nonverbal communication.

Other studies reviewed by Stiff & Miller look at the other side of the coin: what behaviours are associated with lying when it is real? The crucial behaviours that we use are response latency (i.e., the time the person takes before starting to answer a question) and speech errors (i.e., interruptions to the flow of speech). Facial expressions are generally less useful for detecting deception, but they do indicate nervousness. (Remember that in the studies mentioned, the subjects were *pretending* to lie, so had no real reason to feel nervous — unlike

BOX 2.4 Functions of gaze, eye movements, and nonverbal communication

Mutual gaze (when two people gaze or stare at one another) is used as a signal that two persons wish to 'engage' or start a social encounter (Kendon & Ferber, 1973). It is also used — at the correct distance — during the 'salutation' or greeting phase at the start of an encounter. Sometimes, if people see each other from too far away, they will move toward one another but will look away until they are closer, when they will start mutual gaze again.

Speakers begin long glances at the listener just before the end of an utterance (Kendon, 1967). This seems to signal the end of the utterance so that the listener has a chance to contribute and take over, if desired.

Eye contact relates to 'floor-sharing' and the patterning of speech in an encounter (Cappella, 1984); but staring at someone else too much will cause him or her to make more frequent speech errors (Beattie, 1981).

Gaze and eye contact are reduced when a person is embarrassed or when a partner makes unsuitable self-disclosures to the other (Edelmann & Hampson, 1979).

Gaze and eye contact also serve to indicate:

warmth, interest, and involvement in the interaction (Argyle, 1983)

liking for one's conversation partner (Exline & Winters, 1965; Rubin, 1973)

dominance of the other person in the interaction (Exline, 1971) threat (Exline & Yellin, 1969) — even when this is done by an experimenter to a monkey. The monkey becomes quite violent.

Libet & Lewinsohn (1973); Trower et al. (1978), and Argyle (1983) show that clinical populations (depressives and schizophrenics, especially) have disturbed or abnormal patterns of eye movement (see BOX 2.5).

someone attempting to smuggle dope through the customs).
Apparently, deceptive behaviour may use cues different from those we use to judge whether someone is lying.

> Cues which are stereotyped as deceptive behaviours are not necessarily related to deceptive communication. That is, observers tend to rely heavily on visual and vocal cues which are relatively unrelated to deceptive behaviour [Stiff & Miller, 1984].

In a pair of studies where people were filmed telling real lies (i.e., concealing the fact that they had cheated on a test to earn $50), judges relied heavily on the stereotypic vocal and visual cues, but these are not actually related to deception (Stiff & Miller, 1984). Evidently, we tend (foolishly) to interpret any unsystematic, awkward, or nonfluent behaviours as indicating deception, and we sometimes remark on a person's 'smooth-ness' and fluency as a sign of their plausibility.

One feature of real lying is that it involves some concentration ('cognitive load'). We do not merely have to say Yes or No to some experimental question that we care nothing about: we are involved, so we experience emotional stress. We also realize that if we are talking to someone we know, then they may know us well enough to know what behaviours of ours give us away — so we pay close attention to our behaviour and try hard to control anything that might 'give us away', or 'leak' our true meaning or feelings or the true state of affairs. The whole experience is therefore arousing for us. In a clever study looking at these factors, Greene et al. (1985) had subjects lie (about where they had been on holiday) to a confederate of the experi-menter. That was the easy part; many people can lie that they have been to Puerto Rico, as some of the subjects were asked to do. It's particularly easy if you have been told some time in advance that the question will be asked and what you should say. The difficult part — which the subjects were not actually expecting — was what to do when the confederate became interested in the trip and asked all sorts of details about it. What Greene et al. (1985) found when they used this approach was that subjects can control leakage of the fact that they are lying up until the point when they suddenly have to think hard and carefully about what they are saying.

I think that these sorts of results are interesting in themselves, but let us apply them directly to relationships. They are relevant, for instance, to the ways which partners in relationships conduct 'secret tests' of the state of the relationship (Baxter & Wilmot, 1984). Bear in mind that we misjudge other people's 'deceptiveness' whilst I discuss these results.

Baxter & Wilmot argue that partners are often uncertain about the strength of their relationship yet are reluctant to talk about 'the state of the relationship'; they regard it as a taboo topic. Our usual solution is to apply direct and indirect tests — secret tests — as means of discovering how things stand. Such methods involve, for instance, *asking third parties* whether your partner has ever talked about the relationship to them or use *trial intimacy moves* to see what reactions you get as an indication of intimacy. Obviously, this can take the form of increased physical or emotional intimacy, but it can be more subtle. For example, partners often use 'public presentation': inviting the partner to visit parents or friends or talking about their intention to have children some day. The questions in each case are: how does my partner react, and does he or she accept the increased intimacy or the open commitment? Other methods described by Baxter & Wilmot (1984) are the *self-putdown* (when you hope the partner will respond to a self-deprecating statement with a supportive, intimate statement) and the *jealousy test* (when you describe a potential competitor and hope to observe a possessive, committed response by your partner).

Obviously, such ploys are a useful test of partner commitment only if you can genuinely assess your partner's responses and when you make the tests you will be carefully reading all the nonverbal signs described thus far. Nonverbal communication can be relevant to the testing of relationships (and hence to their future) as well as to their conduct and regulation. Consider, however, these are *precisely* the signs that Stiff & Miller's study of deception points out we do not read very intelligently in reality.

Skilful use of nonverbal cues

Nonverbal communication is relevant to relationships in another way also. In chapter 1, I discuss embarrassment and loneliness, whereas in the preceding sections of this chapter, I examine deception, anxiety, and nonverbal behaviour, generally, and draw attention to some nonverbal behaviours that make people hard partners to enjoy (e.g., those of lonely or of shy persons). Shy or lonely people are sometimes lonely because they are difficult to deal with: they are nervous, embarrassed, shy or socially incompetent. Lonely people may possess poor social skills not only of the type discussed in chapter 1 (i.e., inability to stay on the conversational topic or to respond with appropriate verbal reactions to a partner's comments) but also in the present sense: poorly adapted eye movement, smiles, gestures, nods, and the like.

Such poor quality of social skills could take two forms: poor encoding or poor decoding. *Encoding* refers to the ability to put our feelings into practice, to 'do what we mean', if you like (e.g., to act assertively if we want to assert, to look friendly if we feel friendly). Conversely, *decoding* refers to the ability to work out what other people mean, by observing their nonverbal communication and correctly working out their intent. Some people are inept at this; sometimes, you read in the papers that a fight began in a bar because someone was staring provocatively at someone else. Maybe, one was staring (poor encoding) or maybe the other just thought he or she was (poor decoding) or maybe drink caused their social psychological judgements to decline in accuracy.

People with poor social skills

Many people have poor social skills, and this, in particular, is true of depressives and schizophrenics (Argyle, 1983). Such skills deficits not only are symptoms of their problems but may be partial causes (or, perhaps, may exacerbate and increase their problems).

The list of people who show social skills deficits is lengthy. At the extreme end, patients with schizophrenia are very poor at decoding nonverbal signals (Williams, 1974), as are some violent prisoners (Howells, 1981); depressed patients also show similar deficits (Libet & Lewinsohn, 1973). In less extreme ways, the same has been found to be true of alcoholics (before they became alcoholics — afterwards they are even harder to relate to, of course; Orford & O'Reilly, 1981) and children who are unpopular at school (Furman, 1984). By contrast, those who are successful in their careers are better at social skills than those who are failures (Argyle, 1983), and physicians can improve their success in healing patients by improving their social skills (Hays & DiMatteo, 1984). Nonverbal communication cannot be underestimated in importance. Although it usually occurs in the context of verbal behaviour also (see following sections), it has been found (Argyle et al., 1970) that nonverbal cues exert 4.3 times more effect than does verbal behaviour on the impressions formed of a speaker.

For these reasons, correction of social skill problems is often attempted in training programmes. Such social skills training brings about improved social functioning in relationships and also improves the person's feelings about himself or herself, as BOX 2.5 shows.

Speaking Up for Yourself: Using Words

It ain't what you say . . .

The ways in which we use words are just as important as the words themselves. If I shout Fire, then it means more than just 'I can see pretty dancing flames': it means there is an emergency. The structure, use, and form of language carry messages over and above the content or meaning of the actual words that are spoken.

How do people use language and how does it convey extra messages about speakers? We want to know: how accent, speed, volume, error rate, tone of voice, and 'speech style'

BOX 2.5 Social skills training

Some examples of successful social skills training of nonverbal behaviour are:

General 'pepping up' of depressives' responsivity in social encounters is shown in several mental health contexts to contribute to patient recovery and improvement (Trower et al., 1978).

Lonely and shy people can be trained to adopt new styles of social behaviour that enhance the skill of their performance (Jones et al., 1984). Such training can also be directed at conversational turn-taking or topic management.

Nonassertive persons benefit from training related to posture as well as to other behaviours more obviously related to request-making (Wilkinson & Canter, 1982).

Social skills training can be used to train managers to take the chair at meetings, deal with disruptive employees, and sell products (Rackham & Morgan, 1977).

Curran (1977) successfully trained young people to make dates with members of the opposite sex by use of social skills training and related techniques.

---

affect the impact of messages; how power is indicated by a communication's overtones; how to structure messages to maximize their persuasiveness; and the like. Language style conveys more information than is merely contained in the sentence: different actors can give different meanings to the same passage of Shakespeare just by speaking it differently.

An easily observed element of speech is accent. Does this affect evaluation of a speaker? A speaker's accent is evaluated separately from the content of the speech and is probably a more significant influence on the reception of the message (Giles & Powesland, 1975). Accent can be *more* important than either looks or work competence. Seligman et al. (1972) asked student teachers to form impressions of each of eight fictitious

schoolboys on the basis of:
  a photograph (which was attractive or unattractive)
  a tape-recorded speech sample (with a 'good' or 'bad' accent.)
  a sample of the boy's work (either good or bad)

They matched up attractive photos with attractive speech and good work, with unattractive speech and good work, and so on, in all eight possible ways (2 attractiveness × 2 speech × 2 work levels). Using this design, Seligman et al. could work out the relative contribution of accent, looks, and work to the final evaluation of the boys. Boys with good accents were always evaluated more favourably than those with poor ones. As part of this, the well-spoken boys were rated as more intelligent, more privileged, better students, more enthusiastic pupils, more self-confident, and more gentle.

We might expect such general effects to 'wash out' in the long-term relationships of the classroom in real life. The results, nonetheless, indicate that general favourability towards an accent will lead to general favourability towards the person speaking it, at least, in the stage of first impressions. Cheyne (1970) had previously found that Scots and English raters both rated a speaker with an English accent as more self-confident, intelligent, ambitious, wealthy and prestigious, good looking, and clean. Scots accents were rated by Scots listeners as indicating that the speaker was friendlier, with a better sense of humour, generous, and likeable.

Other parts of speech

Accent is not the only noncontent aspect of speech to which we pay attention in social encounters. We already know that the rate of flow of speech, irrespective of its content, is used as a guide to someone's competence, truthfulness, and honesty. Interruptions and speech errors are taken as signs of deception, anxiety, or shyness. Those who talk fast are usually regarded as competent, well-informed, confident, and dominant, unless they hog the 'floor' all the time, in which case they soon become boring (Argyle, 1983).

Amount of speech

A measure of leadership in small group discussions is the amount of speech: the more often someone 'holds the floor' the more will observers assume that the person was leading the group's activities (Stang, 1973). In Stang's study, subjects listened to tape-recorded group discussions which had been arranged so that one person spoke 50 percent of the time, another person 33 percent of the time, and a third spoke only 17 percent of the time. The most talkative person was seen as the leader, irrespective of what he or she said, and the second most frequent contributor was rated the most popular. I find this study sad, in that, if three physicists in 1900 had sat down to discuss physics and one spoke for only 17 percent of the time saying only $E=MC^2$, no-one would have liked him or followed his lead.

Fluency is taken as a measure or indication of mastery, competence, and truthfulness. From a person's verbal fluency, we deduce information about the kind of person that he or she is. The other side to this belief — which actually follows logically — is the assumption that persons' views of themselves, or the kind of person they (think they) are, actually does affect their fluency. Thus, someone who is competent has to speak fluently or our whole logical deductive system about their behaviour will be amiss. So what about the opposite case, those who are habitually nonfluent? Are we correct to deduce that they see themselves as incompetent, worthless, and of low value? There are people in the world who habitually stammer, just as we all from time to time get thrown off our stride by stress. A large amount of work now relates habitual stammering to identity problems (see Box 2.6).

Rules about speech

How does language change as a result of the situation in which the conversation takes place, and what are the influences of language and 'speech style' on social evaluation or on the impressions observers form? Whilst a linguist would be interested

BOX 2.6 Speech fluency and dysfluency

Several pieces of work indicate that fluency of speech is taken as a sign that the speaker is competent whilst dysfluency is taken to show anxiety and tension (Cook, 1971).

Many habitual stutterers have the notion of their being stutterers as a core part of their model of themselves (Fransella, 1968; 1972). To stop the stuttering we must help them to reconstrue themselves and see themselves differently so that they exclude stuttering from their self-concept. How do stutterers' views of themselves, of speech fluency, and of stuttering all change as the stuttering becomes less obtrusive during treatment? They come to look upon themselves in a new way, and more importantly, see fluency as something associated with their concept of themselves (Fransella, 1972).

As an interesting example of this, I have a friend who stutters except on subjects where his self-concept is stronger, namely, his expertise as an orthopaedic surgeon. When describing any medical matter, he ceases to stutter.

in the grammatical rules in a given society (the langue), a social psychologist or sociolinguist is concerned with the ways in which people use language (the parole). Social uses of language do not always follow the strict rules of grammar (e.g., on the radio this morning I heard an interviewee say 'I reckon there's lots of dockers as thinks the same like what I does' — and yet everyone knows what he meant by this).

Language is 'situated' in various ways according to the goals of the interactants. As their goals change, so does their speech (Fraser & Scherer, 1982; Scherer & Giles, 1979). For instance, in a social setting, conversation is frequent and almost any topic of conversation is permissible in a chat with close friends. By contrast, when concentration is required, it seems perfectly natural that people converse less and speech acts will decline or, at least, that speech will be task-oriented. Similarly, university lectures are supposed to contain information about the course, and professors may not normally show holiday slides and talk about their vacation.

Just as in nonverbal communication, a most significant aspect of verbal communication is an appreciation of the social rules that apply. Actors in a conversation must recognize when it is appropriate to raise particular topics and when it is not. They must know when to match their speech acts to the rules, since evaluation of their competence depends upon it. Someone who treats 'Would you pass the salt?' as a question requiring a verbal answer is acting as inappropriately as someone who treats the grammatically identical 'Would you lend me your car?' as if it were *not* a question.

Language is used differently as a result of the goals of the actors. In task-oriented discussions, people are happy with a formal language system containing technical jargon-based forms. By contrast, a conversation between friends is usually not task-oriented but socioemotionally oriented. Because it is focussed on feelings, 'atmosphere', and informality, a different speech style is appropriate — one where grammatical rules are broken and where the transfer of information is less significant than is the aim of keeping people happy and relaxed.

Most cultures have two forms of language code available, a so-called *high form* and a *low form*. The high form is formal, planned, careful, precise, complex, full of jargon, and a little pompous. It appears in educational settings, religion, court-rooms, and on official notices (Argyle et al., 1981). For instance, 'I was proceeding in a northeasterly direction towards my domestic establishment' and 'Kindly extinguish all illumination prior to vacating the premises'. The low form is informal, unplanned, casual, direct and simple. It is the more familiar form of everyday speech. For example, 'I was going home' and 'You guys switch off the lights when you go'.

The two forms are used in different settings in appropriate ways. However, there are occasions when this causes difficulties and we deliberately break the rules to convey a social message, like a joke or a distancing from someone. One example where problems are caused by the existence of the two codes is in the courtroom. Many witnesses either do not understand the formal language used in court and so make themselves look stupid by having to have it explained in low code form or try to adopt the high code but get it wrong. An example of the conveyance of social messages through use of codes is use of a high form in a casual setting to deflate someone. For instance, when a close friend abruptly addresses you as Ms or Mr and starts to use formal language. A calculated misjudgement of the circumstances conveys a *social message* over and above the grammatical content. When the message form or structure is made inappropriate to the form or structure of the encounter (e.g., informal language in a formal setting) the social result is negative (e.g., a judge called by his or her first name by a witness would probably fine the witness for contempt of court).

One other message is conveyed by differences in use of high and low forms of code, and that is power. Powerful and knowledgeable persons use jargon-based high code, while the rest use low code translations. One reason why do-it-yourself auto repairers are usually 'one down' in going to buy spare parts is because they do not know the proper terminology. Asking for 'one of those round things with the bent bit at one end' is a betrayal of low status in such situations. Use of technical terms is a way of claiming status, particularly if it is done deliberately to someone who does not know the terminology. Car mechanics could perfectly well talk about 'round things with the bent bit at one end', but they do not. Psychologists could write about chatting and conversation, but instead they write about 'socially situated speech acts' and 'interacts'.

We have to admit that many of us have used this power ploy. Think back to your first days as a student; can you recall using university abbreviations like GPA, JCR and technical language about courses? A frequent way to put first year students one down is to give them directions in language that is current in the university but not well-understood outside (e.g., 'Go right past the Rec Centre through Fylde res block, cross over SE3 driveway and turn into Challis. The Grease Pit is then on your left and Nightline offices are opposite you over the URB centre. Don't forget your FNU form, by the way'). They *have* to ask you what at least one bit of it means and you are instantly 'one up'.

More about content

The content of speech carries two important social messages, one of which is *power* and the other is *relationship* between speaker and listener. Brown (1965) refers to these dimensions as *status* and *solidarity*. These two dimensions are very similar to two 'messages' conveyed by nonverbal cues also: dominance and liking.

Status

Language conveys different power relations in encounters among persons, differences in power over objects (i.e., ownership), and differences in control of the interaction itself. Relative status of participants in an encounter is an ever-present and powerful dimension of the encounter. One immediate way in which persons reveal relative status and power is by their title, another is by the form of address used to them. Someone greeted as 'The Most Magnificent Eminence, Child of the Sun God, Father and Mother of the Earth, Bringer of Harvests and Lord of the Seas' will obviously not be given the chipped cup to drink from, whereas 'scumbag' may not be given a cup at all.

Yet what is the difference between a Lavatory Attendant and a Comfort Station Hygiene Executive or between a 'terrorist' and a 'freedom fighter'? The terms and titles are not neutral, and as airlines and car manufacturers are aware, titles such as Ambassador, Consul, Executive, and Monarch can be used to attract people to buy status — instead of just buying second-class air tickets or low-range cars. The titles carry social messages and emotional or social meaning. To travel Ambassador Class presumably feels different from merely travelling 'at the front of the plane'.

Particularly important nowadays is the distinction between 'everyone should take his seat' and 'everyone should take his or her seat'. Just as with previously widely used words like 'Negro'

BOX 2.7 Julius Caesar's use of language

The Romans had several styles of address. When talking to the mass of private citizens in the forum, orators would address them as Quirites; *when talking only to senators in the Senate one called them* Patres conscripti; *serving soldiers in the field were hailed* Milites. *Once when Caesar's legionnaires mutinied, he began his speech to them with* Quirites *rather than with* Milites, *thus implying that they were not acting like trained soldiers but like a crowd of private citizens in Rome. Caesar's own account of this event is that this single word was enough to shame the troops and stop the mutiny.*

---

or 'queer', the titles and assumptions built into the use of the word 'his' on its own have now become offensive to us. Hyde (1984) shows that the use of the pronoun 'he' or 'his' on its own to cover both sexes, rather than the gender-neutral 'he or she' or 'his or her', significantly influences a whole range of people, from first graders to college students, to think of male persons *exclusively*. Gender-related pronouns also affected the concepts that children formed of a fictitious occupation ('wudgemaker') and particularly the use of the pronoun 'his' dramatically reduced their perception of a woman's competence to do the job.

Relationships between speaker and listener

In some languages (e.g., French, German, Spanish), intimate friends and relatives are addressed with one pronoun (e.g., *tu, du*) and a different one is used for people whom one does not know or whom one treats with respect and deference (*vous, sie, usted*). Thus the French say *tu* (you) when talking to friends but use *vous* (you) for talking to strangers or parents-in-law. The single word tells everyone about the speaker's familiarity with the other person and gives a clue as to the closeness or distance of relationship between speaker and listener.

In seventeenth and eighteenth-century England, many Quakers were abused for calling everyone thou, which, as in present-day French (*tu*) or German (*du*), had previously been reserved for use only to close intimates, family, and 'inferiors' like servants and children. Brown (1965) notes that a status norm has evolved in countries which persist in using the two forms of address (*tu* and *vous* in French, *du* and *sie* in German, e.g.). The so-called V form (*vous*, *sie*, which are actually plural but may be used to a singular person also) is used to address a person superior to oneself in status. The so-called T form (*tu*, *du*) is reserved for those of status lower than oneself. Persons who are of equal status both use the T form to each other if they are close, but the V form if they are not.

The form of address carries a message about the power relationship between the speakers. The message can be a personal one ('I am superior to you'), a solidarity one ('We are both equals'), or a political one ('All persons are equal; there is no hierarchical structure in society'). During the French Revolution, the peasant revolutionaries purposely addressed the aristocrats as *tu* to reinforce by language the social and political changes that had taken place.

We may like to believe that such linguistic messages are a thing of the past, but they still survive. We still use respectful forms and informal ones. Do you call your professor Professor Surname, or Sally? What do her colleagues call her? Do you call your father by a title (dad, father, pop) or by his first name? What does he call you? In some cases, a fictitious first name is used when one person does not know the proper name, but does not want to accept a lower status by using a general polite form, like sir or madam. Thus, New York taxi drivers call passengers Mac, and Glaswegians call people Jimmy, and — unfortunately for me — many people in northern England call everyone duck.

These points and observations may seem quaint and unreal until you actually try to break the rules. Try calling some of your professors by their first names without permission and see what reaction you get. More interestingly, see how it feels to you personally. If you *really* want an experience then try calling them Mac.

Speech style and power

Speech style can be classified as powerful or powerless according to its general structure (Lakoff, 1973; 1975). Powerless speech uses a high proportion of: *intensifiers* (very, extremely, so very, really); *empty adjectives and adverbs* (wonderful, incredibly, amazingly); *deferential forms* (would you please? may I?); *tag questions* (isn't it? don't you? *n'est ce pas*?); *hedges or lack of commitment* (I suppose, I guess, maybe); *hypercorrect grammar*; *gestures with speech* (suggesting lack of emphasis in the speech itself); *intonational patterns* that seem to 'fuss' and 'whine'; *lack of perseverance* during interruptions and *acquiescence* in simultaneous speech. Note that since many of these forms are 'polite' in our culture, polite speech can seem powerless.

BOX 2.8 Language, titles, status

Staples & Robinson (1974) study the forms of address used by members of a department store to one another in different situations. Title and last name (e.g., Mr Smith) are used in formal situations; for example, in front of customers or when referring to the person to a large group. First-name forms are used in informal settings.

High status persons tend to try to maximize status differences whilst low status persons attempt to minimize them.

Argyle (1983) notes that customs vary across cultures. Americans and Australians move from title and last name to first-name forms much sooner than do the British.

Is women's speech generally powerless? Lakoff claims that women's language contains more intensifiers, qualifiers/hedges, and tag questions than does men's speech. This, Lakoff argues, leads to women's speech being seen as less powerful than the speech style typically produced by men. Use of the above forms of speech by either men or women was assumed to be less powerful, and court witnesses who used it were seen as less trustworthy, less competent, and less convincing (Erickson et al., 1978). Several pieces of evidence confirm that men actually talk more than women (e.g., Argyle et al., 1968), although this may indicate that men take the floor and do not concede when interrupted by women. Women are more likely than men to be interrupted, and those who interrupt them are more likely to be men than women (McMillan et al., 1977).

Using language to relate to other people

One most intriguing aspect of language is the way in which it can be used to indicate the relationship between the speaker and the listener. We have already learned that power and solidarity can be conveyed by such a simple cue as the choice of pronoun style used to address persons (whether the T or the V form). There are other ways in which the immediacy of language can indicate closeness, intimacy, or acceptance (Mehrabian, 1971). Immediacy refers to the amount of positive feeling or inclusion of the other person in the message and to the amount of distance implied in the message. Consider the differences in 'Ms Jones and I have just been for a walk', 'We two have just been for a walk', and 'Jonesey and I have just been for a walk'. What about 'X is my neighbour' and 'X and I live in the same neighbourhood'? And, what of 'I hope your career is successful' as distinct from 'I hope you are successful'? These different phrasings of the same message convey different degrees of interest and involvement.

Such messages also help to create and hold together our relationships with other people. We are all sensitive to the different relational messages conveyed by our forms of speech, and we change them as relationships develop. Processes of growth in a relationship are managed through communication; we can indicate to a partner and to the world at large that we have grown closer simply by subtly changing the way in which we address the person. To become noticeably more immediate is to become noticeably more intimate; to start talking of 'us' is to claim that a relationship exists or is coming into existence; to encourage greater intimacy in language is to instigate greater intimacy in relationship (Morton et al., 1976). It can be a condemnation of a relationship to complain about the language used in it and vice versa. 'We don't communicate any more' is just such a statement.

Equally, partners develop private languages and personal idioms to personalize their relationship (Hopper et al., 1981). For instance, for some partners the single word 'jellybeans' may come to mean 'You're talking over my head and I don't understand' (Berger & Bradac, 1982). In short, language conveys degrees of intimacy, is a powerful developer and definer of relationships, and is used to indicate many privacies in relationships. It conveys messages by its structure as well as by its content, but it does not do it on its own in the course of normal everyday interactions. It is a part of a system that works together. We can be both verbally immediate and nonverbally intimate, for instance, and this could be important in indicating relational intimacy — it could be problematic if the two 'channels' (verbal and nonverbal) do not match up.

Children's use of language

When children are younger than three or four, do they show any awareness of the differences implicit in the different communicative strategies? We have to learn how to convey relational messages and to learn their significance as an extra component to *social* language. So how do children develop them? Children's communications about conflict and compliance-gaining become more complex with age (Haslett, 1983a). In particular, they reflect increasing awareness of an opponent's need for information and their growing understanding of the needs for communication during conflict. At the age of two, the child's conflicts are brief episodes settled by physical force and vocal signals that are not recognizable as words. By the age of five, however, children address conflict through talk and sustained discourse that pays close attention to the triggering event and goes into side issues that also rise. In short, their talk focusses on the causes of the conflict and discussion of its wider context.

Preschoolers show a more general development of communicative strategies also. Communicative functions and strategies in children's conversations change in styles as the children grow up (Haslett, 1983b). At the age of three, children's language and communicative strategies are mostly aimed at the verbal mastery of information about the environment (e.g., 'That's a doggie' — labelling; 'It's a big doggie' — elaboration of detail). However, there is also some expression of needs and ideas (relational function) when the child egocentrically emphasizes self ('I'm hungry', 'I got here first', 'Leave my doll alone'). At the age of three, children show little tendency to talk about monitoring of their own actions or to project to situations not presently being experienced (e.g., they do not say 'Shall we go swimming?' 'When Daddy comes back we are going to have a party'). The three-year-olds seem to be extending control over their environment by verbal means whilst maintaining their egocentric needs.

At age four, by contrast, their communications take in a projective or imaginative function. This involves the predictive, empathizing, and imaginative uses of language and is a more developed form of structure to communication and thinking. They are able to talk about the future, to look forward to events not presently being experienced, to appreciate other people's viewpoints more effectively, and to engage in less egocentric talk. They can also use language more successfully to play 'let's pretend'. Such evidence of projective function continues to develop in five-year-old children also.

This and the other evidence teaches us that the structure of language has important communicative elements, over and above the content alone, and that we adapt our styles of language even as we mature in early childhood. In a later chapter, we shall look at childhood unpopularity and consider whether it is likely that communicative strategies might play a role in this. Could children become unpopular because they fail to adapt their communicative strategies in a way that helps them to integrate into the wonderful world of play with other children?

Switching: the messages of change

An understanding of the role of language style in social relationships leads to our questioning the social functions of 'switching' between styles. What social messages are conveyed by a sudden switch in immediacy or a switch from high to low or from low to high forms of speech? Low form is typically associated with informal, friendly settings whilst a high form goes with formality and emotional distance. A switch from low to high is a distancing strategy that shows disapproval, aloofness, dislike, and hostility. By contrast, a high-low switch is an affiliative strategy that indicates liking, approval, and a desire to be less formal and more friendly.

In an influential theory relating speech to social behaviour, Giles (1977; Giles & Powesland, 1975) argues that we 'accommodate' our language (whether language style, speech style, accent, code, or content) to our interaction partner if we feel attracted. We play down the distinctiveness of our own individual style of speaking and accommodate, or move towards, that of the other person ('convergence'). For instance, parents frequently accommodate the style of their language and talk 'baby talk' to young children whilst adults adopt the code form preferred by one actor in a given setting (e.g., they talk formally to their boss).

On the other hand, when we wish to distinguish ourselves from some other person or group, we accentuate differences in our speech style ('divergence'). For instance, French Canadians prefer their politicians to make public speeches in English with a thick French accent, even if they are capable of speaking perfect English (Bourhis & Giles, 1977). Accommodation is a powerful indicator of group identification (Giles, 1977). The best example is from 1973 when Arab oil producers suddenly switched from issuing their decisions about oil prices in English to doing so in Arabic. That was a powerful message to the world indicating who now had the upper hand and who now had to accommodate to whom.

BOX 2.9 Accommodation in speech

Speakers often adapt their speech to be more similar to that of the partner, particularly when they wish to relax that person or to ingratiate themselves (Giles et al., 1973).

Such 'convergence' occurs at various linguistic levels, involving speech rate, silences, different languages, regional accents, or vocal intensity and loudness (Giles & Powesland, 1975).

In bilingual Canada, there is a norm that a bilingual salesperson is supposed to converge towards the language chosen by the customer (Scotton & Udry, 1977).

The higher prestige language is usually adopted in a bilingual community as long as partners like one another (Giles, 1978).

Divergence is equally powerful (Bourhis & Giles, 1977). When speakers dislike their partner or the ethnic group from which he or she comes, they will adopt extremely different speech styles, occasionally even refusing to speak in the partner's adopted language (e.g., persisting in speaking Welsh to disliked English weekend-holidaymakers in Wales).

Putting Verbal and Nonverbal Together

So far, I have been looking at the components of communication separately as linguistic and nonverbal forms; obviously, they occur together most of the time. They can be consistent with each other or can contradict and cut across each other. I can say nice things and smile — or I can say nice things but frown. How do other people interpret inconsistencies?

Facial messages are the most powerful components of such contradictions (Zaidel & Mehrabian, 1969). They are seen as conveying the real messages and as giving the true evaluation of the person. Words, on the other hand, are assumed to relate to the person's acts or deeds. That is, we tend to assume that the facial expression indicates the speaker's evaluation of the person as a person, while the words evaluate the person's behaviour. 'Well done' said with a scowl, for instance, indicates grudging praise for someone who is disliked. Young children have particular difficulty with such inconsistent messages and tend to treat all such messages as if they were negative, whichever channel conveyed the negativity (Bugental et al., 1970).

Verbal and nonverbal flows can be disrupted together, and, as we saw in looking at deception earlier, nonverbal 'panic' plus

---

BOX 2.10 Some research findings about nonverbal cues and verbal behaviour

Argyle et al. (1970) presented subjects with a videotape of someone speaking a superior/inferior/neutral message in a superior/inferior/neutral nonverbal style. Their findings showed that nonverbal cues had 4.3 times the effect of verbal cues in influencing the ratings made by observers.

If the friendliness/hostility of messages in verbal and nonverbal channels is varied then similar results emerge (Argyle et al., 1972). Interestingly, however, inconsistency between channels when friendliness/hostility was the variable was interpreted as insincerity or instability. Inconsistent messages about friendliness create particularly damaging assessments of the message sender. It is essential, therefore, to convey consistent messages about friendliness towards someone else.

verbal disruption is our best indicator of stress. This, however, has been found in studies of deception that have taken the form almost entirely of studying lying. There are many other forms of 'deception' that occur in social life, some of which help to smooth it all along (Hopper & Bell, 1984). For example, teasing, joking, put-ons, hypocrisy, 'bull-shitting', exaggerations, pretences, poses, embellishments of stories, concealments, half-truths, and innuendo are not really lies as such. We also use ambiguity (rather than lying) pretty effectively to assist social encounters. For example, sometimes we do not tell partners when we do not like their new clothes, because to do so would not help our relationship or their self-esteem. Occasionally, we use truth to deceive, or we allow people to draw their own incorrect conclusions which we do not put right. Also, we sometimes implicitly negotiate deception with partners (Knapp & Comadena, 1979). For instance, we may plot with them to deceive other people or to conceal birthday surprises or the like. Hopper & Bell (1984) point out that most lying is verbal, but much deception is nonverbal (e.g., acting busy to deter others from asking for favours or smiling at people we do not really like).

In real life we do not always seek out deception (unless we are investigative journalists or paranoids) but we recognize that it can occur. The relationship between deception and its detection in real life, however, can be problematic. Deception does not always create interpersonal problems; sometimes it helps surprises to be enjoyed or facilitates the kind of teasing that indicates liking for a person.

So how do people typically understand the word 'deception'? Hopper & Bell (1984) gathered words related to deception, by use of dictionaries and thesauri and the like. They had subjects sort the resultant collections of words and then rate them on various dimensions (e.g., good/bad; socially acceptable/socially unacceptable; easy to detect/hard to detect). Results showed that we have three major dimensions for evaluating deception: an *evaluative* dimension (right/wrong); a *detectability* dimension (hard/easy; overt/covert); and a *premeditative* dimension (planned/unplanned; examples here are forgery, cover-ups and

spying versus white lies, exaggerations and self-deceptions).
Results also showed that six categories of deception are evident
to people.

1 Fictions (exaggeration, myth, irony, tall tales, white lies,
make believe)

2 Playings (jokes, teases, kiddings, tricks, bluffs, hoaxes)

3 Lies (dishonesty, fibs, untruths)

4 Crimes (conning, disguises, cover-ups, forgeries)

5 Masks (hypocrisy, two-facedness, back-stabbing, conceal-
ment)

6 Unlies (misleading, distortion, misrepresentation, false
implication).

Thus, we can see that deception is not carried out entirely by
verbal means, although we tend to act as if that is the 'correct'
channel to use for its detection. Neither is deception necessarily
all bad, at least from the point of view of regularity and
sustaining social relationships and social encounters.

The evidence shows the importance of nonverbal cues in
social behaviour and the extreme subtlety of some influences
upon impressions and social judgements. We know that impression management can depend upon our nonverbal performance, and we have learned that judgments of ingratiation,
liking, intention and sincerity can depend on the way we move
our eyes or distribute our limbs.

Both ordinary language and the silent language of nonverbal
cues convey messages about liking, strength of feelings towards
someone, trust, liking, status differences, and power. Most of
these are relational messages, so in chapter 3 we shall look at
relationships, their growth, decline, and repair.

Summary

Language and nonverbal communication both convey implicit
as well as explicit messages about power, control, liking. Every
time we speak to someone we can convey messages about how
much we like them and what we think is our relationship to
them — not just by explicitly saying so in the content of our talk
but also by the style of the language that we use and the accom-

panying nonverbal communications that we make. Identity management is achieved by both verbal and nonverbal means, and the form of speech is as important as are the minute movements of face, eyes, and body that make up the whole nonverbal system. In chapter 6, we shall see that there are some extremely powerful applications of such work in medicine.

Further reading

Argyle, M. (1983) *The Psychology of Interpersonal Behaviour (4th edn)*. Penguin Books: Harmondsworth, UK.
Duck, S.W. (1983) *Friends, For Life*. Harvester: Brighton, UK.
Giles, H. & Powesland, P.F. (1975) *Speech Style and Social Evaluation*. Academic Press: London.

CHAPTER 3

Interaction and Daily Life in Long-term Relationships

When we are asked what matters to us most in life and gives it its fullest purpose, the majority of people give one simple answer: relationships (Klinger, 1977). Relationships are obvious sources of joy and happiness — we like being with friends, we enjoy the company of others, being in love is wonderful. On the other hand, they can be hell when they go wrong and cause pain.

Relationships with other people are obviously important in childhood and may even be the bases for self-esteem, for ability to relate to others, and for deviant personality (Duck, 1983; Duck & Perlman, 1985). They are also implicated in the effec-

---

BOX 3.1 Points to think about

— *Why do we like some people and not others?*
— *Are dating agencies right to try to fix up partners who 'match' on attitudes and personality?*
— *How do relationships start? How do they develop and what promotes their growth?*
— *We like some people enough to try to start up a friendship with them but why does it not always work?*
— *How should people get out of painful or unsatisfactory relationships?*
— *What are the best ways to put things right for people who want to repair their relationships?*

tiveness of physicians (patients recover faster in the hands of friendly and liked physicians, Hays & DiMatteo, 1984), in the quicker recovery of patients who have lots of friends (Reis, 1984), in successful careers at work (Mangham, 1981), and in general as protection from the pains, stresses, and hassles of life (Cobb & Jones, 1984). The relationship between teacher and pupil affects the rate of learning (Menges, 1969); medical knowledge is transmitted as much by personal relationships between doctors as it is by advertisers' mailings (Menzel & Katz, 1957) and the fashionability of scientific ideas is influenced as much by the relationships of scientists as by the merit or originality of the ideas themselves (Innes, 1980).

However, there is a negative side to relationships. They may cause criminality, violence and aggression, neurosis and depression, illness, shyness, drug and alcohol abuse problems, marital difficulties, divorce, child abuse and 'granny battering' (see various chapters in Duck, 1982b; 1984b; Duck & Gilmour, 1981a; b; c).

The study of first impressions makes theoretical sense as our starting point. In everyday life we are enormously influenced by first impressions. Job applications, interviews, and the whole course of a relationship can be set by the first few moments. In everyday life, we make many snap judgements about people and form instant likes and dislikes. We all know that we create 'irrational' first impressions, sudden lusts and likings, and intense hatreds for strangers. We can like the manner of a person we do not know and can form instant dislikes of someone who has not even uttered a word to us. So the study of initial responses to strangers makes sense as a starting point for understanding personal relationships; it is the point when relationships most often start or fail to start. We may decide (not) to date someone whose appearance does (not) appeal to us, and so we may (fail to) embark on a relationship that could change our lives.

Aside from appearance, *what* makes us attracted (and attractive) to other people? 'We have similar attitudes and personalities'. That is a reasonable thought. How does it stand up to investigation?

BOX 3.2 Exercise on relationships

— *Think for a moment about the people with whom you are particularly friendly. What do you like about them and how did the relationship get started? How does the relationship with each person differ from those that you have with the others? Write out 2 short lists (say 10 items each) giving:*
(a) the features of the other person that you like (7 items) and those that you dislike (3 items)
(b) the sort of activities that you perform or topics you talk about almost exclusively with friends (7 items) and those that you do with other people too, but that are 'better' with friends (3 items)
— *Think for a moment about an attractive person you have seen but not really met — one you would like to start a relationship with if you were completely free to do so. Write 2 short lists (10 items each) giving:*
(a) what you find attractive about them (7 items) and what you find unattractive about them (3 items)
(b) 7 things you would do or talk about with them if you got to know them and 3 items you would definitely not talk about or do.
— *Compare your various lists and try to work out the important differences among them, if any. Consider the differences involved in 'relating' to strangers and friends, and think what it is that changes when strangers gradually turn into acquaintances and friends.*

If we find that friends have similar attitudes, we may congratulate ourselves that we found an answer to the question until we realize that we have not shown whether similarity causes liking or liking causes similarity. (After all, we *do* try to persuade our friends to adopt our ideas, don't we?) The aim is to find a way to alter similarity levels between people and then see what it does to their attraction for one another.

The problem was solved by Donn Byrne. He did a series of experiments on attraction to strangers where subjects filled out an attitude questionnaire and then were given another scale completed (allegedly) by a stranger. Byrne then assessed subjects' responses to the stranger (who was actually nonexistent, i.e., bogus or hypothetical — the method was called 'the bogus stranger method'). The experimental subjects did *not* know that the stranger was fictitious. The subjects would be presented with the information allegedly provided by this stranger, and they would then be asked what they thought of him or her. Byrne carefully arranged the information so that the stranger's attitude scale matched up with the subject's own to a precise degree (say 80% or 65% or 20%).

The work, known as 'Byrne's attraction paradigm', assumed that attitude similarity is an example of 'reinforcement' or reward — something attractive, desirable, and positive that we like to experience. The important point is that it is reinforcement that we like and attitude similarity is usually reinforcing. Note that Byrne does not say that attitude similarity is always reinforcing or attractive (sometimes it may be boring to meet someone whose attitudes are absolutely the same as ours). But usually, Byrne says, attitude similarity will be reinforcing, and so we find it attractive.

When all we know about someone is his or her sex and a sample of his or her attitudes, then we will like that person in proportion to the amount of reinforcing similarity between us; the more similar, the more we like him or her. If we know a little more about the person then the picture becomes more complicated: for instance, it matters whether we have a positive view of him or her (e.g., that we have not found out that the person is obnoxious or mentally ill — unless we are too). It also matters whether: the similar attitudes are important to us; the reasons given for holding them are similar to ours; we believe the strangers are stating their true opinions, and the like. In brief, as the picture becomes more complicated, so the plain and simple commonsense rule that 'similarity is attractive' turns out to be more and more inadequate. In investigating this area,

Byrne (1971) and colleagues established an enormous amount of detail about this particular phenomenon.

We usually like people whose attitudes are similar to our own, so long as we like ourselves and the other people are normal, sensible people stating their true opinion. It is the method used by dating agencies who match partners up by selecting people with similar attitudes and beliefs — the strangers there are *real*, not bogus. Byrne often tested the validity of his work outside the 'laboratory'. He found that bank managers give bigger loans to people with similar attitudes, for instance, that jurors are more likely to be lenient to defendants with attitudes like theirs, and that similarity of attitudes can overcome the prejudices of racial bigots so that prejudiced whites actually express liking for blacks who have similar attitudes (Byrne, 1971).

Is Byrne's work artificial?

Laboratory-based, experimental, manipulated studies of liking may not penetrate real liking. In life we rarely gain such unambiguous access to someone else's attitudes. When was the last time a stranger came up to you and gave you a written list of his or her attitudes? Sometimes, we have to be 'detectives'; we know that people often conceal their true attitudes and we have to uncover them. For instance, they may conceal their true attitudes from us to get something from us or to ingratiate themselves. Also, sometimes, people withhold their 'true' attitudes for other reasons, such as desire to create a positive impression or fear of how their 'true confession' might be received by us. We know that we behave in these concealing ways ourselves.

Social processes operate to ensure that initial encounters (and even later ones) are not always open, frank exchanges of unambiguous information. For these reasons, we have to work at uncovering the true picture — some of us will be more proficient than others. For instance, aside from individual differences in the detecting skills of 'normal adults', it is likely that young children will be less good at interpreting people's

BOX 3.3 Byrne's work

We prefer strangers who are reinforcing for us and this often takes the form of their being attitudinally similar to ourselves (Byrne, 1961). We like strangers who agree with us.

The amount of liking is directly predictable from the proportion of similar attitudes and hence from the reinforcement derived: the more the reinforcement, the greater the liking (Byrne & Nelson, 1965).

Some attitudes are difficult for us to check and validate or gain evidence for. The more difficult it is to validate an attitude, the more we appreciate it when someone shares that attitude with us (Byrne et al., 1966). Uncommon similarity (i.e., similarity on attitudes that are not widely held) is especially attractive (Lea & Duck, 1982).

'Coke dates' arranged on the basis of attitude similarity are more successful and partners can remember more about one another several months later (Byrne et al., 1970).

Similarity to unreinforcing strangers (e.g., mentally disturbed persons) is not attractive (Byrne & Lamberth, 1971): reinforcement matters more than similarity does.

Attitudinal similarity affects electrical skin conductance but not heart rate. Disagreement makes us more aroused than agreement, but both are arousing (Clore & Gormly, 1974).

The inferences we draw from similarity may be what makes it attractive. Duck (1975a) reports that the underlying extent of similarity mattered: that is, it is more attractive to be similar to someone who gives the same reasons as yours for holding the attitude than it is to be similar to someone who holds the attitude for different reasons. When we find attitude similarity attractive, it may be because we assume that the person will share many other underlying values with us and will be generally rewarding.

People will actually return to a laboratory to work with an attitudinally similar stranger (Gormly & Gormly, 1981).

attitudes as will be some psychologically disturbed patients. These extreme examples merely make the point that differences in detecting skills can exist. Maybe, the shy and lonely 'normal adults' are at the poor end of the scale when it comes to determining whether someone has similar attitudes, and so they get off to a bad start with strangers. The effects of 'detective work' are likely to be less important than those of other conversational skills.

When strangers are introduced — even in the laboratory — to have a conversation, the effects of attitude similarity 'wash out' (Sunnafrank & Miller, 1981). Similar subjects do not like one another any more than do dissimilar ones after they have had a brief interaction. Also, dissimilar partners who interact like their partner more than do dissimilar ones who do not interact. Interaction has a positive effect on liking, and it modifies the effect of dissimilarity on its own. When communication exceeds a 'one-off' conversation and is extended over time and to explicit discussion of attitudinal issues, then again it is the *dis*similar stranger who gets a better rating (Sunnafrank, 1983).

What about relationships?

Students of initial attraction are usually well aware that they are studying a small part of a broader set of issues (e.g., Clore & Byrne, 1974). Often, they are both startled and hurt by critics who effectively said 'This work on strangers is silly because it tells us nothing about marriage'. Work on obstetrics tells us little about senility, but that is not a reason for not doing it. *Many* real-life examples make initial attraction an obvious and important area of concern. What we must bear in mind, however, is that not all attractions lead to relationships (Byrne, 1971).

'Attraction does not mean relationship'

There are a myriad of reasons why we do not set up relationships with every attractive person we meet, the most significant being: lack of a wish to do so (e.g., married or engaged, going steady, not enough time, too many commitments); inapprop-

riateness (e.g., differences in status, circumstances not condu-
cive); or, perhaps more poignant, incompetence. Many people
who report being lonely or shy feel unable to carry out their
wishes to set up desired relationships. Occasionally, I get letters
about this, saying things like 'I am a 25-year-old male and have
this inability to converse, communicate, or form any sort of
relationship with the opposite sex. It is a long-standing
problem. Girls do seem attracted to me but as soon as it gets
down to speaking, conversing, etc. it goes no further' (actual
letter). Obviously, we might begin by looking at the social skills
of such persons (see chapter 2), but the commonness of the
problem is significant. It is the most frequent problem dealt
with by the various Crisisline/Nightline services on university
campuses. 'If you can't deal with strangers you won't get
friends'.

Even so, attraction to strangers is the starting point for all
relationships that do eventually start. We need to know why we
select between strangers, why we prefer some to others, and
what happens once we move on from our initial attraction. A
problem with laboratory work on attraction is that it 'freezes'
situations out of context: subjects go to a room for an experiment, meet a stranger (or don't meet a bogus one), and then go
home. This might lead us to think of all interactions as frozen
and context-free — like separate snapshots rather than single
still frames from a continuous movie. Life is not made up of
such separate snapshots. In life, one meeting with a person
often leads to another — or it can. When we know that, it
probably affects what we do and how we treat the strangers we
may see again and get to know better. So we must expect that
our reasons for initial attraction are not necessarily those that
influence long term development of relationships or help us to
stay in relationships. Why should they be?

Acquaintance is made up of several different parts, each with
its own influences as things proceed. Acquaintance is a *process*
(Duck, 1977). Long-term acquaintance is probably not caused
by, say, physical attraction even if that is what interests us
initially. The development of relationships is not caused by
initial attractions. Relationships do not work like electric

motors — which just start and run whenever we press the right switch. That simile, surprisingly, is widely held ('we just clicked'), even though it is an absolutely stupid idea. Of course we have to do something in the long term to make relationships work: we do not just 'sit there looking pretty' in the hope that the rest is automatic. Relationships do not develop just because two people start out with 'compatible personalities'. Rather than dismissing the impact that attitudes and personality may have on relationships, we need to understand their role in our lives, just as Byrne (1971) and Clore & Byrne (1974) urge us to.

How do attitudes and personality affect what we do to make relationships work?

Sometimes, we act as if two people *are* similar and that's that. It is not so simple. What do we have to do to find out that we are similar to someone else? Does it take time and might it not be quite difficult in reality? Most of us have thought that we were similar to someone else and then found out that we were not as alike as we first thought. That two people *are* similar to one another is a 'cognitive' fact; that they *learn* that they are similar is a 'social' fact. To discover that we are similar to someone else we have to do something and so do they. We have to communicate effectively, draw the right conclusions, manipulate and process the information correctly, and recognize what it means when we see it. Byrne's work shows us what happens when the information is already easily available, but what are the real-life processes by which we make it available? How do we bring it out in the course of normal social life? Byrne tells us about the cognitive stimuli that may be attractive, but not about the social processes by which they are pulled into the open in interpersonal interaction. One-sided attractions do not explain relationships; acquaintance is a two-sided venture in which both persons take an active role. We communicate. We adapt.

One major area of adaptation and communication in the development of relationships concerns nonverbal behaviour and the 'microstructure of interaction'. Each person's nonverbal behaviour changes in response to changes in the other person's behaviour (Cappella, 1984). How, then, does nonverbal interaction affect the ways in which we feel about one another in relationships? Cappella (1984) argues that

> attraction between persons ought to be found in the interactional structures they exhibit, how they fit in with or adapt to one another's communicative styles, not just in the communicative styles that they exhibit independently [p. 241].

In line with the argument that I am developing here, Cappella argues that relationship formation is interactional; it is predictable not from the way in which two persons happen to 'click together' but from how they *make* the 'pieces click together'. We never see the internal states or attitudes of other persons directly so we can only infer them from nonverbal and verbal behaviour. Because of this, the meshing of nonverbal behaviour will be crucial to this inference process and highly significant in acquaintance. The microstructure of interactions does change as relationships develop, so nonverbal behaviour does reflect and illustrate growth of relationships.

How do we reveal (and detect) information in the acquaintance process?

Precisely how and why do we go about choosing information about ourselves so that we can communicate it to other people who can use it? To answer this, let us look at the work of negotiating and creating a relationship out of all the information that partners manipulate in interactions.

The information that we get from others usually helps us to reduce uncertainty about them and to form a clearer picture of them and their relationship to us (Berger & Bradac, 1982). Sometimes, when we learn about another person's past relationships or attitudes or feelings for us, then we become more certain about the future of our relationship and also feel we know the person better. New information, sometimes, does not 'fit', and we have to rethink what the other person is like.

Not all the information that we receive from others comes directly from their words or intentional communications (as we saw in chapter 2). Not all the information that we get fits with our (initially sketchy) model of them. When we learn things that surprise us then we have to re-evaluate our model of their personality and what they are really like. Basically, our aim in real-life acquaintance is to make a good model of the other person and to assess how it matches up with our own personality (Duck, 1977; 1983). *Then*, we have to make the relationship work.

Social life helps us in these tasks by reducing uncertainty for us in many subtle ways. For instance, other people's suitability for us is sometimes socially determined. We do not have the complete freedom of choice we like to believe we have. For example, whether it is socially desirable that it happens, research consistently shows that people choose partners who come from their own racial, religious, economic, intellectual, and social background (Kerckhoff, 1974). One reason is communicative: it is easier to talk to people whose background helps them to understand and share the experiences we describe. Another reason is sociological: every relationship is conducted in a context of other relationships. Our family, for instance, often feels it has some right to approve our dating or marital partner, and families tend to prefer people who are from the same background as themselves. A third reason why 'like is attracted to like' is because we dislike uncertainty; every similarity between us and a partner reduces uncertainty. We feel surer about a partner and of our relationship's future the more like us they are.

Does new information always reduce uncertainty? Sometimes, new information makes us more uncertain about our partner (Planalp & Honeycutt, 1984), as when we learn that he or she has been 'cheating' or has a side to his or her character that we had not seen before. Those discoveries increase uncertainty for us.

Also, we must not assume that uncertainty reduction is a culmination; we become acquainted by an extended process of uncertainty reduction that continually shifts its focus and moves on to new, unknown areas (Duck, 1973). When we understand a person at a superficial level, we look more deeply and broadly into other parts of his or her make-up. When we know someone's attitudes to sport, we may want to know more about his or her deep personal feelings about parenthood, for instance. We keep turning to new areas of his or her personality or value system. The process of getting to know someone is the process of reducing uncertainty in as many ways, as many places, and as many levels as we can.

Changing our focus to different matters as acquaintance progresses is generally called 'filtering' (Kerckhoff & Davis, 1962). We can see why: it is as if we have a sequence or series of strainers or sieves and when a person passes through one they go on to the next. Our first 'filter' may be physical appearance. If we like the other person's looks then we will want to go on and see what his or her attitudes are like and whether we enjoy those. 'Attitudes' would then be the second filter, and so on. We assess our acquaintances within a progressive series of 'tests': those who pass one test go through to a deeper level of friendship — and on to the next test.

In my own model (Duck, 1973; 1977), such tests are subtler and subtler comparisons of one's own attitudes, beliefs, and personality compatibility with the partner. We start out in a gross way ('Are they extrovert or introvert like me?'), and become more and more fine in our 'tuning' as the relationship goes on. What specific values do they hold most dear and are they the same as mine? What little things upset them when they are in a bad mood? What 'personality knobs' can I press to cheer them up and what sort of comforting works best with them? What are their deep, deep, deep fears about themselves? We work through such filters because we wish to understand and create a thorough picture of the partner's mind and personality in as much detail as possible. The tests, or filters, help us to reduce uncertainty and draw our partner's personality in finer and finer detail as the relationship deepens and develops.

Filtering theories are more sophisticated than the 'switch on' models that suggest that relationships are caused by one simple feature, like attitude similarity or physical attractiveness. While filtering theories overemphasize thought and cognition, they really only propose a more sophisticated sequence of motors to be switched on and say little about the other processes that go into developing a relationship.

Much research into other aspects of acquaintance shows that acquaintance is not an accident but often happens by design (Duck, 1977). Two important lines of work are: the ways in which we form and carry out the intention to become related; and the strategic use that we make of self-disclosure, that is, revealing personal information about ourselves as a sign of growing intimacy and trust of our partner. Self-disclosure occurs usually by words but occasionally by nonverbal means. We self-disclose when we tell someone how we have been upset by something recently or 'What I am most ashamed of about myself' or 'What I dislike most about my parents'. We self-disclose when we tell secrets or give other people access to private attitudes that we share with very few others. We can also self-disclose nonverbally by 'giving ourself away', for instance, bursting into tears unexpectedly or suddenly blushing.

In most social psychological work, self-disclosure refers to verbal intimacy — particularly the messages that are so disclosed. This work assumes that we can tell how intimate others are merely by examining the words they use, the topics they talk about, and the subjects they introduce to a conversation. Such topics have occasionally been listed and rated for intimacy level. For example, Davis & Sloan (1974) put 'How I react to others' praise and criticism of me' at the bottom of their list and 'My feelings about my sexual inadequacy' at the top of their list for very intimate topics.

Remembering the discussion in chapter 2, you may find this a bit dissatisfying: in life, there are more indicators of intimacy than just words; nonverbal cues as well as the relationship between the partners help to define and communicate intimacy. For this reason, Montgomery (1981a) talks of 'open communication' rather than just self-disclosure. She describes it as composed of five elements, some of which occur more often in some types of relationships whilst others appear more frequently in others. *Negative openness* covers openness in showing disagreement or negative feelings about a partner or situation. *Nonverbal openness* relates to a communicator's facial expressions, vocal tone, and bodily postures or movements (see chapter 2). *Emotional openness* describes the ease with which someone's feelings or moods are expressed and his or her unconcealment of emotional states. *Receptive openness* is a person's indication of his or her willingness to listen to other people's personal information. *General-style openness* refers to the overall impression that someone creates (Norton, 1978).

Even if we look at just the content of speech then we can split openness into different elements, of which topic intimacy is only one (Montgomery, 1981a). Intimacy of a topic is not the same as 'intimacy of topic in a relationship'. For instance, what is said about a topic can make it intimate or nonintimate and the target of the disclosure likewise. Thus, the question 'How is your sex life?' looks like a promisingly personal and intimate topic unless we reply 'pretty average' or if it is our physician who asks us about it. In short, even intimate-sounding topics can be discussed nonintimately, or in nonintimate contexts. Other factors that make for intimacy in conversation are, as we have learned before, verbal immediacy, nonverbal accompaniments and relational context. Openness, then, includes both verbal and nonverbal aspects of behaviour and deals as much with the function of a message as with its medium (Montgomery, 1984). When we look at open communication in context, what does not discriminate between high and low open communicators are content and topic intimacy alone.

How strategic are we in making acquaintances?

Has it struck you how passive much of the work assumes that we are? Do we actually try to make other people like us sometimes or do we just sit back, smile, flash a few attitudes around and hope that they will react positively? I believe that we actually spend quite a lot of time trying to get other people to like and appreciate us. We become upset when we fail to create positive feelings in other people; it is a great source of personal distress and dissatisfaction. We must have strategies for making others appreciate us and an awareness of 'how we are doing' (Bell & Daly, 1984). Take a moment to think about the strategies we might use (BOX 3.4 gives the answers that Bell & Daly found). Note here, however, that Bell & Daly assume that liking between two people is not an accident, as some of the work I have just been discussing might seem to imply. At least they point out that if attraction is like a switch on an electric motor then people might actively try to *find* the switch and power it up. Occasionally — or perhaps frequently — we are affinity-seekers; that is, we initiate an 'active social-communicative process by which [we] attempt to get others to like and feel positive toward [us]' (Bell & Daly, 1984, p. 1).

If we are successful in attracting someone to us, what happens to deepen the relationship? Recall the earlier discussion of self-disclosure. Some self-disclosure is a sign of good mental health and influences the course of relationships: a certain amount of intimate disclosure is *expected* in our culture, as an indication that we genuinely trust another person. We are supposed to say a few disclosing and revealing things in order to 'open out'. Women are particularly 'expected' to self-disclose and are often pressed into doing so if they do not do so voluntarily; 'closed' women are asked direct questions that make them open out (Miell, 1984).

Reciprocity of self-disclosure is also expected. If I self-disclose to you, you will self-disclose back. It confirms a desire to develop a relationship since the person could have chosen not to reveal the information, especially if it is quite personal (Schlenker, 1984). Conversely, we could hold back a relationship, if we wanted, by not revealing something personal to our partner if our partner did so to us (Duck et al., 1984). Self-disclosure is used strategically both to develop relationships (Davis, 1978) and to hold them back or to shape the relationship into one form rather than another (e.g., to keep someone from getting too intimate, too fast, or to protect the relationship from straying on to taboo topics; Baxter & Wilmot, 1985; Miell, 1984, see BOX 3.5).

The material in BOX 3.5 helps us to see that we do play an active part in our own lives and are not simply corks floating on a sea of reinforcement. We actually choose certain courses of

BOX 3.4 Affinity-seeking strategies

There are 7 groups of strategies of affinity-seeking used by persons who impress us as likeable, socially successful, and satisfied with their lives (Bell & Daly, 1984).

Control and visibility. *Strategies here are aimed at taking control of the other person (e.g., by showing our personal autonomy and independence, by being rewarding, and by taking charge of the conversation) or else at becoming noticed (e.g., by appearing dynamic, interesting, and physically attractive).*

Mutual trust. *Two strategies are used here. One (trustworthiness) is designed to make one trustable whilst the other is intended to make one look trusting (openness).*

Politeness. *This strategy is characterized by conversational rule-keeping.*

Concern and caring. *This involves confirming the other person's self-concept, listening carefully, being sensitive, supportive, and altruistic and encouraging the other to talk about himself or herself.*

Other involvement. *This strategy is intended to draw the other person into things by facilitating enjoyment and nonverbal immediacy.*

Self-involvement. *This strategy serves to integrate one person into the activities of the other person and signals a desire for a relationship.*

Commonalities. *This strategy, well-worn in cocktail parties with employers, involves appearing comfortable and relaxed in their company, accompanied by the pointing out of similarities between ourself and the other person. When that person is not a superior, the strategy is buttressed by an attempt to assume equality. Appearing superior is a fatally non-affinitive method (unless you really are superior in some way, in which case everyone should be directing these strategies at you anyway).*

BOX 3.5 Strategic self-disclosure

Partners use self-disclosure as a tool for the control of relationships (Duck et al., 1984; Miell & Duck, 1985). For instance, we will occasionally overdo a disclosure so that we plunge our partner into a 'norm of reciprocity' requiring him or her to respond with something equally intimate and revealing.

Acquainting persons frequently use false disclosures to provoke an argument or debate (Miell, 1984). By doing this we find out what our partner really thinks (i.e., we induce partner to self-disclose by a devious means rather than by a direct question asking for partner's views).

Self-disclosure serves an important role in creating relationships and helps partners to construct a story of the origin of a relationship (Duck & Miell, 1984). Partners begin to construct 'relational disclosures' to make to outsiders to indicate depth of involvement.

There is a reverse side to this, however. There are 'taboo topics' that we recognize and respect (Baxter & Wilmot, 1985). Some themes are 'dangerous' ones to explore (e.g., partner's past relationships; the present state of our relationship). Lack of self-disclosure can thus sometimes be strategic and can help to preserve the relationship because it keeps us away from topics that can be inherently threatening.

---

action thoughtfully and for strategic reasons, when we want to develop a relationship.

How much do we think carefully and how much do we just react?

Acquaintance is not entirely orderly, always 'cognitively driven', or utterly strategic. Many of us have sensed that we did not know how a relationship would develop; many have been in chaotic relationships; all have been in uncertain ones. Although some theorists represent acquaintance as rational, orderly, and well-planned logical, decision-making, we know that they are probably wrong if they think that acquaintance happens like that all the time.

Frequently, we 'follow our noses' and follow social rules unthinkingly (Bochner, 1983). Relationships have ritual elements, and we often do things because they are expected rather than because we want to (e.g., shaking hands with someone). Social interaction, generally, is structured for 'symbolic bonding' to occur; that is, we do things which make us look sociable and friendly when we may not necessarily be feeling either. We have many formulae in social life ('Hi! How are you today?') which make us appear to be emotionally attached or 'bonded' to or really interested in someone. When, in fact, the formula is emotionally insignificant, we feel little or nothing for the other person (Harré, 1976). Many conversations are started by asking how someone is; this is a 'formulaic question'. We do not usually mean it as a genuine request for a detailed report. People who respond with an emotional or physical 'shopping list' of their latest medical symptoms would be regarded as eccentric.

Not all apparently intimate and concerned questions show that we are really 'bonded' to people, forcing us to determine when they are genuine and when they are merely polite. For such reasons, it is sometimes difficult for us to assess our real closeness to someone else (particularly at the start of relationships).

Furthermore, there is a cultural taboo that frowns on us telling someone explicitly that we like them. Because of this, 'liking messages' are usually wrapped carefully in enigma, shrouded in ambiguity, and concealed in the more obscure language of nonverbal cues (see chapter 2), especially at the start of acquaintance. We smile at the person; look interested or intrigued; show concern; and listen carefully. From that, the person is supposed to deduce that we like him or her — a task made harder by the fact that those self-same behaviours are what we do when we are being 'polite'.

Establishing, Developing and Maintaining Relationships

What is the psychological relationship between liking and long-term liking? How do we convert 'gut attraction' into a working relationship? What are the processes through which one becomes the other?

In life, my experience is that we plan to meet people; we share points of contact; predictable routines bring us together frequently with those we know well. If we study only meetings between interchangeable, anonymous strangers in contextually sanitized laboratory environments, we miss the point that our real life encounters are not usually unforeseen, unexpected and accidental but predictable, anticipated and (often) prearranged. Because meetings are like this, they are based on coded memories and we have 'stories' about the relationship in which they arise: stories about where the relationship came from, what it means to us, and where it is going. We create these stories according to our own sets of beliefs and by reference to shared knowledge of rules for relating in our culture. Before attraction becomes a relationship, we need a story (Duck & Sants, 1983).

Relationships are often buried in daily routines

Some theories (e.g. *Equity Theory*, Hatfield & Traupmann, 1981; *Exchange Theory*, Huesmann & Levinger, 1976) claim that relationships depend on the past, present, or future levels of reward which we receive, vis-à-vis our partner. I think that this approach makes one fundamentally wrong assumption: we are continuously sustaining our relationships by conscious acts of reinforcement, testing, or strategic development once they are established. Most of the time daily life is remarkably humdrum, routine, predictable. We take our long-term relationships for granted in some way most of the time and assume that the partner we slept next to will wake up still feeling like a partner tomorrow. We do not go through a ritual each breakfast time where we treat each other like strangers and run through a whole range of rewarding techniques to re-establish the relationship and take it to where it was the day before: we behave that way only with friends we have not seen for ages.

The remarkable fact about daily life is that continuities exist and do not have to be worked for, once the relationship is defined and established. Although most friendships are not like this, they can feel as if they exist and continue over years and miles without any contact except the occasional 'phone call, Christmas card or letter — as long as reward levels do not wander too far.

Relationships have their permanence *in the mind*, on the basis of beliefs not just of behaviour. They survive distance, climate, revolt, pestilence, and Act of God, as long as we both *think* they have.

Relationships which have major effects are of this perpetual but dormant kind: parent-child relationships, marriages, friendships, collegial relationships at work. They are part of the unchallenged and comfortable predictability of lives made up of routine, expectation, and assumptions that most of tomorrow will be based on the foundations of today. They are not composed of perpetual recreations founded on a social psychology that begins each day as a blank tablet.

These predictabilities help to explain why breakdown, development and repair of relationships are disruptive. Distress at disruption and loss of relationships is often precisely because they are so humdrum that they become built into the other routines of our lives. These taken-for-granted routines build in ways that we do not always realize until they are removed. Their loss takes away unspoken and unrealized parts of ourselves.

Thinking about relationships

What do we think relationships are like, then? One influence on our thinking is the social rules that govern our relationships. How does our knowledge of them affect or afflict our success in relating? How do we pattern our lives to reflect these beliefs? Do we really follow the rules? Do we behave differently in the company of friends, do different things with them and structure our lives around the relationship — or do we just *think* we do?

A relationship takes its existence from the partners thinking that they have one and represent that belief in their behaviour toward one another. Such behaviour can change; our views of a partner or friend can alter; attitudes about the relationship can be affected by mood, circumstances, and the state of the rest of our lives. Accordingly, relationships should be regarded not as permanent 'things' that we investigate clinically, but as potentially changing mental and behavioural creations of participants and outsiders. Researchers explore the mental maps that people have of them and how these change with relational growth or decline. They also look at the ways behaviour changes in relationships across time.

Relationships do not just automatically pop out of strings of interactions or strings of rewards; neither is it interactions (as opposed to relationships) that people complain of when things go wrong (Duck & Sants, 1983). Instead, we transform our views of partners as we get to know them better, and behavioural changes (e.g., increased intimacy) are indicators of such mental changes (Cappella, 1984). Partners' views of themselves, their partner, and the relationship develop in parallel with the development of the relationship itself.

Do partners always agree about their relationship?

Discrepancies of interpretation — even between close partners — are an inevitable part of everyday social life (McCarthy, 1983). When we find such disagreements, it should surprise us less than it does. Our own and everyone else's cognitive processes are inaccessible to us; if we do not know what other people are thinking, we can depend only on guesswork and we often guess wrongly (Nisbett & Wilson, 1977). Secondly, we seldom discuss our views of relationship openly and explicitly with our partners except when we think something is wrong (Baxter & Wilmot, 1984). So we do not get much experience of seeing explicit agreement about it, and the experiences we do get will emphasize the discords.

The problems with relationships are more likely to be visible, accessible, and familiar than are the smooth parts. In particular, we misperceive other people's feelings in one important respect: we tend to be uncertain about partners' commitment to relationships and assume that they might change their mind — we are their friend for only as long as they think we are (Duck, 1983). More importantly, partners probably each see different events as crucial in the relationship, so there is no good reason to expect partners to be in total agreement about the nature or course of the relationship (McCarthy, 1983).

Partners' 'mental creations' of the relationship matter significantly and play an important part in creating and sustaining relationships. Yet they are not more than a part of the whole. For one thing, only part of my mental creation of my relationships comes from within myself; other parts come from what my partners think, how they act, and how I respond to that; other parts come from the reactions and behaviour of outsiders. Such differences are what distinguish between fixed and tentative relationships, between public and secret relationships, between cooperative and competitive, between open, trusting and closed, threatening relationships.

Does it matter what 'outsiders' think?

Much research shows that we are aware of outside influence on relationships (Boissevain, 1974) and that outsiders can affect the course of a relationship. For instance, parents' attempts to discourage a relationship between a given boy and a given girl could actually lead to the couple feeling *increased* love for one another (the Romeo and Juliet effect, Driscoll et al., 1972).

Outsiders have influence in two other ways. First, as we pull into one new relationship we correspondingly have a little less time for our old friendships (Milardo et al., 1983). New friendships disrupt old ones. Second, outsiders, in the shape of the 'surrounding culture', give us clues about the ways to conduct relationships. We try to hide affairs but we are happy to publicize marriages, for instance.

As partners become more involved in a courtship, so this

adversely affects their relationships with friends (Milardo et al., 1983). Respondents in the later stages of courtship interact with fewer people, relative to persons in the earlier stages of courtship, and see them less often and for shorter periods of time. However, the most noticeable changes in rates of participation occur with intermediate friends rather than close ones. Changes in frequency and duration of interactions subsequently lead to a decrease in the size of network. In other words, as we see our date more, so we see our casual friends (but not our close friends) less until they finally drop out of our network altogether, if the courtship progresses satisfactorily (Milardo et al., 1983). Courting partners are thus less of a substitute for close friends than for casual acquaintances. In brief, emotional commitment to one person affects the structure of the larger network to which we belong.

Every culture has certain views about the nature of relationships and the 'rules' for conducting them. Some of the preceding developments mean that the relationship begins to have meaning for other people, too, to become an 'organization' over and above the feelings that the partners have for one another. Whilst social psychologists explore the ways in which feelings for one another pull partners together, and communications scientists explore the ways in which those feelings are expressed and communicated, sociologists are interested in relationships as social units over and above the two members in them (McCall, 1982).

Think for a moment how often we have heard people say 'It was too intense' (i.e., the relationship was), 'It wasn't going anywhere' (i.e., the relationship wasn't), 'We have a nice relationship where we both feel relaxed', and the like. Sociologists have noticed that persons develop a sense of membership to 'a relationship' and that the formation of interpersonal liking bonds is not the complete story. 'Institutionalized social forms' of relationships affect our relating and acquainting also (e.g., we know what our culture thinks 'a friendship' is as distinct from an 'extramarital affair', and we know that professors and students are 'permitted' to have one form of relationship but not the other).

Each real life form of a relationship creates some tension with the social blueprint, as it were, in that we may become aware of discrepancies between our own relationship and the cultural expectations for it ('I guess it wasn't a "perfect marriage"'). Third parties, particularly in-laws, it seems, exert 'audience effects' on relationships by commenting on the partners' attempts to implement the social blueprint.

Another part of a developing sense of togetherness is that partners develop a set of 'intimate idioms' or private language characteristic of that particular relationship but not of others. So, once again, the joining of the relationship itself creates effects on our thoughts, feelings, and behaviours. In particular, membership of a relationship necessitates role differentiation and the division of labour, that is, part of the job of setting up a relationship is the issue of 'who does what?'

The wanting to enter into a relationship, therefore, means that we have to do more than just like our partner. There are factors, beyond the purely dyadic ones (e.g., the liking), which affect and exert influence on a relationship and the partners in it. There are cultural rules for relationships and our execution of the rules will affect the picture that people form not only of our skills as a relater but, to some extent, of our intentions during the early stages of relationships, for instance, if we break the rules we may seem too pushy or too shy.

Relationships, then, are not mere reactions to the qualities, properties, or attributes of another person. Other influences such as time, viewpoint, strategy, the wider culture, and skill are all relevant. Against this background, what do people actually do?

Making sense of relationships

I am convinced that a large number of the findings reviewed here point to one startlingly overlooked fact: sometimes people think about their relationships and sometimes they do not. We may do this when we are face-to-face with our partner, but we also do it frequently when they are not there. We can plan the relationship; we can think back over encounters and try to work out what went wrong with them or what we can learn from them (Duck, 1980). We can learn about our partners by thinking things over in this way since we can easily pick up on some crucial point that may have escaped us before. This 'out-of-interaction' fantasy, or thought work, is a very important aspect

---

BOX 3.6 Rules and skills of relationships

There are 13 rules that apply particularly to friendship (Argyle & Henderson, 1984). Examples are 'Show emotional support', 'Trust and confide in the other', 'Don't criticize the friend in public', 'Don't nag', 'Respect privacy'. Although some 43 rules altogether were expected by subjects to apply to friendship, most of them did not apply very strongly.

There are cross-cultural differences in friendship rules, too, and friendship is not the same the world over. Argyle & Henderson (1984) conclude that there are central 'friendship rules' whose breaking will dissolve the friendship, but also that there are 'general rules' to distinguish friendship from other relationships and 'quality rules' to differentiate ordinary friendship from high quality friendship.

Within a particular culture, we know the characteristics that make up a friendship and that make it different from casual acquaintance (Davis & Todd, 1985). For instance, enjoyment, trust, mutual assistance, respect, understanding, and intimacy are all-important, defining features of friendship.

There are also skills of friendship based on the social skills we learned in chapter 2 (Duck, 1983). Better adjusted people have greater relational competence and a larger repertoire of social skills that they use more appropriately than have poorly adjusted people (Burns & Farina, 1984). They know the rules and they follow them. Intriguingly, Burns & Farina (1984) show that such skills run in families, and it looks as if we learn friendship skills from our parents.

of both the building and destroying of relationships. I believe that it has been overlooked because researchers have not yet asked people how they spend their time. I am quite sure that we spend a lot of our time thinking, musing, and daydreaming. Maybe we can plan our relationships to make them work better then.

One essential feature of relating is the need to provide a 'story' about it, and, clearly, these stories could be readily made up in the course of such out-of-interaction thinking. Try keeping a diary of how you feel about your partner, then you'll know what I mean. This kind of musing also might help us to create a sense of continuity — a sense that the relationship is a lasting venture, not a temporary phase. That sense of continuity, by means of humdrum routines, and the dispositional language mentioned in chapter 1, is what sustains our beliefs in the continuity of the relationships to which we belong. It is functional in that it preserves us from the need for continually re-establishing new relationships or continually re-enacting our existing ones on each new day.

Beliefs, routines, and future projects are central to everyday life, but we are not always completely sensible, thoughtful people. I see myself making mistakes and wrong assumptions, being inconsistent, losing my temper, taking unreasonable dislikes to people, unfairly teasing people, feeling uncertain, embarrassed, and ashamed occasionally. Yet it is all too easy to overlook these little foibles and assume that no-one else does these things. It often looks to me as if the rest of humanity is going around soberly and seriously processing information in the manner of true scientists, in rational, statistically defensible ways, reaching conclusions, being competent, liking people who are well-dressed, attitudinally similar, and who order their arguments properly. Yet, I know I am often persuaded by people not for these reasons but because I cannot be bothered to argue about some issues, do not think of the effective debating point till I am halfway down the street, am in a rush to do something more important to me, or I simply do not know enough about the topic to challenge them adequately.

As in the rest of life, so I think we can easily misunderstand what really goes on in relationships. It does not feel to me as if the world is full of relationships where perfect strangers grasp one another's collars in breathless attempts to shake out the other person's attitudes in a search for reinforcement. Neither do I see people in long-term relationships going round giving marks to partners for their every action and calculating whether the arithmetic works out well enough for them to stay in the relationship for the next ten minutes. Not every encounter is a surprise; not every person a blank slate upon which rapid calculations have to be performed. Not every member of the family has either just fallen in love with you or is about to file for divorce, is either a young child with a tendency to initiate violent acts or an elderly incontinent who feels lonely.

Relationships are a part of life, and everyday life is a part of all relationships. As those lives change through our ageing, so do the concerns we have and the things we do. Our friendship needs vary through life as do our opportunities for getting them and our bases for seeking them (Dickens & Perlman, 1981). In teenage years, the main search is for a group of friends and for sexual partners; later, most people become committed to one partner and their network of friends stabilizes for a while. If we marry the partner and have children, then our friendship needs are affected by these circumstances and by career developments. When the children leave home, parents often become involved in the community more extensively and start up new friendships in the middle years of life, and so on. As life develops new demands and new routines so we change friendship 'work'.

A consistent element of these lifelong routines consists of trivia, and we apparently waste a lot of time doing seemingly unimportant things. For example, we spend much of our time talking about other people, gossiping, and giving views of one another (Emler & Fisher, 1982). Behavioural measures of friendship are better predictors of relationship growth than are purely cognitive ones (Hays, 1984), and what we do together matters more than what we think about. For instance, people do not sit down and check up all the time on whether their attitudes or personalities are similar — at least, not directly or explicitly. Frequently, they are being active together but in seemingly unimportant ways.

People 'outside the laboratory' are not engaged in the kinds of activity that have often been supposed, and one major difference is that our encounters are not usually unforeseen and fortuitous. They are more likely to be preplanned and foreseeable because they fit in with the other routines of everyday life such as living in a family or an institution where events have predictable sequences (e.g., meal times, habits, patterns).

Interactions in social relationships are not interchangeable, because of these chains of routine that keep us together. Routine makes us predictable for one another and defines some of the sorts of behaviour that will (not) occur between us (e.g., I won't sit and watch TV with my colleagues in the department but will do so with my family).

Routines are not only predictable but they tie people together behaviourally — ensuring that the relationship continues, as part of those other routines. For instance, we meet friends because we have arranged it, and these routines and appointments are not trivial and unimportant in developing relationships; they are the bases of the normal day.

One crucial aspect of developing a relationship is that the partners start doing things together, sharing time, acting as a unit, and going around with one another (Hays, 1984; Huston et al., 1981). The ways that they manage to do this and their success or failure at it are not predictable from just their liking for one another. Partners who are deeply attracted to one another from the start do not necessarily bind themselves together any more effectively than persons who are less sure about their feelings for one another (Huston et al., 1981). Equally, some people become more fond of one another because they spend more time together rather than vice versa.

When things go wrong

The rosy picture of relational progress drawn so far is only part of the truth. Things often go wrong in relationships in all sorts

---

BOX 3.7 Social participation

Wheeler & Nezlek (1977) devised a method (called the 'Rochester Interaction Record') for recording people's daily social interactions. Essentially, the method is a structured diary that records, for instance, whom the subject met, where, for how long, what was talked about, and how the subject felt about the interaction.

They find that 56% of interactions that last more than 10 minutes are with persons of the same sex. The women subjects spend more time in interaction in the first part of their first university year than do men, but by the second part of the year this difference disappears. This may show that women adjust to the stress of their new arrival at university by seeking to involve themselves in social life.

Reis et al. (1980) show that attractive men have more social interaction than less attractive men. For women, there is no relationship between their physical attractiveness and their level of social participation, somewhat surprisingly. However, both attractive men and attractive women report greater satisfaction with their social interactions than do the less attractive persons.

---

of ways and cause a lot of pain when they do. How does it happen?

There are several parts to acquaintance, and we would expect there to be several parts to the undoing of acquaintance during relational dissolution. This is not only because relationships exist in time and take time to fall apart, so that at different times different processes are taking a role in the dissolution. It is also because, like a motor car, a relationship can have accidents for many reasons, whether the 'driver's' fault, mechanical failure or the actions of other road users. Thus, in a relationship, one or both partners might be hopeless at relating; or, the structure and mechanics of the relationship may be wrong, even though both partners are socially competent in other settings; o. outside influences can upset it. All these possibilities have been explored. However, I am going to focus on my own approach to these issues and refer you elsewhere for details of the other work. One reason for doing this is that my own theory of relationship dissolution is closely tied to my theory of relational repair (Duck, 1984a) as well as to my theory of the development of acquaintance (Duck, 1977) and so provides links between what has gone before and what follows.

The essence of my theory of relational dissolution is that there are several different phases, each with a characteristic style and concern (Duck, 1982a). Thus, as shown in Figure 3.1, the first phase is a *breakdown phase* wherein partners (or one partner only) become(s) distressed at the way the relationship is conducted. This generates an *intrapsychic phase* characterized by a brooding focus on the relationship and on the partner. Nothing is said to the partner at this point: the agony is either private or shared only with a diary or with relatively anonymous other persons (e.g., barstaff or secretaries or counsellors). Just before exiting from this phase, we tend to move up to the scale of confidants so that we start to complain to our close friends — but do not yet present the partner with the extent of our distress or doubts about the future of the relationship.

Once we decide to do something about it we have to deal with the problem of facing up to the partner. Implicit — and probably wrongly implicit — in my 1982 model was the belief that partners would tell one another about their feelings and try to do something about them. Both Lee (1984) and Baxter (1984) show that people often leave relationships without telling their partner, or else by fudging their exits. For instance, they may say: 'I'll call you' and then not do it; or 'Let's keep in touch' and never contact the partner; or 'Let's not be lovers but stay as friends' and then have hardly any contact in future. Given that my assumption is partly wrong, it nevertheless assumes that partners in formal relationships like marriage will have to face up to their partner, whilst partners in other relationships may or may not do so. The *dyadic phase* is the phase when partners try to confront and talk through their feelings about the

FIGURE 3.1: A sketch of the phases of dissolving personal relationships

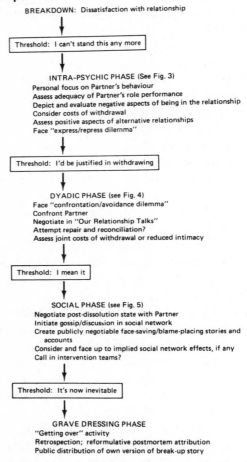

BREAKDOWN: Dissatisfaction with relationship

↓

Threshold: I can't stand this any more

↓

INTRA-PSYCHIC PHASE (See Fig. 3)
Personal focus on Partner's behaviour
Assess adequacy of Partner's role performance
Depict and evaluate negative aspects of being in the relationship
Consider costs of withdrawal
Assess positive aspects of alternative relationships
Face "express/repress dilemma"

↓

Threshold: I'd be justified in withdrawing

↓

DYADIC PHASE (see Fig. 4)
Face "confrontation/avoidance dilemma"
Confront Partner
Negotiate in "Our Relationship Talks"
Attempt repair and reconciliation?
Assess joint costs of withdrawal or reduced intimacy

↓

Threshold: I mean it

↓

SOCIAL PHASE (see Fig. 5)
Negotiate post-dissolution state with Partner
Initiate gossip/discussion in social network
Create publicly negotiable face-saving/blame-placing stories and accounts
Consider and face up to implied social network effects, if any
Call in intervention teams?

↓

Threshold: It's now inevitable

↓

GRAVE DRESSING PHASE
"Getting over" activity
Retrospection; reformulative postmortem attribution
Public distribution of own version of break-up story

Source: Duck (1982b, p16) *Personal Relationships 4: Dissolving Personal Relationships* Academic Press: London. Reproduced by permission.

relationship and decide how to sort out the future. Assuming that they decide to break up (and even my 1982 model was quite clear that they may not decide to do that), they then move rapidly to a *social phase* when they have to tell other people about their decision and enlist some support for their side of the debate. It is no good just leaving a relationship: we need other people to agree with our decision or to prop us up and support us. Other people can support us in ways such as being sympathetic and generally understanding. More important, they can side with our version of events and our version of the partner's and the relationship's faults. ('I always thought he/she was no good', 'I could never understand how you two could get along — you never seemed right for each other'.) This is the *grave-dressing phase*: once the relationship is dead we have to bury it 'good and proper' — with a tombstone saying how it was born, what it was like, and why it died. We have to create an account of the relationship's history and, as it were, put it somewhere so that other people can see it and, we hope, accept it.

Those are the main elements of the approach, although it took thirty pages in the original to expound it properly. How does other work support (or not) this set of proposals? I have already noted that Lee (1984) and Baxter (1984) produced results that support it in some ways, but not in others. BOX 3.8 gives some detail of their work.

Gossip plays a key role in the social and grave-dressing phases: in a dissolving relationship, we actively seek the support of members of our social networks and do so by gossiping about our partners (La Gaipa, 1982). In some instances, we look for 'arbitrators' who will help to bring us back together with our partner. In other cases, we just want someone to back up and spread around our own version of the break-up and its causes. A crucial point made by La Gaipa (1982) is that every person who leaves a relationship has to leave with 'social credit' intact for future use: that is, we have to leave in such a way that we are not debarred from future relationships. We must leave with a reputation for having been let down or faced with unreasonable odds or an unreasonable partner. It is socially acceptable to say 'I left because we tried hard to make it work but it wouldn't'. It is socially *un*acceptable to leave a relationship with the cheery but unpalatable admission: 'Well basically I'm a jilt and I got bored dangling my partner on a string so I just broke it off when it suited me'. That statement could destroy one's future credit for new relationships.

Accounts often serve the purpose of beginning the 'getting over' activity essential to complete the dissolution (Harvey et al., 1982). A large part of this involves selecting an account of

BOX 3.8 Dissolution of relationships

Lee (1984) reports on work examining a framework to explain the sequences that we go through when we break off long-term romantic relationships. He identifies 5 stages:

D (Discovery of dissatisfaction)
E (Exposure of the dissatisfaction)
N (Negotiation about the problem)
R (Resolution of the issue)
T (Transformation of the relationship)

Not all dissolutions involve the partners in explicit disclosure of each of these stages. Sometimes people move to T without N (e.g., they leave without making any attempt to put the relationship right).

How do partners disengage themselves from a relationship? Baxter (1984) found that there are 6 distinct elements to a disengagement:

(1) onset of problem;
(2) decision to exit;
(3) initiation of unilateral disengagement action (e.g., expressing the desire to get out);
(4) initial reaction to broken-up-with party;
(5) ambivalence and repair scenarios where partners try to reconcile but find they cannot;
(6) initiation of bilateral disengagement — when both partners accept that it's all over.

These stages are evident even in divorces. If partners are to have an orderly divorce (i.e., one where we both successfully cut ourselves off from not only our feelings about our partner but our attachment to the routines of the marriage and also the feeling of being married) then there is a need for 'lee-time' (Hagestad & Smyer, 1982). This means that we need time to prepare ourselves for being divorced and to get away from our old relationship. Mostly, the authors found, it is the wife who takes charge of this process.

dissolution that refers to a fault in the partner or relationship that pre-existed the split or was even present all along (Weber, 1983). This is the 'I always thought she/he was a bit of a risk to get involved with, but I did it anyway, more fool me' story that we have all used from time to time.

However, accounts also serve another purpose: the creation of a *publicly acceptable* story is essential to getting over the loss of a relationship (McCall, 1982). It is insufficient having a story that only we accept: others must also endorse it. As McCall astutely observes, part of the success of good counsellors consists in their ability to construct such stories for persons in distress about relational loss.

Putting it right

If I wanted to put a relationship right then we could decide to try and make it 'redevelop'; that is, we could assume that repairing a relationship is just like acquaintance, and we need to go through the same processes. This means that we have to assume that break-up of relationships is the reverse of acquaintance, and to repair it, all we have to do is 'rewind' it. This makes some sense: developing relationships grow in intimacy whereas breaking ones decline in intimacy so perhaps we should just try to rewind the intimacy level.

In other ways, this idea does not work. For instance, in acquaintance we get to know more about a person and in breakdown we cannot get to know less. We probably just reinterpret what we already know and put it into a different framework, model, or interpretation ('Yes, he's always been kind, but, then, he was always after something').

I think that we need to base our ideas about repair not on our model of acquaintance but on a model of breakdown of relationships. I think that my model of breakdown is a good starting point.

My approach to relational dissolution has a built-in theory of relational repair (Duck, 1984a) that is consistent with the principles governing formation of relationships in general. Research on relationships has begun to help us understand what precisely happens when things go wrong. By emphasizing processes of breakdown of relationships and processes of acquaintance, we have the chance now to see that there are also processes of repair. These address different aspects of relationships in trouble. This, I believe, also gives us the chance to be more helpful in putting things right. Bear in mind the theory just covered, as you look at Figure 3.2, and you will see that it is based on proposals made earlier. There are phases to repair of relationships and some styles work at some times and not at others (Duck, 1984a).

If the relationship is at the intrapsychic phase of dissolution,

FIGURE 3.2: A sketch of the main concerns at different phases of dissolution

Dissolution States and Threshold	Person's Concerns	Repair Focus
1. Breakdown: Dissatisfaction with relationship	Relationship process; emotional and/or physical satisfaction in relationship	Concerns over one's value as a partner; Relational process
Threshold: I can't stand this any more		
2. Intrapsychic Phase: Dissatisfaction with partner	Partner's 'faults and inadequacies'; alternative forms of relationship; relationships with alternative partners	Person's view of Partner
Threshold: I'd be justified in withdrawing		
3. Dyadic Phase: Confrontation with partner	Reformulation of relationship: expression of conflict: clearing the air	Beliefs about optimal form of future relationship
Threshold: I mean it		
4. Social Phase: Publication of relationship distress	Gaining support and assistance from others; having own view of the problem ratified; obtaining intervention to rectify matters or end the relationship	*Either*: Hold partners together (Phase 1) *Or*: Save face
Threshold: It's now inevitable		
5. Grave-dressing Phase: Getting over it all and tidying up	Self-justification; marketing of one's own version of the breakup and its causes	

Source: Duck (1984b, p169) *Personal Relationships 5: Repairing Personal Relationships* Academic Press: London. Reproduced by permission.

for instance, then repair should aim to re-establish liking for the partner rather than to correct behavioural faults in ourselves or our nonverbal behaviour, for instance. These latter may be more suitable if persons are in the breakdown phase instead. Liking for partner can be re-established or aided by means such as keeping a recо̄ ᴜ, mental or physical, of the positive or pleasing behaviour of our partner rather than listing the negatives and dwelling on them in isolation (Bandura, 1977). Other methods involve redirection of attributions, that is, attempting to use more varied, and perhaps more favourable, explanations for the partner's behaviour — in brief, to make greater efforts to understand the reasons that our partner may give for what is happening in the relationship.

At other phases of dissolution, different strategies of repair are appropriate, according to this model. For instance, at the social phase, persons outside the relationship have to decide whether it is better to try to patch everything up or whether it may serve everyone's best interests to help the partners to get out of the relationship. Figure 3.2 thus indicates that the choice of strategies is between pressing the partners to stay together or helping them to save face by backing up their separate versions of the break-up. An extra possibility would be to create a story that is acceptable to both of them, such as 'It was an unworkable relationship'.

Essentially, this new model proposes only three things: relationships are made up of many parts and processes, some of which 'clock in' at some points in the relationship's life and some at others; relationships can go wrong in a variety of ways; repairing of disrupted relationships will be most effective when it addresses the concerns that are most important to us at the phase of dissolution of relationships which we have reached.

That is the theory. How does research align with it? Let us start with the point that partners can differ in their views of relationships.

Different perspectives are possible in a relationship, and partners may have fundamentally different ways of looking at their breakdown, at what matters most in the relationship, and at what is most important to put right. In 1983 it was pointed out, for instance, that retrospective data on relationships are not necessarily biassed and erroneous just because they look back on relationships after the event. Nor is there only one 'true perspective'. Retrospections are different perspectives, whose place in the whole pattern is not clearly apportioned yet (Duck & Sants, 1983). We should not just dismiss them as errors until we can say what is *not* error: so we should look at the relevant psychological processes through which views of relationships are normally transformed as time goes by.

The ways we change our 'stories' about a relationship provide important psychological data, and they indicate the dynamic nature of the help that outsiders have to give to relationships in trouble. Different parts of the story need to be addressed at different phases of breakdown. Is one, and the same, kind of intervention appropriate at all stages of a relationship's decline? Probably not. It makes more sense to look for the relative appropriateness of different intervention techniques as those dynamics unfold (e.g., Kressel et al., 1980; Duck, 1982a; 1984a).

Clinical psychology and relationships

If a person has troubled relationships, should we treat the person or the relationship? How do troubled relationships impact on the rest of life and vice versa? A major emphasis of early clinical work was on individuals or, at best, on couples, but social psychology now has a growing awareness of outside influences on individuals and couples. Researchers have learned more about the ways in which friendship groups, the quality of friendships, and the state of a marriage impact on a person's physical and mental health (Gottlieb, 1981; 1985; Cobb & Jones, 1984; Reis, 1984). Also, some family therapists now treat systems and relationships instead of dealing only with 'problem individuals' in a family (Orford & O'Reilly, 1981). It is also clear now, that relationships interact with clinical symptoms, and if depression is not actually caused by relationships with other people, it can be exacerbated by them (Coyne,

1976). Perhaps, treatment of depressives should involve treatment of relationships and relational partners, not just the depressed person alone. Similarly, Lewis & McAvoy (1984) show that treatment of opiate abuse (particularly, heroin users) often takes the therapist into knotty relationship issues where pathological relationships can be either the result or the cause of opiate abuse. Some addicts turn to drugs through loneliness, but most addicts develop relational difficulties after they become addicted, anyway. Opiate abuse itself can become a central 'resource' of the relationship and a focus for its existence (e.g., when one person turns to pimping, prostitution, or stealing to provide drugs for the other person or when the relationship works only so long as one person is an addict and so 'needs' the partner). In some cases, the partners prefer it when the addict is quietened down with heroin so they resist attempts at a cure and subtly reinforce and sustain the addiction. In such cases, cure of the drug abuse will adjust the relationship dynamics and could well torpedo the relationship entirely. Treatment of the 'clinical' problem involves treatment of both the 'social' and relational problem.

How else does relationship work interact with the problems that counsellors and clinicians solve? Patients respond better to therapists whom they like (e.g., Takens, 1982), but some clinicians now believe that disturbed sexual relations, prejudice, and aggression can be viewed as consequences of relational disturbance or relational incompetence (Howells, 1981; Yaffe, 1981). Lonely and relationally incompetent men have a higher tendency towards rape, for instance (Check et al., 1985). However, a major issue for many of us is the break-up of close personal relationships and researchers have learned how their disruption leads to a number of serious consequences, ranging from unhappiness to death (Lynch, 1977; Bloom et al., 1978; Stroebe & Stroebe, 1983). Such breakdowns cause major physical and psychological upsets of a type that often bring the people into the care of counsellors and clinicians, and we do not often understand how to handle these situations on our own to avoid the negative consequences. As social psychologists develop a fuller understanding of the dissolution of relationships, so they can help provide guidance on repair (Duck, 1984a).

There are few 'scripts' for handling break-up of relationships and many intriguing research questions surround the actual processes by which people extricate themselves (or can be helped to extricate themselves) from unwanted relationships. For example, Miller & Parks (1982) look at relationship dissolution as an influence process and show that different strategies for changing attitudes can help in dissolution. It is now a major aim in the personal relationships field to explain dissolution and repair of relationships.

Summary

The new field of personal relationships is different from the old field of interpersonal attraction.

In looking at personal relationships a view broader than that of strangers, thoughts and uncertainty is needed. Early work on attraction to strangers is useful, provocative and too narrow; other work on acquaintance assumes too orderly a process and puts too much emphasis on thought. New emphases are present in the more recent work in this field. A current emphasis is on the view that relationships are continually developing processes rather than static states begun and defined purely by partners' initial psychological make up or reward levels. There is emphasis on: the *creation* of relationships; the effects of time and process; the interaction of beliefs with social skills and behaviour; and the role of perspectives and influences from outside the relationship. Decline, dissolution and repair of relationships must be considered in tandem with the role of everyday routines.

Now, we can look at the family and at children's relationship, perhaps the two most important kinds of relationship in life for us all.

Further reading

Duck, S.W. (1982) *Personal Relationships 4: Dissolving Personal Relationships*. Academic Press: New York & London.

Duck, S.W. (1983) *Friends, For Life*. Harvester Press: Brighton.

Duck, S.W. (1984) *Personal Relationships 5: Repairing Personal Relationships*. Academic Press: London & New York.

Duck, S.W. & Gilmour, R. (1981a) *Personal Relationships 1: Studying Personal Relationships*. Academic Press: London & New York.

Duck, S.W. & Gilmour, R. (1981b) *Personal Relationships 2: Developing Personal Relationships*. Academic Press: London & New York.

Duck, S.W. & Gilmour, R. (1981c) *Personal Relationships 3: Personal Relationships in Disorder*. Academic Press: London & New York.

Haley, J. (1978) *Problem Solving Therapy*. Harper & Row: London.

Hinde, R.A. (1979) *Towards Understanding Relationships*. Academic Press: London & New York.

Minuchin, S. (1978) *Families and Family Therapy*. Tavistock: London.

CHAPTER 4

Relationships with Relations: Families and Socialization

What sort of picture comes to mind when you think of the typical family? Two youngish parents with 2.4 children driving in an average-sized car to an ordinary supermarket to buy their normal breakfast cereals, right? The advertisers love families. So do politicians. Even average people in ordinary families like typical families. There are many aspects to family functioning that fascinate psychologists, too, and relationships in families — particularly as they form the basis for a child's beliefs about relationships with other people in general — raise a number of particularly interesting issues for us.

Kinship and membership of a family is a biological and genetic relationship, but it is also a social one. It is the social aspect of family life that concerns us here. What is social life like in the family? Yours may or may not be typical. Most families seem to be enjoyable and safe environments in which to live or grow up and our adherence to the hobby of keeping family albums and family trees testifies to most people's wish to remain in a family and to see themselves as a part of it through their life. There are other aspects to families, too.

Outside of the armed forces, the family is the most physically violent group or institution that a typical person is likely to encounter (Straus, 1985). We are more likely to see, commit, or be a victim of violence within the family than in any other setting. We are more likely to be murdered, beaten, or physically abused by our mother, father, or siblings than by a random stranger (Gelles, 1974), and every year a large number of people are permanently relieved of the pressures of daily life by a family member's violent and fatal burst of rage. Despite the cosy family photographs, there is a dark side to families. Partly,

BOX 4.1 Points to think about

— *How does the interaction of married partners influence the family that they create and how far does it depend on their courtship?*

— *Is it sensible to treat individuals for their problems or should we look deeper and explore their experiences in the family setting?*

— *How far do children's experiences with parental caretakers affect their future relationships?*

— *Are our later social lives predetermined by what happened in the family when we were kids, or do playground experiences at school matter also?*

— *Do some people stay disturbed because they stay in their family?*

— *Why are some children unpopular? Do they lack social skills that can be corrected?*

this is because we spend most of our time there, but it is also because of the intensities of emotion, both positive and negative, that are learned and experienced there.

Nearly half of all marriages will end in divorce (Cherlin, 1981) and by the time they are eighteen years old, one out of every two children will experience an upbringing in a single-parent household (Shorr & Moen, 1979). Whilst the Victorian family was something of an emotional iceberg (Shorter, 1975), the recent trend is towards families expected to be emotional refuges and strongholds. These shifting demands couple with new economic and social conditions to place new strains and demands on the family as a unit. Spouses are now asked to be satisfying lovers, caring friends, and even mutual therapists in a society that forces the marriage bond to become the closest, deepest, most important, and most enduring relationship in one's life (Slater, 1968). At first, we might see this as a welcome development, but the increased importance has the paradoxical effect of making it more likely that the members of the family will fall short of the emotional demands placed upon them (Slater, 1968).

People who live continuously in proximity to one another will interrupt one another's goal attainments frequently, so we should be less surprised about the turmoils inherent in family life than we often are. Cooper's (1970) radical critique of the family argues that when it functions best, the family is the ultimate destroyer of people by social means. It draws people together through a sense of their own incompleteness, it impedes the development of an individual's identity, it exerts too strong a social control over children, it indoctrinates family members with elaborate and unnecessary taboos. Other views are more accepting of the family and see it as a primary source of stability in society. It is true that many people find the family to be their greatest source of support in times of stress and their greatest comfort in life as a whole. However, the two views exist. Take a look at your own family album, and make your own choice.

Developing the Bonds

From first date to marriage

The family usually starts with a marriage and a marriage usually starts with a courtship. In a sense, then, each nuclear family starts on the first date between the two partners who eventually marry, though obviously not all first dates have those consequences.

It may seem strange to start with courtship, but if we are interested in the effects of parental divorce upon the children, for instance, we need to know something about the causes of broken marriages. Some current research is beginning to find that 'faulty' courtship predicts faulty marriages. It would be too simplistic to claim that all divorces are consequences of mistakes in courtship but a couple's courtship history does have some relevance here.

Are marriages made in heaven or do we have to do some of the work ourselves? Current work indicates that there are different routes, pathways, or trajectories through courtship, and some of them seem to bind the couple together more effectively than do others. How do new couples organize their relationships and does it matter? Yes, particularly in marriages, we are concerned with the ways in which partners make a good working living partnership and their ability to do this in courtship is not only an indication of courtship progress but a measure of the success of the relationship.

You may have noticed that I headed this section 'Developing the bonds'. 'Bonds' is a metaphor that implies tying, connection — chains, even. When we talk of a 'couple' we are actually using a similar metaphor. How do people tie themselves to someone else through the restructuring of their daily routines and thus become part of one another's life? As I pointed out in chapter 3, it is such involvements that make relationships, rather than mere feelings for one another that do so. Feelings start the process, but it is the meshing together of routines that is the creative part of forming relationships. Initial selection of friends and marital partners may well be due to their attractive looks or nice qualities, but long-term acquaintance and courtship are complex interpersonal processes.

How does courtship work?

Not all courtships follow the same track, and important differences have been found among four basic types (Huston et al., 1981). The four distinct pathways to marriage are associated with a different pattern of partner involvement in one another's daily routines. BOX 4.2 gives details of the study and others in similar vein.

BOX 4.2 Pathways to marriage and the decision to wed

Huston et al. (1981) found 4 different pathways towards marriage. They report on the development of a premarital and marital activities checklist which assesses 3 basic domains of the relationship: affectional activities, leisure activities, and instrumental activities such as household chores. They also developed a graphing procedure by means of which they could track the paths taken by couples towards marriage: essentially they asked married couples to think back over their courtship and indicate the points where they noted changes in their confidence that they would eventually marry. The resulting graphs identify 4 courtship types:

1 Accelerated-arrested *begins with a high level of confidence in the probability of marriage, but slows down in its final progression to marital commitment.*

2 Accelerated *starts off more slowly than type 1, but proceeds smoothly and directly to certainty of eventual marriage.*

3 Intermediate *evolves quite slowly and gradually, with the most turbulence and difficulty occurring at the last stages.*

4 Prolonged *courtships develop slowly and uncertainly, with much turbulence and difficulty.*

Partners in the intermediate courtships are the most independent of one another, particularly as regards feelings and joint actions (i.e., the so-called affectional and instrumental domains). They show less affection and joint activity. Partners in prolonged courtships report less affectional activity and lower proportions of leisure activities done together. Accelerated courtships are characterized by close affiliations and high, strong levels of liking, but partners are not necessarily more cohesive or bonded together when it comes to activities and time shared with other people.

Couples in the different types of courtship give different styles of explanation for why the relationship developed at given turning points (or why they were seen to be turning points). For committed relationships, partners give a higher percentage of explanations in dyadic rather than circumstantial terms (Surra, 1984), that is, they say they get together because they want to rather than because of circumstances, chance, or things over which they have no personal control.

Partners give more dyadic reasons for upturns in the probability of marriage ('we both were keener on it'), but more individual reasons for breaking off a relationship themselves ('I became bored'; 'my partner found someone else') according to Lloyd & Cate (1985).

Patterns of conflict and activity management in courtship predict stability in the marriage several years later (Kelly et al., 1985). Specifically, couples with high conflict in courtship do not seem to learn to handle it any better and continue to be highly conflictive in later marriage.

The feelings that partners have for one another are not necessarily a good predictor of their success at creating a sound relationship. Couples who are deeply in love may nevertheless fail to relate effectively, may become frustrated at the length of time it takes to carry out courtship successfully, or may give up and either leave the relationship or marry anyway and just hope that it will all work out. Bonding takes place through time and affects the activities and routines with which the couple intertwine themselves. Those that lead to greatest satisfaction with the courtship are those in which the couple's daily lives become most fully entwined as the routines of their day get more closely interlocked (Huston et al., 1981).

There are good and bad kinds of conflict to have during courtship. Some conflict seems to help the relationship but some of it most decidedly does not (Lloyd & Cate, 1985). 'Good' conflicts which facilitate the courtship are those about negotiation of tasks or activities or roles in the relationship. Couples may expect to argue about who does what, who goes where how often, what I shall do for you if you do this for me, who decides who does what, and the like. By sorting out these issues, even if it causes a few arguments at first, the couple is actually binding itself together more effectively as the two separate individuals start to function as a social unit. So those kinds of conflict (and their resolution) can be helpful. Those that are not helpful are the ones that centre on incongruent goals or inconsistency of desired outcome in the relationship. If we argue about the nature of the relationship (marriage vs friendship, e.g.) rather than who does what in it, then we are in trouble.

If partners handle these aspects of their courtship successfully, they lay the foundations for handling them successfully in the later marriage where tasks and duties shift and new problems occur (e.g., during the transition to parenthood — Lips & Morrison, 1986). The effects of conflicts or unresolved negotiations at this stage do not always show up until later into the relationship (Markman, 1979; 1981). Even serious conflicts in a courtship do not necessarily prevent couples from carrying on and developing the relationship, but these conflicts predict dissatisfaction with the marriage five years later (Kelly et al., 1985).

What about sex?

One difficult aspect of courtship is the question of sexual behaviour. In this context, too, there are different paths to follow and Christopher & Cate (1985) identify four typical pathways towards sexual intimacy, as indicated in BOX 4.3.

Sexual behaviour can be a source of pleasure and mutual satisfaction in a couple, but it has to be 'managed'. Questions arise as to frequency, initiation, context, and type of sexual activity agreed or permitted in the relationship. How often should it occur? Should it grow only from mutual desire or may either partner initiate it? What styles and variations are acceptable? Such matters are negotiable, and lots of conflict in the creation of a couple centres on these negotiations and behaviour (Christopher & Cate, 1985).

We often find that we are arguing about (or, at least, discus-

---

BOX 4.3 Pathways to sexual intimacy (Christopher & Cate, 1985)

There are 4 different pathways to sexual intimacy through the stages of (a) first date, *(b)* casual dating *, (c)* considering becoming an exclusive couple, *to (d) partners seeing themselves as an* established couple:

— Rapid involvement. *Here couples begin their sexual interaction at a high level during the early stages of dating, often having intercourse on the first date.*

— Gradual involvement. *This is characterized by a slow incrementation of sexual activity from first date to the 'couple' stage with orgasmically oriented sexual interaction starting typically at the stage when the couple was contemplating becoming 'a couple'.*

— Delayed involvement. *This is characterized by a gradual incrementation that nonetheless starts from a level lower than that of gradually involved couples. Sexual intercourse is typically delayed until after the couple see themselves as 'a couple', at which time there is a dramatic rise in the average level of sexual involvement and in varieties of sexual activity.*

— Low involvement. *Here couples start at a minimal level of sexual involvement on first date, and, by the time they become 'a couple', they are still at a preorgasmic level of sexual intimacy.*

Rapidly involved couples report high conflict but also high levels of love at the early stages, and, for the other types, increases in sexual involvement are associated with increases in both conflict and love.

---

sing) sexual matters as both the relationship and our expectations develop. Satisfaction with the level of sexual activity runs hand-in-hand with overall satisfaction with the relationship, whilst sexual dissatisfaction is a major source of unhappiness in marriage leading to arguments and extramarital affairs (Buunk & Bringle, 1986).

Getting the relationship organized

Thus far, we have learned more about the relatively obvious point that: families, marriages, and courtship have a history; the different parts of the history have to be established by agreement and negotiation; and they are quite likely to influence one another. The family, the marriage, and the courtship involve at least two of the same persons right through, and the different labels ('courtship', 'marriage') mean that only some parts of the relationship are new or different at each turning point. The partners are the same, though, and live life in many of the same old ways throughout. For this reason, many of the same sorts of issue and problem recur for the couple throughout that interconnected history from courtship to marriage (and, maybe, to divorce).

Therefore, a marriage is influenced not only by the *endogenous (or 'internal') factors* (e.g., how the two partners progress in interactions, communicate, feel about one another at a given time) but by some *exogenous (or 'external') factors* that do not arise specifically in interactions (e.g., the relational history). There are other exogenous factors, such as societal views about the ideal forms of relationships. When partners are married, they become a socially recognized unit ('the couple'; 'the happy couple', even), and the rest of us often treat them as one 'entity' that is invited everywhere together (by only one invitation, as opposed to individually), expected to do things together, has the same address, television — and status.

Relationships become organized and take on many of the properties and qualities of other organizations, such as shared history, private jokes and languages, distribution of labour and a sense of belonging, as we saw in chapter 3 (McCall, 1982). These are additional to the feelings that the partners have for one another, but they are just as important. Relationships can succeed or fail as much because they become disorganized as because the partners stop liking one another as people. For instance, we have all heard people complain about relational organization; for example, 'The relationship was too intense' or 'The relationship wasn't going anywhere' or 'We liked one another, but the relationship just didn't work out'.

The formation of the bonded unit, or married couple, has to be handled in its own right, and this often proves difficult. The couple's attempt to 'become a socially recognized unit' is not an automatic consequence of their liking, and they have to work at it and handle it. Even the honeymoon has this kind of role (Hagestad & Smyer, 1982): it helps the couple make the important transition between one couple type (engaged) and another (married). Immediately after being formally joined by the marriage, the couple go away from all the friends and relatives who knew them as 'unjoined' individuals. When they return, they return as a couple and the honeymoon period has given everyone the chance to adjust to the transformation.

Equally, the transition to parenthood is an important time of adjustment for the married couple, both in attitude and in distribution of time, activities and the ways in which they view themselves and each other (Lips & Morrison, 1986). It is particularly associated with an increased focus on family issues, and I noticed that when they were expecting a first child, many of my friends developed an interest in tracing their family tree, just as I did in the same circumstances. One gets a sense of belonging to a larger enterprise. Thus the transition to parenthood is a developmental process not only in obvious ways in respect of the family but also in less obvious ways in respect of the parents themselves.

The ways in which the relationship is worked out and organized in transitions, such as courtship, will eventually affect the way the marriage and the family work out.

The Working Family

Marriage: who does what?

Major factors that influence a couple's satisfaction are exogenous to the relationship, as noted earlier. They come from outside and are not part of its workings or of the feelings that the partners have for each other. Such factors could be, for instance, knowledge of the average statistics for frequency of sexual intercourse, which may affect the partners' views of whether they are behaving 'normally'. More important examples come from societal definitions of the 'proper' distribution of labour in marriage.

If a society generally believes that the 'good husband' carries out certain duties whilst the 'good wife' performs other quite distinct duties, then the couple who arrange things that way will feel that their marriage is ideal in that respect. But, if the society generally expects both partners to share all duties equally, then the same couple (or one member of it) will feel aggrieved and dissatisfied. The difference in the two cases is not the actual work or duties carried out but the context of attitudes in which they are carried out. What counts as a perfectly acceptable distribution of labour in the 1980s bears no resemblance to that in the ideal marriage in the 1890s. Couples from the two times who felt perfectly contented would probably look on each other's marriages with incredulity.

Part of the feeling that a marriage is working well depends on what the partners expect and expectations can come partly from the beliefs that society has about marriages (Sabatelli & Pearce, 1986). Partners can see how their marriage matches up to society's ideals for the relationship. If they see themselves carrying out their roles well then they will be satisfied. Dissatisfaction can be created by partners' feelings that their relationship does not live up to the societal ideal. Most of us are guided in our feelings and behaviour by some such influences, but some people actually take the lead almost entirely from social norms. Norms show them where they stand and increase their satisfaction with the relationship since they make it easier to know what is required of them.

Exogenous factors matter as much as the factors we usually assume to be significant, the endogenous factors, in marital satisfaction. The partners' feelings for one another, communication style, and relative power are examples of endogenous factors. The three really represent one and the same: expression of affection is done through communication and power is a communicative concept, too. When we talk of power in a relationship, we are describing partly the way in which one person's communications affect the other person and partly the way in which that other person responds. As Kelvin (1977) points out, power does not 'reside in' a person: you do not have power unless someone else treats you as if you do. It is a relational concept and depends on the acceptance of a person's power ploys by the person to whom they are directed.

Communication and satisfaction

How does this all impact on a couple? When one person acts and the other responds in a couple, they have accommodated, or adapted, to one another. Dyads, or pairs of people, communicating to one another do accommodate in various ways (outlined in chapter 2). Couples communicate in terms of their ability to resolve conflicts, express affection for one another, be open in self-disclosure of thoughts and feelings, and the like. Satisfaction is related to these communicational variables, and the primary predictor of marital satisfaction and dissatisfaction is the communication that occurs between partners. Most forms of communication between partners are reciprocal or couple-based which we have seen is true of power.

Therefore, the communication style of the couple should be far more important for their satisfaction and success than, say, demographic background and the personality matching of the partners are. In any case, the social meaning of any personality characteristic comes from the way that 'personality' is operated by the communicative behaviour of the persons (Duck, 1977). For many years, sterile debates took place about the role of similarity or oppositeness (i.e., complementarity) of personality in predicting success of marriages. But, these abstract personality variables do not predict marital happiness: happiness is predicted by the concrete ways they are put into practice through communication.

BOX 4.4 Marital satisfaction and communication

Happy couples give more positive nonverbal cues than do unhappy couples (Rubin, 1977).

Happy couples express more agreement and approval for the other person's ideas and suggestions (Birchler, 1972).

Satisfied couples confirm and support one another whilst dissatisfied ones reject and disconfirm one another — not only in respect of verbal statements but even in their very existence, often making statements that seem to imply 'You are nothing to me'; 'You do not exist for me'; 'Your comments and opinions do not matter to me'; 'I don't care' (Watzlawick et al., 1967).

Happier couples try harder to avoid conflicts (Raush et al., 1974).

They are more willing to reach compromises on difficult decisions (Birchler, 1972).

They express agreement more often than they express disagreement with the spouse during problem solving or conflict (Gottman, 1979; Riskin & Faunce, 1972).

Happy couples are more consistent in their displays of nonverbal affect (Noller, 1982).

Distressed couples are more likely to reciprocate negative communications than are happy couples (Gottman et al., 1977).

Different strokes for different folks

Are there different types of communication in marriage? Fitzpatrick (1977; Dindia & Fitzpatrick, 1985; Fitzpatrick & Badzinski, 1985) has developed a typology of marriage based on differences in communicative style. In the typology, there are three basic definitions which apply to individuals and thence to couples: traditional, independent, and separate.

In a *traditional* individual, communication is characterized by interdependence and expressiveness, and the person has conventional views about marriage and family life. Such persons seek regularity in their use of time, prefer stability to change, and confront rather than avoid conflicts, but they do so with some degree of social restraint. Such persons intertwine their life with their partner, release their emotions in limited ways, and are traditional in outlook.

Independent persons are only moderately interdependent in their marriage and have nonconventional views about marriage and family life, but, more so than Traditional persons, are very expressive in communications with their spouse. They share and confront conflicts, preferring to be frank, open, and unrestrained by social factors, but they like to explore novelty and change in marriage.

Separate persons are not particularly interdependent, have ambivalent views about marriage and family life and are not at all expressive in their communications with their spouse. They emphasize autonomy, differentiation of space, emotional distance, and avoidance of conflict.

From these three basic definitions for individuals, we can obviously make nine possible couple types (3 possible husband types × 3 possible wife types). In the three cases where husband and wife are both the same, Fitzpatrick speaks of the relationship as a *pure type* (traditional, independent, separate), and some 60 percent of couples are like this. The remaining 40 percent are distributed across the remaining six mixed types of relationship.

There are different relationships between communication styles, or patterns, and satisfaction with marriage, depending on the type of marriage — particularly in the pure types (Sillars et al., 1983). Independent couples are more likely to enjoy informational exchanges (e.g., self-disclosure, descriptions and discussion of conflict, etc.), and so they are more likely to be satisfied with an open, frank, and direct marriage that would be a source of great dissatisfaction to a separate couple. Separates are satisfied by denial of conflict or by refocussing onto other issues that serve to avoid conflict rather than to explore it. Thus conflict avoidance is more satisfying to separates than to independents. Satisfaction, then, is not necessarily created by any particular style of communication, per se: different couple types are satisfied with different types of communication style.

Satisfaction and behaviour

Relational behaviours predict satisfaction and create the inter-connectedness of different parts of the courtship/marital history of a couple. Communicative and negotiative work is necessary to forge the bonds that turn pairs of 'starry-eyed' individuals into a satisfactory, socially recognized unit. Enduring aspects of the relationship are the expressive behaviour, and these continue through courtship to marriage — and into the family that follows.

A couple's communication influences their level of satisfaction and affects the atmosphere in the rest of the family they have. If courting partners mesh their routines together, they improve the chance of working out ways to deal with new relational routines that become necessary (e.g., to cope with the birth of children). Kelly et al. (1985) study couples before marriage and then follow them up after their marriage to see whether features detected during courtship are predictive of marital stability, and, if so, which ones. Make your own predictions.

What is the best premarital predictor of marital stability? It is the ability to deal with conflict in the time before marriage (Kelly et al., 1985), which is a communicative factor rather than an individual one. On the other hand, ineffective nonverbal communication is associated with marital dissatisfaction (Pike & Sillars, 1985), and nonverbal cues provide a context for verbal communications. Nonverbal affective patterns (i.e., showing affection by smiling, touching, etc.) are more important than verbal disclosure and explicit verbal attempts to avoid conflict.

Obviously such work as the preceding studies helps marriage (and premarital) counsellors trying to prevent marital problems. Their effort is to try and create in courtship a stable basis for the subsequent marriage over and above the intention to increase the couple's satisfaction with their courtship (Ridley & Nelson, 1984; Markman et al., 1982). Some couples, for instance, volunteer for 'enrichment programmes' without feeling that their relationship is in serious difficulties, but they merely want to get more out of it in the present or future (Ridley & Nelson, 1984). Nonetheless, Markman (1979; 1981) shows that the more positively couples rated each other's communication during negotiation exercises, the more satisfied they were with their relationship later on (both 2 and a half years and 5 years later on). This was so even when the degree of positivity/negativity of communications was not related to partners' satisfaction at the time when the assessments were initially made. In other words, our future satisfaction is predictable from how we feel about present communication patterns, even though we do not notice it at the time.

So, we could begin to see that families are made in marriages, marriages are made in courtships, and maybe courtships are made in activities and routines. What background do the partners' activities create for their future relationship as a family? Who 'does best' out of marriage, men or women?

Marriage as a background for the person's life

Men benefit more in the traditional marriage. Over sixty years ago, men reported being more satisfied with their marriage than their wives were, and women were more seriously disappointed (Hamilton, 1924). Marriage, or the status of 'being married', tends to be associated in men with decreased rates of suicide and a higher health status even very recently (Bernard, 1972).

Although compared to women, men are more liable to heart problems, ulcers, and earlier death, the rates for married men are lower than those for single men and so are rates of alcohol abuse and drug problems. We might immediately think of one criticism of these points: perhaps, it is the healthier men who are able to attract spouses in the first place, so that figures are unfairly inflated. Maybe; but that idea is based on the same mistake the attraction literature made in assuming that the 'entry qualifications', such as personality profile, set the relationship forever. As we saw in chapter 3, it is unwise to ignore the behaviours of acquainting since these affect the relationships, too. Equally, we can expect the behaviours in marriage to be more important than the initial entry qualifications, like health and good looks. Maybe we have to be healthy to increase our chance of marrying, but good health does not guarantee that the marriage will 'work'.

Men suffer more severely from the consequences of death of the spouse or from disruption of their marriage by separation or divorce (Stroebe & Stroebe, 1983). Bereaved husbands suffer higher rates of sudden death and severe health difficulties following the death of their wife than women do after the death of their husband. The period of separation or divorce from a wife, children, and family is particularly stressful for men (Bloom et al., 1978) and a whole retinue of health problems ensues, ranging from tonsillitis to heart disease. The existence of a marriage is good for men and its loss is bad for them.

Relationships with women actually correlate with good health (Reis, 1986) and the more women we meet in the day, the healthier we feel. It is understandable, then, that a husband gets benefits from marriage that the wife does not obtain within the marriage, but may obtain from her female friends.

What can we deduce from those facts? Maybe, they show the deficiency of marriage for women; or, perhaps, they show the positive effects of marriage for men. At present one has to decide this issue for oneself. However, it points out that the emotional investments of family members in a marriage are unequal and so are the needs for each of the family members. In traditional marriages, the 'resources' are often unfairly distributed, in that one partner (the husband) has more extensive control over them than does the other (the wife). We should bear this in mind whilst recalling that power is a relational construct that depends not just on control of resources but on control of information, communication style, and various 'couple variables', already discussed.

These differences in power, needs, investments, and outcomes are important for the two adult members obviously, but are also relevant when we take a broader look at the family and include the children. Children have low power in families; they are subject to control by parents; yet their relationship with parents can act as a model for their own relationships with other people later in life.

Caretakers and children

There has been enough thinking about the impact of parental upbringing on 'life chances' for truisms to have reached the popular media as far back as the 1950s (e.g., 'Hey! I'm depraved on account I'm deprived' in West Side Story). Such truisms stem in part from the important pioneering work of Bowlby (1951), who claims that an infant's relationship with the mother is predictive of later adolescent relational success. In brief, Bowlby's claim is that an infant separated from the mother developed psychological complexes that impaired subsequent relationships and could lead to delinquency in adolescence and adulthood.

This is almost commonsense nowadays even though the work was revolutionary in its time. How often have we heard people say that their relationship with their mother is responsible for later life events? But, do they mean to blame a relationship that happened before they could even speak? Do we really believe that people turn into delinquents just because their relationship with their mother was inadequate for four to six months?

This work has been seriously questioned (Rutter, 1972). One problem is that the 'maternal deprivation hypothesis' seems to assume that everything that happens between the ages of one year and thirteen years does not have much effect. By contrast, we should be looking at the activities that occur during the rest of childhood and the impact, on the child's social life, of its view of itself as a social being. Self-esteem influences our views of our attractiveness and so has a major effect on our relationships. So, let us take a good look at the experiences in the family which affect self-esteem and give us the basis for our relationships with other human beings.

The specific variable of parental style of control in a family not only can affect the child directly but can provide a model for the child's subsequent social relationships. It lays out foundations for future relationships through its effect on the child's self-image. Fitzpatrick & Badzinski (1985) conclude that 'there is little doubt that making a child feel loved, supported and comfortable in the presence of a parent leads to the development of a large range of socially valued behaviours in the child'.

There are essentially three styles in which parents treat children (Baumrind, 1972). The *authoritarian* parents try to control and evaluate the behaviour of a child using some absolute standards of behaviour. They stress obedience and punishment — often physical punishment but this also frequently takes the form of withdrawal of love or psychological blackmail. Secondly, *permissive* parents relate to the child's behaviour in nonpunitive and accepting ways, often consulting the child about its behaviour, offering rationales for the standards that are used, and relying on reason rather than punishment in child-rearing. Finally, *authoritative* style is one based on direction of the child through reason but not on the basis of equality or, necessarily, of acceptance of what the child is doing. Such a parent exercises firm control, but does so by verbal interchange. This style of parenting is more successful in producing children who are independent, cooperative, friendly and achievement-oriented.

These different styles affect the happiness and character development of the child and also provide different models for the child's own perception of the world and relationships between people. A child who is taught by example to be obedient to adults or authority figures is more likely to become authoritarian in relationships with superiors and inferiors (Adorno et al., 1950).

The different parental styles probably indicate differences in parental attitudes to one another also and are not simple products of parents' personalities. For example, reconsider Fitzpatrick's (1977) system of classifying married couples into traditionals, separates, and independents, and note that as a classification system it contains some 'echoes' of the Baumrind model. This is so despite the fact that Fitzpatrick dealt with partners' communications with one another, whilst Baumrind looked at parents' communications with their children. For a style to develop in a family, it has to be created, negotiated, and shared. When the two parents have different approaches to child-rearing, we can expect to find problems for the child and the parents. For instance, a child is likely to become confused by inconsistencies (although this could itself be useful training for life, where inconsistencies are a far more frequent experience — in both ourselves and other people — than we might prefer to believe). Equally, two parents with different approaches are increasing the risks of their coming into conflict with one another, thus causing family distress — which itself is likely to upset the child in question. Finally, inconsistencies of parental treatment between one child and another are sources of both family tension and personal anguish for that child who feels aggrieved or neglected.

Can we classify family functioning?

There are systematic stylistic differences between 'deviant' and 'normal' families (Burgess, 1981), although the problem, by its very nature, may take years to develop. The features of family life that may exist once the problem has come to light could be different from those that 'caused' it.

An unsatisfactory, or dysfunctional, style of bonding in the family takes five forms:

1 The negative side of things is accentuated (i.e., there is a critical, punitive style focussing on poor performances rather than praising good ones).

2 The parents are poor observers of their children's behaviour and do not make good discriminations between different performances of the same acts (e.g., they may not notice slight improvements, may take little note of the amount of effort put into achieving the outcome, etc.).

3 The parents are highly inconsistent in their use of punishment, sometimes ignoring transgressions altogether but at other times inflicting dire retribution.

4 The parents establish low levels of positive contact; that is,

they do not act particularly warmly or affectionately to the child in general and certainly do not go out of their way to do so.

5 The emphasis of their relationship to the child is on power, force, and coercion. In this context, the model they present is one that tends to reward the child for being aggressive.

Such behaviours probably confuse the child and cause stress not least because of the child's lowly place in the scheme of things. Most of those dysfunctional behaviours have the obvious effect of devaluing the child, and, at early ages, it would be surprising if this did not lead to a paralysingly low self-esteem (Duck, 1983). If this occurs, then we would be likely to find the child experiencing difficulties in other relationships because:

(a) the child has no reliable models of how to conduct good relationships;

(b) the child has a low opinion of his or her own social value to other people.

Problem children in nursery schools (aged 3–5 years), are of three basic types (Manning & Herrman, 1981):

Aggressive: such children present management problems for the teachers and are dominating, rough, defiant, and spontaneously violent.

Dependent: these children are anxious to please, are demanding of teachers, want everything done for them, and are timid with other kids.

Withdrawn: these children do not enter games with the others but keep to themselves, often looking on longingly at the other children playing.

We cannot derive each of these styles directly from one particular parental style, but the possibility remains that some connection exists. As I have suggested, the dependent or withdrawn child may have developed low self-esteem coupled with fear of other people whilst an aggressive child may come from a home where aggression is rewarded or where parents are aggressive or abusive to one another and so act as models for the child's own style.

There are clear elements of children's beliefs about themselves which could stem from their experiences in the family, even if the sort of connection is not exactly as proposed by Bowlby. Whether a direct connection is assumed, relationships between people in the family setting provide the easiest examples for children to follow. If the family is happy, the children have a better chance of developing into sociable adults themselves. Conversely, problem children usually come from problem families.

Happy Families?

How can we assess the quality of the family and its success?

We could ask whether the family accomplishes major family goals, whether the organization of the family violates societal principles, and whether the family contains a 'diseased' member. Riskin & Faunce (1972) once claimed that the least studied family unit is the family itself. Most work that claims to explore 'the family' actually explores particular dyads or pairs within the family, such as the marital pair, the mother-child pair, the father-child pair, or the sibling-pair. Few works look at the family as a unit, and most of that is work on disturbed families (Fitzpatrick & Badzinski, 1985).

By considering the family all together, we can see the ways in which the parts influence one another. For example, we could bring families to the laboratory to discuss a problem or engage in a task that obliges them to interact whilst the experimenter records and then transcribes the interaction for later analysis (Bochner, 1976). As one instance of this, some clinical therapies have an exercise where the family gets together to work out a family tree and the therapist takes note of 'who knows what'.

When we look at families in this way, we usually find that abnormal children or adolescents (say, aggressive, delinquent, or schizophrenic individuals) come from families in which positive, nurturant, and encouraging or supportive behaviours are either less frequent than normal or else excessive and stifling, such that the child feels smothered and wants to do something to escape. For this reason, argumentative, noxious, negative, primitive, or aggressive interactions are much more frequent in such families than are normal interactions (Fitzpatrick & Badzinski, 1985). This may occur because negative parents serve as poor models for their children, who may not only learn wrong behaviours from them but also develop many negative feelings towards them and towards other authority figures. More likely, children affect parents, too, so that disruptive children cause disruptive responses from parents.

Whilst all this may be true, it is an 'individual' way of looking at things: it assumes that individuals are just influenced by other individuals. It does not emphasize the context of other interactions available in the family system. Yet, the relationship between any two people in a system influences the other interactions that can take place in that system. If a father has a favourite child, for instance, then that fact may affect the relationships between the children, may cause jealousies, could make the mother 'compensate' towards the other child(ren), and so on. The system-based nature of the family is important, and the parts are interdependent one upon the other (La Gaipa, 1981). With family problems, the systems approach is turning up some intriguing findings.

Who causes an individual's problems?

'Individuals have problems and individuals should be treated for them' was, and in some places still is, the usual motto when a person developed aberrant behaviour, such as, alcohol problems, drug abuse, depression, or schizophrenia. That the person could be not only an individual but also a man or woman, a husband or wife, a sibling, a daughter or son tended to be given lesser importance.

In many cases, such a view may be quite right, and it would be correct to conclude that the social context for psychological problems is not necessarily important. If a person is depressed because he or she cannot establish relationships with other people, then his or her personal lack of social skills may be far more important than the family background — although we

---

BOX 4.5 Family relationships and social, personal or physical problems

Some persons show depressive symptoms that are intended for a specific audience, that is, members in the family (McPartland & Hornstra, 1964). If someone withdraws, shows irritability and agitation in a family setting, it is difficult for the family members to ignore. It disrupts the social functioning of the family as the depressives' attempts to throw the burden of their problems onto other people become more strident and obscure.

Unhappily married people, relative to the divorced or happily married, showed more neurosis, depression, chronic illness, and disability (Renne, 1971).

Men who felt unsupported by their wives were more likely to suffer physical and psychological disturbances after an involuntary job loss (Gore, 1978). Specifically, they showed changes in cholesterol, illness symptoms, and affectivity (or emotional instability).

Psychosomatic diabetic children have exaggerated 'turn-on' of free fatty acid (FFA) rates that relates to emotional arousal and the first step in the occurrence of a diabetic symptom pattern (Minuchin et al., 1978). The authors found these FFA turn-on rates are uniquely elicited within the family context and that they suffer an impaired turn-off ability following the child's participation in a family conflict.

---

may enquire whether the deficiency in such skills results from experiences within the family. What is needed in such cases could be simply an individualized training programme in social skills, focussing on the kinds of nonverbal and verbal communication that are covered in chapter 2.

However, it is faulty to assume that a person's problems have an individualized locus without taking the necessary scientific steps to ensure that the social and domestic context *is* irrelevant (Feldman & Orford, 1980). A social context can 'cause' the problem (e.g., in a family where interaction is usually negative and causes much stress). On the other hand, it may just reinforce an existing problem (e.g., when one partner in a relationship is dependent on drugs or alcohol and members of the family are happiest, in some sense, when the person is calmed or stupefied by the substance).

Relationships and depression

Depression is a good example of an 'individual' problem that can have a basis in relationships. Relationships can both cause depression and reinforce it since other members of the family tend to treat the depressed member in a stilted, spurious or 'careful' way (Coyne, 1976), which in itself may reinforce the person's sense of insecurity and fragility. This can make depression become a self-perpetuating interpersonal system: all persons in the environment end up creating a system where feedback cannot be received or given properly. The depressed person keeps getting misleading feedback that says 'You're not normal' but no-one does anything to help. The behaviour system thus only maintains the problem.

A woman's characteristic pattern of social relationships could act to increase her vulnerability to depression (Brown & Harris, 1978). Absence of close confiding relationship with a husband or boyfriend is associated with higher risk of developing depression after a big loss or major disappointment. It looks as if a poor social relationship network — or, rather, absence of confiding relationships — is a major 'vulnerability factor'; it deprives people of the armour with which to defend themselves against severe blows or disappointments in life (Brown, 1984; O'Connor & Brown, 1984). In the absence of such blows and disappointments, the vulnerability is insignificant on its own; it is only when the person is 'stretched' and tested that the problem cannot be well handled.

An individual level of analysis is not necessarily wrong in all cases (e.g., some forms of depression result from metabolic disturbance in the person, Johnson, 1984). However, we must take account of social relational issues in the equation, especially when the nature of the problem creates relational consequences.

Family problems and family relationships

Family problems and interpersonal relationships usually go hand in hand (Burgess, 1981). The variables most associated with life-satisfaction are relational variables like marital happiness rather than, say, socioeconomic factors like income level. Equally and conversely, conflict and individual deviancy are directly 'traceable to contingency histories located within the family itself' (Burgess, 1981). In other words, we are happy when family relationships are going well, but we, and probably other people too, develop side-effects when things go wrong. Such side-effects can be as simple as stress or as complicated as physical and psychological conditions which appear to be totally unrelated to the family problem. Relational difficulties are suspected to underlie some cases of, for instance, anorexia nervosa, cancer, heart disease, and even sudden death (Lynch, 1977).

Let us, for the moment, look at a couple of detailed instances where family relationships appear to be influential in creation and extension of social problems (BOX 4.5 gives more instances). Such cases help us to see that when an individual has problems we should, at least, look at the domestic, social and relational context of that individual. We may find nothing, or we may see the root of the problem.

Alcoholism, drug dependence, and relationships

How can alcoholism or drug abuse possibly have anything to do with the family? The heavy (problem) drinker is not merely an individual who happens to have impact on a family (i.e., it is not adequate to see the drinkers as 'the problem'). Although there are such impacts (e.g., on children of parents who drink excessively — Wilson & Orford, 1978), there are some problems with this kind of interpretation. For one, a large proportion of families are quite resistant to improvements in the family member with the problem (Orford, 1980). Spouses themselves sometimes break down when their partner's drinking problem is cured (Orford & O'Reilly, 1981). Also partners sometimes describe 'the other person when drunk' in terms more favourable than they describe 'the other person when sober' (Orford, 1976). In particular, wives often describe their 'drunk husbands' as more masculine and dominant than they describe their 'sober husbands'. Orford et al. (1976) even found that unfavourable 'when sober' perceptions of a spouse were predictive of poor outcome for the drinking problem over the subsequent twelve months. If we prefer partners drunk it is unlikely we shall substantially support their attempts to stay sober.

The feelings of one family member towards another who has a problem can help to sustain the problem and interfere with attempts to solve it.

What are the links between relational factors and 'individual problems' with drugs? Partners and children of opiate abusers are frequently called on to structure their lives in a way that, as it were, depends on the addiction of a family member. For example, the partner and children may spend the day routinely stealing money to pay for the drug. Such routines of life are important to us as frameworks in which to conduct ourselves. Suppose the addiction is treated. How does that alter the way in which the addict's partner and children need to spend their routine day, and does that change their attitudes to themselves? In a sense, they are no longer needed: their functions have become redundant. As we might predict, these people frequently resist the therapeutic exercise and lead the addict back to the addiction, thus restoring their routine usefulness (Lewis & McAvoy, 1984). In such cases, treatment for opiate abuse often includes treatment for the abuser's family. Treatments strive to provide some alternative structure and routine for the abuser's family so that the addict's return to normality does not simply empty their lives together (Lewis & McAvoy, 1984).

Distress and family interaction

Happy families have pleasant interactions and unhappy ones do not: it is not just that they like or dislike one another. The problem is behavioural and routine. The habitual styles of interaction in a family are good indicators of the levels of distress, unhappiness, and dissatisfaction.

Even when distressed families are not arguing, there are still disturbed aspects to their interaction, so this is not just a circular argument. We would not expect distressed families to show just distressed patterns of interaction almost by definition, if we believe that 'internal distresses' or unhappy feelings are reflected in transactional distress or behavioural routines.

The style of management of conflict may be as important as its rate, intensity, or seriousness. The interactions of distressed families are noteworthy; they are rather ritualized (Haley, 1964). They are characterized by low meshing (i.e., partners' behaviours do not fit well; e.g. one may talk about one topic and another replies by talking about another). As one example, distressed families have high rates of monologue-silence-monologue-silence (Ferreira & Winter, 1968).

Distressed families generally show lower frequencies of affectionate and supportive behaviour (Gottman, 1982) but this is not quite as 'obvious' as it might sound, since this obtains even when they are not in a distressed episode or argument. People in distressed families are habitually and routinely unsupportive and lacking in displays of affection. It seems, then, that distressed families are more rigid and predictable. They are much more likely to reciprocate negative affect or emotion than they are to do with positive feelings. They are more likely to behave unconnectedly, and their 'conversations' are more like two tape recorders running in parallel rather than being two people meaningfully interconnecting their speech and communication.

Splitting up

All through this I have written about distressed families that stay together nevertheless. Many couples, however, become divorced — something near 40 percent of all marriages since 1970 will end in divorce, and the figure for those since 1975 may be considerably higher. That means conversely that 60 percent of marriages endure through the years despite a multitude of factors that work against long-term marital satisfaction. But, as I note at the start of the book that social psychologists assume the positive and 'explain' the negative, so there has been less acknowledgement of this side of the question.

What 'causes' divorce? Answers range from demographic factors, like race and religion, to personality factors like achievement motivation and extraversion (see BOX 4.6).

We must avoid treating divorce as an event for which a cause should be found. Rather, divorce is a transitional process *not* an event, and researchers are now looking for those causal factors which combine to fuel the relentless unforgiving development of that process. Divorcing takes so long because there is more to it than just 'falling out of love'.

There are at least three parts to marriage that have to be unpicked in divorcing (Hagestad & Smyer, 1982). As we saw in discussing courtship, partners have not only to love one another (one part) but to be successful in meshing their activities and daily routines together (second part). As their relationship becomes well-bonded and the routines, work, or division of labour in the relationship are sorted out, so the partners develop attachment to the role of spouse — the 'being a husband or a wife' (third part). These three things (love for partner, attachment to established routines, attachment to the marital role) all are built up in courtship and marriage. All have to be disassembled during divorcing. There are many types of divorce that are identified (Hagestad & Smyer, 1982). The first distinction is between orderly and disorderly divorce.

In orderly divorces, the partners detach themselves success-fully not only from their feelings for one another but from their attachment to the role of 'husband' or 'wife', from their involvement in an established set of daily routines, and from the legal role. They have to decide that they do not love their partner, do not want to be 'a spouse', do not miss the routines of

---

BOX 4.6 Some findings about marital breakdown

Marriage at a young age predicts a lower degree of marital happiness and adjustment (Bentler & Newcomb, 1978). It is also associated with a greater likelihood of divorce (Mott & Moore, 1979).

Individuals with gross psychiatric symptomatology have low marital adjustment and happiness, as do those with rigid defensive personalities (Murstein & Glaudin, 1968).

Men who saw themselves as extraverted and invulnerable, with a high need for orderliness, more often are divorced than are men without those views (Bentler & Newcomb, 1978).

The more premarital sexual partners that a person has, the less marital happiness he or she is likely to report (Athanasiou & Sarkin, 1974). Premarital pregnancy is another predictor of low marital happiness (Furstenberg, 1979).

Heterogamy (i.e., unequal matching on age, race, religion, etc.) is strongly related to poorly adjusted and unhappy marriage (Newcomb & Bentler, 1981).

Couples who have cohabited before marriage report fewer barriers to terminating their marriage (Cole, 1976).

The presence of children consistently lowers the marital adjustment felt by both men and women (Renne, 1970).

There is a gradual decrease in happiness over the first 10 years of marriage (Rollins & Feldman, 1970) but it increases after the children leave home (Argyle & Henderson, 1984). This could result from the emerging effects of many of the preceding factors.

---

their daily life together, but do want to be legally divorced.

Disorderly divorces are those where at least one aspect of these disengagements is not successfully completed. For instance, one partner may stay in love with the 'ex', or may find it impossible to adjust to 'not being married'. Hagestad & Smyer (1982) list seven types of disorderly divorce, ranging from 'business as usual' — the couple want to be legally divorced and do not love one another but continue to stay in the same house and do the same sorts of things in daily life as they have always done — to 'I wish it hadn't happened' — partners' daily activities are disconnected from one another but one partner still feels love for the other one.

Three important points about divorce

First, divorce is a stressful process with both physical and psychological side-effects. It affects and disrupts the partners' daily lives, routines, and sense of identity as well as just making them unhappy. Second, the divorce of two persons has consequences for many more people than just the two persons who are separating. It obviously affects the children of the marriage. Since we are looking at the family as a system, we should think about those effects. Third, to become divorced, couples have to separate — that is, to unpick, 'brick by brick', the relationship they have put together and to do this they have to undo both the internal ties (e.g., affection) and the external binding (e.g., family and societal pressures and forces that may keep them together). Just as society creates exogenous influences on couple's courtships and marriages, so it creates barriers to the dissolution of marital relationships. Two obvious ones are:

1 'Divorced' is a negatively valued state that people do not like to have to apply to themselves. One adjustment that divorcees have to make is to the sense of shame and failure that often is felt by the person or imposed by outsiders. In our society, it is believed that a divorce is a *failed* relationship (rather than, say, a courageous and honest response to an unworkable partnership).

2 Society is organized in a way that 'expects' people to belong to couples, so that it is actually regarded as embarrassing, say, to invite a single person to a dinner party without inviting another 'single' of the opposite sex to balance things out. What may seem right to the hosts, however, can sometimes be embar-

rassing to the 'single' guests who probably take mild offence at being crudely paired off like that.

Children and divorce

Divorce is an extended transition that inevitably 'affects the entire family system and the functioning and interactions of the members within that system' (Hetherington et al., 1982, p. 233). The outcome and experience of the divorce affect different members of the family differently, and the problems faced by the divorced parents are likely to be different — and to require different skills — from those faced by the children. There is no such thing as a victimless divorce (Hetherington et al., 1982) — that is, one where no member of the family reported any distress or exhibited disrupted behaviour.

Children in distressed families, particularly those that experience separation and divorce, develop certain personality styles or views of themselves and also manifest social-behaviour problems when interacting with other children. Children experiencing parental divorce tend to suffer from depression and psychological disturbance, such as excessive feelings of their own guilt — they particularly tend to assume that their parents' divorce is somehow their fault (Hetherington, 1979).

In the first year, particularly, of the divorce, children from divorced families are more oppositional and obstructive, more aggressive, lacking in self-control, distractible, and demanding than are children from families that are still together. This is true even if the intact (i.e., undivorced) families are showing high rates of marital distress and discord. The divorce itself is a significant factor.

Being labelled 'the child of divorced parents' is something that children find difficult to cope with (e.g., they may get a 'hard time' at school for 'having no mother or no father'). In an attempt to explore this issue, Gottlieb (1983) reports a programme in Canada designed to deal with the aftermath of parental divorce. By introducing children of divorced parents to one another, Gottlieb was able to establish support groups for them. The support group shows them they are not alone in their experience and helps them to share and develop ways of coping with their problems. This technique makes use of what we now have learned about children's friendships outside the family.

Outside influences

After it was realized that a mother's relationship to her infant in the first six months did not necessarily predetermine the rest of the child's social life, researchers looked first in two main directions: to adolescent gangs and to family life (Duck, 1983). Two other major areas also opened up: the impact of peer or sibling interactions, and the relevance of style of fathering. Researchers began to realize that brothers, sisters, fathers, and friends — and childhood — had somehow been omitted from the earliest thoughts on this issue.

Are children essentially passive and receptive to various significant forces that stamp themselves on the developing person, or are children active persons who exert their own individual influences? Maybe, they are interactive. Maybe, the child is an active participant exerting influence and effects on others as much as being influenced and affected by them.

In our first interactions with our parents, development is a basic framework for understanding and evaluating our own personal worth. From this base, children work out their own value to other people as a social object; an understanding of the nature and structure of relationships between people; and the kinds of relationship that they are best at establishing with others. Such thoughts can be formed by influences as subtle as the mother's speech style (Garrard & Kyriacou, 1985). Mothers who use a language code based on awareness of others' feelings increase the child's social sensitivity, the ability to comprehend others' feelings in friendship, and the awareness of others' needs and goals in social settings.

Many influences on a child's willingness to relate to others are equally subtle — even, for instance, the age of the parents. As adults mature through their own life cycle, so their pattern of friendship alters in various ways (Dickens & Perlman, 1981; Reisman, 1981). Their networks expand and contract as a result of the pressures on them from careers, family, and age itself. At some ages (usually mid-20s to mid-30s), parents' own friends have young children and these, therefore, make good playmates for one another. If, however, a pair of parents are of unusual ages for parenthood (say they are much older than usual) then their friends may not have young children any more. There, a natural shortage of playmates exists for their own children, who may thus be exposed to fewer social experiences with other children.

Perhaps, it is a small point then, but as a child develops, so do the parents and other members of the family system, who have their own life-tasks and concerns. Anderson (1985) shows that both mothers and fathers show sharp increases in role stress when their eldest child first enters school. For the average pair of parents, however, a child's entry to kindergarten or infant school presents them with a new range of friends themselves. Childrens' parents are sometimes enabled to become friends with one another just because the children meet at school and become friends. The parents' paths cross more frequently, and they begin to share common interests and concerns.

This is an important change because very young children play with other children only if they are pointed at them. Obviously, they do not have the resources or mobility to go round choosing or visiting friends. They play with those who are 'put in front of them'. Yet, even at young ages the child probably needs experience with other children. The smiling encouragement of caring parents is not enough; even when it paves the way, the way has to go somewhere.

Peer influences

If you were unpopular at school you are more likely to become an alcoholic, a depressive, a schizophrenic, a delinquent, a dischargee from the army, or a psychotic (Putallaz & Gottman, 1981). Who says that children's friendships with each other do not matter? Recognizing their importance, researchers have begun to explore the bases of children's friendships, the ways in which they change with age, the ways in which they go wrong, and the most effective means for putting them right.

Cognitive bases of children's friendships

It seems to make sense to ask whether children's friendships are based on their general mental development. In other words, is social development related to cognitive development? Children acquire moral reasoning and intellectually manipulated skills in a predominantly systematic and progressive fashion. Are their friendships based on similar principles? Is there a predictable sequence in children's approaches to friendship?

In a single sentence, children become less egocentric and instrumental in their friendships between the ages of zero and six, develop relationships based on cooperation during the ages five to ten, and begin to appreciate more fully the value of a friend's deep psychological qualities, like character, from about the age of nine. These developments and sophistications continue in adolescence (Duck, 1975b). To put it even more briefly, the focus shifts from 'Me and what you can do for me' to 'You and Me and what we can do together' to 'Us and how we can help one another to grow as people'. Figure 4.1 gives a comparison of two major approaches and shows the various labels that have been given to the stages behind my preceding short summaries.

Children initially (i.e., ages 3–7) define friends in terms of proximity and availability (Selman & Jaquette, 1977). Somewhere between the ages of four and nine children acquire an ability to differentiate another child's viewpoint from their own, but a friend is still valued for what he or she can do for me rather than on any reciprocal basis. Between six and twelve ('fair weather' cooperation), children come to appreciate reciprocity in friendship and realize that the other person has rights, needs, and wishes also. However, these are still seen as self-interested rather than mutual, and a child will satisfy a friend's needs only if it suits. From around nine, the child realizes that friendship is collaborative: mutual and common goals are important. Only around the age of twelve does complex

FIGURE 4.1: Two major theories of children's friendships

Selman & Jaquette[a]			Bigelow & La Gaipa[b]		
Stage	Friendship awareness	Perspective-taking	Stage	Dimension	Grade at onset
0 (3–7)[c]	Momentary physical playmate	Undifferentiated; egocentric	I.	Situational 1. Common activities 2. Evaluation 3. Propinquity	2 3 3
1 (4–9)	One-way assistance	Subjective; differentiated	II.	Contractual 4. Admiration	4
2 (6–12)	Fair weather cooperation	Reciprocal; self-reflective	III.	Internal-psychological 5. Acceptance 6. Loyalty and commitment 7. Genuineness 8. Common interests 9. Intimacy potential	4 5 6 7 7
3 (9–15)	Intimate-mutual understanding	Mutual; third person			
4 (12+)	Autonomous independence	In depth; societal			

[a] Adapted from Selman & Jaquette (1977) and Selman & Selman (1979).
[b] Adapted from Bigelow & La Gaipa (1975) and Bigelow (1977).
[c] The numbers in parentheses are rough guidelines of the age range in each stage.

Source: Dickens & Perlman (1981) in Duck & Gilmour (1981b, p96) *Personal Relationships 2: Developing Personal Relationships* Academic Press: London. Reproduced by permission.

appreciation of friendship appear and begin to take a more adult form, namely, recognizing that autonomy and independence can go together with friendship (e.g., the other person will need other friends and that fact does not threaten our friendship).

Do the stages of children's friendship development reflect the stages of adults' friendships or acquaintance (Duck et al., 1980)? There are many parallels. For instance, adults get to know one another first on the basis of physical cues, then behaviour, then attitudes and detailed structures of personality. In comparable fashion, children at younger ages form friendships on the basis of physical and outward signs, then in terms of (cooperative) behaviour and then, in adolescence, on the basis of character and personality.

Children's behaviour and friendship

Friendship is not all 'cognitive' as we found in adults: behaviour has a major part to play, and behaviour changes as the child grows up. It is through behaviour, particularly through reciprocity and cooperation, that children begin to learn about relationships (Youniss, 1980). In particular, they come to know about other people through social collaboration. Our knowledge of ourselves and of other people comes from an increasing understanding of social relationships built up from social interaction. Earlier I was claiming that a child establishes a level of self-esteem from early interaction with parents and Youniss' (1980) more sophisticated view of the interactions of peers is entirely consistent with such a view.

The interaction of thought and behaviour is only one side of the coin: even if children do develop through stages at a reasonably steady rate, we need not assume that they all start with the same levels of abilities: some are tuned in to friendship and some are not. Children scoring high in friendship motivation are different from other children in their detailed understanding of friendship (McAdams & Losoff, 1984). They also show very sociable behaviour (which is independently classified by teachers as 'friendly', 'affectionate', 'cooperative', 'sincere', 'happy' and 'mature'). Those with higher scores on

BOX 4.7 Children's friendships

There is a relationship between a child's conception of friendship and behaviour with friends (Sants, 1984). Children with a highly developed friendship conception are more likely to ignore other children, to try to organize them or control them, and are more successful at doing so than are children with less developed concepts. 'Highs' are less likely to be the victims of all forms of negative behaviour. Sants also shows that level of friendship conceptions is positively related to IQ scores.

Girls and popular children of both sexes have a higher level of interpersonal understanding than do boys and unpopular children (Schofield & Kafer, 1985). However, the advances in ability to understand friendship are not uniform. Some aspects of friendship concepts seem to develop in different ways consistent with a gradual generalization of knowledge rather than with the idea of a strict sequence of stages. Most girls and all popular boys show a higher level of interpersonal understanding, and results of the study generally confirm the idea that the higher the level of a child's interpersonal understanding, the higher is his or her popularity.

motivation also have deeper friendships and they are very stable in best-friend choice.

On the opposite side of the popularity chart, we can distinguish between actively rejected children and those who are merely neglected; these are different sorts of unpopularity (Asher, 1984). Neglected kids are ignored whilst rejected kids are actively disliked and tend to get rejected in new groups too if they are placed in them without training. In particular, they are much more likely to complain of feeling lonely than are neglected children or those with low social status, and they are more 'at risk' for feelings of inadequacy and low self-esteem (Asher & Wheeler, in press). What, then, differentiates them from other kids or, to put it another way, what do they do wrong?

Actively rejected children have unusual ways of explaining the causes of social events (Sobol & Earn, 1985). These differ from the explanations given by children who are merely isolated by neglect (i.e., nonparticipants who are not necessarily rejected) or controversial (i.e., frequently accepted by some peers but equally strongly rejected by other peers). Unpopular, rejected children see the world in more stable terms and, therefore, they see their rejection as quite likely to persist, more or less irrespective of what they do.

Self-esteem, acquired in interactions with parents, sets the scene for later feelings about friendship as represented in friendship motivation. This affects behaviour in social settings which interacts with beliefs about our popularity and acceptability to others. Together this affects our approach to explaining our social successes and failures.

How do we put it right?

The first question really is 'what are we trying to achieve when we try to "cure" unpopularity?' Is it adequate to assume that all we need to do is treat the unpopular child and implant some magical, 'spray' attractant, or should we take the whole children's group and deal with the complexities of their interconnections as a system?

There are many different kinds of skill involved in successful relating in childhood, and hence there are many levels at which difficulties can arise (Furman, 1984). For instance, the child's behaviours may be inappropriate — in which case some form of social skills training may help — or the child's motivation for relationships may be low. Alternatively, the child may lack the relevant social knowledge about behavioural routine or the nature of relationships. The child may be deficient in internal feedback and poor at evaluating his or her own behaviour or general capabilities. The appropriate way to tackle the problem will depend first on correct identification of the underlying problem causing the behavioural inadequacies (Furman, 1984).

By implication, no general style of approach will be universally effective.

Let us start by looking at the separate ideas suggested, before we look at the way that Furman integrates them. One approach we could use is based on 'targetting' the child who has social difficulties, then training the child in various skills that may otherwise be lacking. For instance, some children do not talk enough to their peers or do not engage in cooperative play or never take the initiative in entering games. Direct coaching of such children can be beneficial (Oden & Asher, 1977). In the Oden-Asher programme, children are trained for ten sessions in: participation in other children's play; cooperation and methods of collaborating rather than competing with others; communication skills of listening and talking; validation, support and nonverbal reinforcement by means such as looking, smiling, and offering encouragement. We know from chapter 2, what a stupendous impact such skills have on the flow of social behaviour and on our acceptability to other people. We also know that these skills are usually acquired at random, because efforts to train and guide children in them are so haphazard. Ironically, governments spend vast amounts of money on teaching children academic skills, but ignore those relating skills which are just as important to adult happiness and success.

Such programmes of social skill training are obviously beneficial, but they may not be enough on their own. Even if the unpopular child is trained, the child's peers may not notice. The child's reputation for unpopularity might still exist in the minds of the child's classmates, and they may not notice the child's improved style of behaviour. In that case, merely training the unpopular child may be ineffective if the *classmates'* behaviour is not affected, too. What is then required is a method that involves the classmates also (Walker & Hops, 1973). This method centres on reinforcing peers for interacting with isolated children: the peers are encouraged to approach and play with the previously rejected or ignored child, thus giving the child the experience of acceptance and joint play. In another instance, nonhandicapped children were encouraged to

BOX 4.8 Social skills training for children

LaGreca & Santogrossi (1980) identified children who are accepted by their peers and gave a group of them training in social skills whilst 2 other groups served as controls. Relative to these controls, the training group shows improvements in skill, knowledge, and performance in structured settings or initiations of play. However, on its own, the training does not increase popularity.

Gresham & Nagle (1980) extend such ideas to test out a training/coaching programme, a modelling programme (where unaccepted children watch skilled ones and are taught to identify key aspects of their performance), and a mixed coaching/modelling programme. All 3 methods improve the 'play with' sociometric/popularity ratings of the children.

Unaccepted children can be taught specific conversational skills, and they improve in ability to perform the skills until the follow-up four weeks later (Ladd, 1981). Popularity also increases for these children at that time.

Siperstein & Gale (1983) specifically selected rejected children, rather than those who were ignored or unaccepted, as in the preceding examples. After coaching, such children increase in popularity and also show a decrease in the amount of self-isolation or bystander-onlooker 'hovering' behaviour outside groups of other children (when the child becomes an onlooker of a group he or she obviously wants to join but dares not do so).

play with handicapped children by the direct means of teaching them how (Guralnick, 1976). 'Normal' children can be taught to persist in engaging withdrawn children in play even if they had initially met with a cool and withdrawn reception (Strain et al., 1977). As Furman (1984, p. 115) concludes, 'peers can be effective therapeutic agents'.

Another strategy is to encourage mixed-age social interaction. An immature child given experience of play with younger kids can learn to take control, to have responsibility, and to direct the activities of others. Furman et al. (1979) successfully used such a technique to improve the interaction rates of withdrawn children. For later ages, however, the reverse strategy is proposed (Duck et al., 1980), namely, giving socially immature children the chance to observe older children's friendships so that they can use these as models. With aggressive children, this may have the additional effect of bringing them up against the dangers of using aggression against 'stronger opponents', so that they are encouraged to develop nonaggressive strategies for interaction.

In other cases, it is more suitable to train the child in techniques of entry to groups of other children. A particular characteristic of neglected and rejected children is that they 'hover' on the outside of groups as bystanders or onlookers and do not show effective means of getting themselves admitted to join in (Putallaz & Gottman, 1981).

For a child with problems that persist across situations, and who is obviously the major source of the difficulties, various techniques have been tried. Bierman & Furman (1982) attempted to coach such children in conversational skills by making videotapes about peer interaction and giving the children 'practice' in how to do it. Children are taught social skills based on reinforcements for increasing interaction, for talking to other children, and the like. But these forms of training are combined with group experiences where the skills are practised (under expert observation) in the environment where they will ultimately be used by the child alone. Such subject-oriented and peer-oriented combination programmes seem likely to prove effective in the long run (Furman, 1984).

Summary

Complex interrelationships affect our social behaviour. Relationships, like people, have a history and have come from somewhere, often taking a long time to emerge and develop. A marriage can be affected by the style of the preceding courtship adopted by the partners; a family, as a whole, can be influenced by the kind of marital interaction between the two spouses in particular; the child at school can be affected by the quality of interaction in the family home. The learning that the child gathers about relationships from the family environment can carry over and influence the child's approach or avoidance with other children.

A second, but somewhat hidden, theme in this chapter is that unhealthy family functioning can lead to unhealthy psychological functioning in individuals within the family. By extending this idea to relationships in general, the final chapter begins to apply relationship research to broader (and seemingly unrelated) social issues, such as health.

Further reading

Asher, S. & Gottman, J. (1981) *The Development of Children's Friendships.* Cambridge University Press: Cambridge.

Duck, S.W. & Gilmour, R. (1981) *Personal Relationships 2: Developing Personal Relationships.* Academic Press: London and New York.

Filsinger, E.E. & Lewis, R.A. (1981) *Assessing Marriage: New Behavioral Approaches.* Sage: Beverly Hills, CA.

Gottlieb, B.H. (1981) *Social Networks and Social Support.* Sage: Beverly Hills, CA.

Macklin, E.D. & Rubin, R.H. (1983) *Contemporary Families and Alternative Lifestyles.* Sage: Beverly Hills, CA.

CHAPTER 5

Dealing with Strangers, Acquaintances, and Friends

Social predicaments, like the poor, are always with us. When we go about our daily business, we are often confronted with unexpected situations that force us to deal with awkward strangers, usually to get them to stop some behaviour that is offensive to us — strangers who light a cigarette in a No Smoking area, who jump ahead of us in a queue, who irritate us in launderettes, or may even sexually harass us. On other occasions, the problem is to deal with people whom we know a little, but not very well, and ask them to do something for us that they may be inclined to resist. Our regular bus driver may have to be persuaded to accept and change a large bank note; we may have to ask our class instructor to extend the deadline for an assignment; a person in our large dormitory block may need to be asked to turn down the stereo system; we may want to ask a classmate to come out on a date with us. Sometimes we may even want to persuade a friend to do us a troublesome favour.

In each case, we need to persuade or encourage someone to do something that he or she may be reluctant to do or something where we cannot predict the response. They are instances of the everyday business of 'compliance', or getting people to do things for us. How does this effort get affected by relationships? In each of the cases of strangers, of acquaintances, and of friends, the issues are somewhat different. When dealing with strangers, we have to assume that they are average, sensible members of society about whom we know only what we can see; we have to assume that they will be influenced by the average things, such as, power and likeability, and that they have average attitudes. We react to them just as we would to any other strangers; they are contextless for us, and we have no knowledge of their personal characteristics. Since we have no relationship with them except as one anonymous human being to another anonymous human being, there is no special knowledge on which to draw.

By contrast, with acquaintances, we attempt persuasion and compliance in a different context: we probably do want to emphasize that they know us a little and that they should consequently treat us as persons with individual character-istics. That they do know us means that we can claim special treatment: we are not 'just another person who wants some-thing done in a hurry'. They have a minor obligation to treat us differently.

With friends, we use whatever special knowledge we have about them, but are probably concerned to preserve the relationship between us. However, friendship is a source of obligations, and part of the role of 'friend' is willing acceptance of chores, duties, and favours that help the other persons. We do unwelcome or inconvenient things for them precisely because we are a good friend.

In looking at persuasion and compliance, I shall avoid consid-ering grand issues like political persuasion, voting behaviour, advertising effectiveness, the campaign for/against nuclear

---

BOX 5.1 Points to think about

— *What* general features of people *tend to make them more persuasive?*
— *What* overall techniques and strategies *tend to increase the effectiveness of persuasions in general?*
— *What* message structures *are most persuasive?*
— *How does the* relationship between persuader and target *affect persuasiveness? How does it modify the effects of any of the other things above?*
— *How easily can we employ this knowledge in the living reality of everyday social encounters?*

arms, or the general attempt to persuade people to give up smoking. When it comes down to it in everyday social life, we just want to get someone to change what they are doing (i.e., to comply with our desires) rather than to change their attitudes forever on a key topic. Furthermore, since this is a supplementary text, I merely sketch out some approaches because I want to emphasize the role of social relationships in compliance rather than to repeat a review of attitude change research that can be read in any introductory text.

Dealing with Strangers

In dealing with strangers, we usually lack knowledge about their particular characteristics. What we see is what we deal with. Accordingly, we are likely to pay attention to different aspects of the persuasive context from those we use when we deal with acquaintances or with friends. For instance, we may be concerned about other outside observers' views about the episode. If our behaviour towards a stranger causes a 'scene', we may be concerned about our appearance to any other people that are present; when dealing with friends, we probably have their feelings and interests in mind as much as our own. Consider this example.

Strangers on the train

At the time when I was beginning work on this book, I had to go to London for two days to record a television programme on friendship with a man who specializes in assertiveness training. The journey back involved a three-hour train ride, which, on this occasion, took more than four hours because of poor weather. I always choose a No Smoking section, which is clearly marked with a red circular notice on every window, showing a cigarette crossed out, the words No Smoking, and a statement of the penalty for violating the rule. The carriage filled up with another thirty-one passengers, and off we went. I looked around at the strangers who were my fellow passengers.

Directly opposite was a girl who looked as if she were a student and a young man who was stapling together leaflets about solvent abuse, warning teenagers about the social, health, and legal disadvantages of glue sniffing. He soon started chatting to the student and it turned out that he was a vegetarian who jogged every day and helped to run a youth sports centre. I began to see why he had chosen a No Smoking section: he cared about health. Across the central corridor of the open-plan compartment was a table occupied by two hungry people who began tucking vigorously into a selection of 'junk food' bags. I sat reading a paper about loneliness in college students (Shaver et al., 1985, illustrated in chapter 1) whilst I listened to *The Lark Ascending* by Vaughan Williams on my personal stereo. I could keep an eye on things by 'looking out of the window' since it was a dark winter's evening and the carriage lights reflected the carriage events clearly. These cameos continued amiably enough along their own paths for some hour and a half, interspersed with announcements from the guard/conductor and bar steward.

Then one of the big eaters lit a cigarette.

I drew his attention to the fact that it was a No Smoking section and asked him to go to a different section of the train. He replied that someone further down was smoking but, as a computer manager from Manchester pointed out to him, that did not actually contradict my point that *he* was sitting in a No Smoking section. Out of the other thirty passengers just that one man joined in the argument and supported my request whilst the others looked on with a mixture of amusement and embarrassment.

What about these other passengers? The solvent/health man later left the section for a while and returned to place a pack of cigarettes and a lighter in front of him. He had said nothing, I assume, because he felt divided loyalties. On the one hand, he smoked, but on the other hand he recognized the need to consider other people's rights whilst doing so and had himself left the No Smoking when he wanted to smoke. His behaviour did raise an interesting issue, though, since his other actions and statements pointed to a concern over health and a care for others; so why did he smoke? The student was a nonsmoker who said that she always chose nonsmoking compartments, so why did she say nothing?

When the smoker would neither put out his cigarette nor move there flashed across my mind one of the points from the television programme: stick to your guns. However, it was with something of a sense of failure that I went looking for the guard/ conductor who asked the man to move, which he then did.

Analysing the problem

Some psychologists would point to the smoker's attitude structure: his beliefs about smoking, his beliefs about the legitimacy of his action, and, given that he could see others smoking, his consequent beliefs that he was being unfairly singled out. Some would argue that he felt his freedoms were being constrained and so he reacted against the constraint. Others would look at the structure of my request and its evident ineffectiveness. Some would point to other relevant circumstances, such as the passivity of the others in the compartment. Some of these ideas have been applied generally to all persuasive contexts, but I think that some are more likely to be important in this setting and others elsewhere. Some matter in dealing with strangers and some do not; some are more important in dealing with friends, for instance.

Being noticed

When dealing with strangers, the first essential is to be noticed and have them pay attention to our request. To do this we have to present ourselves in a way that makes it clear that we have the right to have our request dealt with. By contrast, when dealing with friends, our right to be heard and noticed is built into our relationship: they heed us because they know us. With strangers, however, we might need to use some guile and devices.

Attention to a persuasive message is a critical factor for persuasion to occur (Hovland et al., 1953). People attend more closely to a credible source, that is, one that appears to justify our attention, one that has authority and can be trusted or believed. In the 1950s, when Hovland's studies were conducted, it was found, for instance, that Robert Oppenheimer, who headed the team that created the atom bomb, was believed more readily by a US audience than was *Pravda*, the Russian newspaper, whether or not the topic was nuclear bombs.

Source credibility is freely manipulated in advertisements. Advertisers like to say 'Doctors recommend' or 'As used in hospitals' as a way of tying their product to credible sources. When persons are shown recommending drugs or pharmaceuticals, they are frequently figures in white coats ('scientists') or smart business clothes ('executives') — with greying hair if they are male ('authority'). They usually wear glasses ('intelligent'), carry clipboards ('data'), are seen giving other people instructions ('power') against a background of test tubes ('science'), and they use fountain pens ('class'). The same person saying the same thing on a football field in sports gear would probably appear less credible even if the message, the facts, the words, the con, were all the same precisely. What we respond to are the cues in the context: all are cues carefully prepared to suggest credibility. Here credibility is produced by expertise (or, in the case of adverts, assumed expertise: after all, most viewers would realize that the 'expert' is not an expert but an actor playing that part — yet we still might believe what is said).

In dealings with strangers, source credibility is one of the most important factors. I could claim such credibility in a number of doubtful ways ('Hey, I'm a brain surgeon/fighter pilot . . . please stop smoking') or in one of two other more effective ways. These are physical attractiveness and similarity: if we are attractive and are like the stranger in ways that are relevant to the message (e.g., if we wear sports gear when trying to persuade a sporting audience) then we are more likely to be persuasive, according to studies by McGinnis (1970) and by Berscheid (1966) respectively. We are not all physically attractive (although people who appear in adverts usually are — presumably because they are selected for the job as being more credible), but we can improve on Nature if it is important and we have the time and the forewarning to make those adjust-

---

BOX 5.2 Source credibility

Credibility of a source affects a listener's likelihood of changing his or her attitudes (Hovland et al., 1953).

Expertise, trustworthiness, attractiveness, and similarity to the target are important elements of source credibility (Petty & Cacioppo, 1981).

A person is more credible when he or she argues against his or her best interests, perhaps, because it is taken to indicate trustworthiness (Walster et al., 1966).

The racial origin of a communicator can influence the speaker's credibility especially for prejudiced audiences (Aronson & Golden, 1962).

A communicator who takes a predictable line (e.g., a fervent Catholic who speaks against pornography) is less persuasive than one who speaks in contrast to the direction one would expect to be taken (e.g., a fervent Catholic who speaks for the cathartic value of pornography, Eagly et al., 1978).

---

ments. If we are able or willing to do so, then we can also take some steps to become — or to seem — similar to the targets of our persuasion attempts. For instance, we dress up smartly for interviews with important people and take care over our appearance to impress people. We may also go to considerable lengths to agree with them and support their ideas (i.e., we ingratiate by appearing to be similar to them).

The findings on source credibility are helpful with strangers when we have time to prepare, but as researchers soon began to find, source credibility alone is not enough to explain persuasion nor is it always a helpful guide. We are quite often thrown into persuasive contexts quite unexpectedly by the unpredictable actions of other people, and we need to influence them then and there. 'Please serve me next, I was here before this person'; 'Please move your car, you're blocking my exit'; 'Please stop smoking, you're in a No Smoking section'; 'Please turn down your stereo, I'm trying to work'. Everyday life is not always conveniently arranged yet we have to deal with the context in which we find ourselves. If we happen to be nicely turned out, and wearing spectacles then we may have influence but we may happen to be in running gear or a bathrobe or to have just (been) woken up. In any case, appearance alone does not guarantee persuasive success.

Knowing, liking, and being persuaded

Before we go further, think back to chapter 3. What has social psychology found that physical attractiveness, similarity, trust, and status, all 'produce' in observers? Liking. These results point out that we are persuaded by people whom we like or feel initially attracted to. My hunch is that the preceding effects are mediated by liking: the source credibility of strangers is based on cues that make us feel positive about them first.

When we deal with and are familiar with people we know, however, what about source credibility then? When friends and family want to influence us in those circumstances, credibility comes not from the usual cues of clothing and the rest, but from what we know about the person, his or her relevant competences, and how we feel about him or her. If I know my brother is an expert economist, I am more likely to credit his statements on economics. Also I am more likely to credit the arguments of someone I love or have come to respect, even if he or she does not dress well and is not outwardly similar to me. Those I have come to know as irritatingly incompetent probably will not persuade me, however they dress up. Relative power positions are also well known in our everyday encounters and are significant in this context. Over a period of time, we get to know who has authority or credibility and who has not; which friend is the group leader or gives reliable advice; what student in class is bright and a good 'consultant' about classwork; which colleague is an authority or has a strong political base in the department.

Those real-life cues based on personal knowledge affect our perceptions of credibility in everyday life much more than the business clothes or the glasses. A friend is credible to me because I know and trust him or her, not because of the clothes. In everyday life, power, credibility, and trust are based on vibrant, familiar relationships, not on the fripperies of the advertizing image. When familiarity is lacking and we are with a stranger, a shopkeeper, a bus driver who will not give change for a large note, or a sexist waiter who gives the bill check to the man in the party when the woman booked the table, then we probably cannot rely on source credibility alone and need other strategies, like appearing friendly ('Hey, pal') or choosing words carefully, or appealing to bystanders for their help, assistance, and intervention.

The apathetic context

Our predicaments in social life often involve us in taking a stand on some matter when other people are there to see, like other people standing in the line that someone tries to 'jump'. In the No Smoking compartment I found myself in that embarrassing public situation: my request to the smoker was uttered before an audience of other people who were also affected by the smoker's behaviour. No-one else did anything and no-one else (bar one) took my side. That means that there were twenty-eight people sitting around saying and doing nothing whilst the two-act melodrama went on in their midst. In particular, it meant that the smoker was not being made to defend himself or being publicly 'boxed into a tight corner' by social pressure. This provided an important psychological context for my persuasive attempt.

Awareness of the reactions of strangers or friends, whether physically or only psychologically present, often guides our action and helps us to feel good or bad about the situation. We may well be guided in our actions and words by thoughts of 'What would the neighbours think?' or 'What do these other people think of all this?'

It is an important fact, not just a coincidence, that we live our lives as members of social and psychological communities which provide such contexts against which to evaluate our actions, thoughts, and beliefs. We are strongly affected by the views and actions of relevant other people, and we habitually compare our behaviour, dress, attitudes, and beliefs to other people's (Festinger, 1954). The essential argument of the 'social comparison theory' is that we are all inclined to assess ourselves against a relevant group of other persons to see if we compare equally, if not favourably, and we prefer to be liked and accepted rather than disliked and rejected. Have you had the experience of turning up to a party dressed in the 'wrong' kind of clothes? Then, you have experienced the consequences of social comparison theory. Festinger argues that we compare our attitudes, opinions, and emotions also: when we want to know if we are acting or thinking in an acceptable manner or making a sensible emotional response then we compare ourselves with other people to see how they react. If they do as we do, then we are 'OK'.

Festinger's point is vital because it is such a common part of human life: we are *always* comparing ourselves to other people and we want to be accepted or acceptable. For instance, as students, we often want to know what sorts of exam/test/essay grades everyone else got, so that we can evaluate our own performance more thoroughly. Just knowing our own score may not be sufficiently reassuring. Whenever we feel the urge to compare our own jogging times, test grades, body weight, or salary against average figures, we are experiencing the phenomenon of social comparison. It guides us as we attempt to find out if we are normal or right and can even be used as an argument in persuasion as any parent of an adolescent knows: 'Can I stay at the party till 12.00? Everyone else is going to'.

If we look at what happened – or, rather, what did not happen — in the No Smoking section of the train, we can see social comparison at work, telling me I am in the wrong. For one, the smoker's first response was to indicate a comparison group elsewhere to 'make his behaviour right' (i.e., others were smoking in the train). Second, a more subtle comparison was that only one person was concerned about the smoking and no-one else reacted. The smoker may look round and think, 'This smoke doesn't bother anyone else or they'd be reacting. I'm "doing OK". The guy here is overreacting'. I look round and think, 'I am upset by the smoking but no-one else is saying anything. Perhaps my reaction is inappropriate'. Since people tend to assume that others are similar to them (Stotland et al., 1960), a nonreaction is equivalent to support for the status quo rather than for a new proposal. Through apathy, the others are supporting the 'smokus quo' rather than the proposal that it should stop. The message from the comparison group to me, then, is 'You care and we do not, so you are wrong'.

How could I have reinterpreted their indifference so that it becomes supportive of me and provides me with a comparison group? A careful piece of oratory or a well-structured message directed at the apathetic bystanders might have energized a bit of support that could have changed the balance of opinion for comparison. The stratagem would be to make the other people feel good about themselves, and so to interpret their apathy as something positive and supportive of me. For instance, I could have tried suggesting that they were all too nice to speak up as I had done. ('These other people are too polite to say so but they are offended too'.) If they are *really* apathetic, then they will not contradict and say 'No, I am not just being polite; I am really not offended', but they *might* and then my position would look a bit limp.

The dog owner's dilemma

Another useful incident showed me the power of comparison with other people's behaviour and also when fate can intervene to correct bystander apathy. I took Christina (9) and Jamie (4) to the children's playground where a special section for the under-fives is fenced off and has a sign: 'Dogs are not allowed in this area'. There were about twenty parents there, each with at least one child, when one turned up with two small children and a dog, which he brought in and allowed to run strenuously around. Apathetically, the rest looked from one to another, spoke to one another about 'dogs' and made social comparisons: no-one else reacted, so why should I be the first? We all did nothing, all expecting someone else to take the initiative, and all unwilling to risk the dog owner's reactions, since he had a cauliflower ear and a generally uninviting look about him. We all were transformed into nonapathetic good citizens, however, when the dog started to chase one of the children and several of us united to draw the dog owner's attention to the sign. His response was one of those staggeringly brilliant retorts (it is given below) that no-one ever expects and cannot handle. The occurrence of the dog's extra contribution to the incident is what forced us from feeling good about ourselves in one way (tolerant, openminded, unofficious) to doing it in another way (good citizens protecting children from danger). That was the crucial change that led to our intervention.

What did the dog owner say when we pointed his good eye at the notice? With marvellous aplomb, he said 'It's only a small dog; they don't count'. This points to something that is missing from the accounts of predicaments given so far: any reference to the fact that the *target* of our persuasion has a mind — in this case quite an inventive one. He probably felt about himself, as most people do, that he was a normal, rational human being, who is basically all right, acts in a reasonable way, and has an above average sense of humour. How might this have affected his actions and accounted for his beliefs about the dog?

People seem to feel better about themselves when they act in a way which they feel is consistent (Heider, 1944; 1958). Note my careful wording of that statement: it does not state that we are consistent, but that we like to think we are. Consistency theorists suggest that we prefer consistency or 'balance' among our different attitudes. When we become aware of imbalance or inconsistency among them, then we shall be motivated to change something.

In Heider's model, there are usually two persons (P, O) and one object about which they have an attitude (X). P and O can feel + or − about each other and about X. Balance is the result if the signs all come out positive when multiplied algebraically (i.e., +++ or − − +), and imbalance is the result of negative product (i.e. ++−). So in our case, we have me (P), the dog owner (O) and the presence of the dog (X). Things would be imbalanced for me if I liked the dog owner (+); I disliked the

FIGURE 5.1

Balanced states

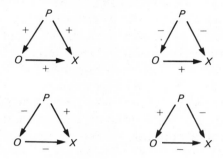

Unbalanced states

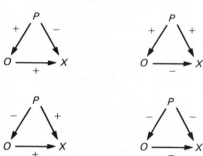

dog's presence (−); and the dog owner liked the dog (+), that is, if the algebraic product of the +/− signs comes out as negative over all. (+) × (+) × (−) comes out negative, according to rules of algebra. However, I did not like the dog owner (−), so I am in a balanced state: the overall algebraic product of (−) × (+) × (−) is positive. So I shall not change my attitudes and I shall continue to believe that the dog should go. The dog owner is balanced too: he does not know or like me (−); he knows that I dislike the dog (−); but he thinks that the dog is nice and too small to count as a dog (+). Once again, then, (−) × (−) × (+) comes out positive, so he is balanced, and he will not move the dog from the area.

On this model, I have to create imbalance for the dog owner, so that he will be motivated to restore balance. I want to change his attitude to the dog's presence by this method, so I must create imbalance in him by affecting one of the other two items of the three. If he knows I dislike the dog but does not care, then he will not change, so I must make him care about my opinion. If I make him like me then he will feel imbalanced. I need to create the following thought system: I like P ($+$); P does not like the dog being here ($-$); I want the dog to stay ($+$); this comes out negative overall ($+$) $\times$ ($-$) $\times$ ($+$), so the dog owner would be imbalanced and would want to change something — for instance, his attitude towards the dog's presence. I should make him like me first; *then* tell him to take his terrier elsewhere.

Critics of consistency theories have noted that it's not so simple. How do I ensure that the attitude he changes is the one towards the dog's presence and not the positive attitude to me that I have induced him into having? Heider's theory, unfortunately, cannot predict which one of the two will be altered to restore balance (Newcomb, 1971). Since his newfound liking for me would have been a recent attitude whilst dog-loving is an old established one, it's much more likely the dog owner would restore balance by changing from liking me to disliking me and would hang on to his belief that the dog can stay. One difficulty with Heider's approach here, then, is that the relationship between the two persons is as likely to be affected by the persuasion attempt as is the attitude I want to change.

In face-to-face attempts at influence, *either* the two parties do not know one another (so they will not care a great deal about their attitudes towards one another and are very likely to change those attitudes quite capriciously) *or* the two parties know one another well and will not want to bicker over a silly attitudinal disagreement, so they might agree to differ. In either case, the relevant attitude probably will not be altered, and balance theory has to be reconsidered or reformulated somewhat.

Another model, Festinger's (1957) dissonance theory, focusses on the attitudes of the target person (P) only (not those of P *and* those of O) and also admits P's behaviour into the equation. (Note: this is different from Festinger's social comparison theory.) In brief, it argues that a person will be motivated to restore balance (or, in Festinger's terms, to restore 'consonance') when the person holds two attitudes which lead to psychologically inconsistent conclusions or when the person's behaviour and attitude about it do not accord. Thus, if we disapprove of smoking but find that we have just lit a cigarette, we ought to experience dissonance.

A more striking and familiar example, perhaps, is the one we have all experienced: we go into a shop to buy something but cannot decide between two equally attractive alternatives. After a long agony, we pick one, pay for it, and walk out. I think that we have all experienced the dissonance that follows from this: they were both equal, yet we picked one. What happens next is that we start to convince ourselves they were not really equal. Sometimes, we might start to believe that we picked the wrong one and we go back to the shop to exchange it. Most often though, we convince ourselves that we really got a bargain because the one we did not pick was obviously rubbish/too big/ too small/wrong colour/wrong height/would not go with the overcoat/would not look right on the shelf/and the like. BOX 5.3 gives some findings about dissonance theory.

Dissonance theory appears in all the psychology textbooks, although its original findings have hardly ever been unambiguously replicated (Stroebe, 1980). It is a striking theory and many of the results from studies into it are striking, too. People have lied for small amounts of money but not for large amounts (Dissonance: I lied; the money did not justify it; therefore, it was not a lie). They have bamboozled themselves (Dissonance: I find this group very boring; I went to a lot of trouble to join it; therefore, it is not a boring group).

Dissonance was probably felt by the solvent/health man in the No Smoking section. It takes two forms: I am a health enthusiast, but I smoke; I am a smoker, but I am sitting in a No Smoking section. We know how he resolved the second simple instance: he moved elsewhere when he wanted to smoke and thereby removed that particular bit of dissonance. As to the first case, it is much more interesting. It would have *created* or increased dissonance for the health enthusiast to support me (I am a smoker telling someone else to stop) *and* for him to support

---

BOX 5.3 Dissonance theory

'Counterattitudinal advocacy' creates dissonance: that is, if you publicly argue against something in which you happen privately to believe, you are quite likely to change your mind on the private attitude (Festinger & Carlsmith, 1959). This is a particularly likely result if there is a poor justification for your making the public statement (e.g., if you are paid a stingy amount for doing it).

Betting punters are more confident of their horse's chance of winning after they place their bet (i.e., after commitment) than they are as they stand in line to place the bet (i.e., before commitment, Knox & Inkster, 1968). Voters' estimates of their chosen candidate's likely success before and after casting of the vote show a similar pattern (Frenkel & Doob, 1976).

Sales for a new product are higher when it is not offered at a discount before the price is standardized (Doob et al., 1969). This may be the result of not dissonance but a move from discount to standard price which represents an increase. It all depends which group of subjects — standard-standard or discount-standard — primarily accounts for the observed effects.

---

the smoker (I am a smoker advocating smoking in a No Smoking section when I care about other people's rights). Hence his silence.

How would dissonance work with the dog owner, though? To get him to change his behaviour, we have to create dissonance in him somehow. Our blatant attempt to do that ('You have a dog here' 'You're in an area where dogs are prohibited') failed. We could have tried to affect other attitudes of his. For example, there is the positive attitude that he probably holds about himself. We could have tried to make his positive view of himself inconsistent with his actions. I once heard this used effectively on a plane: 'If you put your bag in that overhead rack it might fall on me and I know you'd feel bad about that. I'd prefer you not to feel bad so why don't you put it somewhere else?' It worked in that case. We could have pointed out what dissonance he would feel about himself, what a cad he would think he was, if a nice chap such as he did something to upset a lot of other people, for instance, by letting his dog loose in a children's play area. But, because he is a stranger to us, we do not really know, just by looking at him, how much dissonance he can tolerate. Maybe, he has a high threshold and can easily withstand it. Relevant to his tolerance here, is the fact that, if he takes his dog away, he would have to move himself and his children and all his bags of shopping and the baby stroller. If it comes to dissonance versus inconvenience, he may choose to tolerate the dissonance. As it turned out, in another brilliant stroke of ingenuity (proving that he obviously got his cauli-flower ear on a diplomatic mission somewhere), he picked up the dog and put it inside his coat, thus stopping it running around (that keeps us happy), but did not move it from the play area (that kept him happy).

The dog owner's behaviour (bringing in the dog, and letting it loose) is what creates the difficulty and permits us to apply the principles of dissonance theory. What if he had not brought the dog in before we spoke to him — that is, what if we said our piece after he got his children out of the baby-stroller but before he let the dog through the gate?

A key element of a person's attitudes to anything is provided by behavioural intentions (Fishbein & Ajzen, 1972). That is, the best predictor of someone's eventual performance of an action is not that person's expressed attitude to the act but his or her intention to perform it. So the best place to exert persuasive pressure is on the intention to perform the act rather than on the act itself. Once he had let the dog in he was committed and a whole range of new psychological processes was triggered. Before he admits the dog, his intention to do so has not been put into effect, and we could influence his behaviour by influencing his intention.

Undoubtedly, our mistake was to wait until he had committed himself to bring the dog in with him. By attempting to get him to stop — rather than attempting to prevent him from starting — we affected his sense of freedom, and we initiated *reactance* (Brehm, 1966; Brehm & Brehm, 1981). Reactance is a motivational state brought about by the feeling that our freedoms have been constrained. When reactance is aroused, so the theory goes, we attempt to restore our lost freedom, to restate our right to enjoy it, or to regain our control over things. Research shows that reactance can lead people to do exactly the opposite of what they were requested to do — just to show that the persuader does not have control over them. 'This person told me to do X. Right, then, X is the last thing I'll do'. We have all seen other people do this, and, probably, we have all acted that way too. The dog owner was only being human: we should have acted sooner to prevent his reactance.

Problems with these ideas

In sum, then, even though I give these approaches sketchy coverage here because you can read them more fully in your main text, you can see that there are problems that have led to them being discarded. To use their principles, we must know in advance just what would be 'consistent' for the target, and, therefore, how to inject enough uncomfortable inconsistency into their personal situation so that the person will be sufficiently disturbed to want to remove it. When dealing with strangers, this is precisely the kind of knowledge about them that we never have. On the other hand, if we know the other person well, we can take account of individual personal styles.

A second reason why consistency theories are problematic is because they misrepresent us. We are not actually consistent, but often wish we were or try to represent ourselves as if we were. People have all sorts of double standards and can happily do things that to an outside observer appear to be inconsistent or illogical. From the inside, however, the blinding logicality and consistency of our own actions is only too apparent ('Small dogs don't count, so I'm being consistent'). Consistency theories will, in my opinion, never be accurate predictors of all behaviour, but they will often predict the ways in which people will report behaving or would like to behave, or would like to see ourselves — rather than what we actually do. They are of little use when we meet strangers, except in extremely vague and general ways. We have to know people better before we know how to create specific feelings of inconsistency without having them simply decide to dislike and ignore us.

When we know people better and have more time then we can do things differently.

Dealing with Friends and Acquaintances

Acquaintances, however casually we know them, we know them all the same and probably want to emphasize that knowledge in dealing with them or getting favours from them. Also, we often have more time to get them to do things for us, so we can be a bit more strategic and longer-term in our persuasion. Several well-studied aspects of persuasion seem to fit in here, especially those dealing with more than one message from *us* (persuaders) to *them* (targets).

Techniques of persuasion

In any situation, the pattern of the messages that we choose is fundamental. Some message structures are more persuasive than others. There is the 'foot-in-the-door' technique (i.e., asking for a small favour before asking for the big one), or the 'door-in-the-face' technique (i.e., asking for a big, unreasonable request, being refused, and then settling for a small request, which was actually the one you wanted all along). Thirdly, there is the 'low-ball' method, a technique that gets a person committed to something on the basis of false information (e.g., by quoting the costs as lower than they are). Once a person feels committed, however, he or she is likely to carry on with the behaviour even when hidden extras or increased costs are then revealed.

'Foot in the door'

Door-to-door sales people uses a method of trying to put a foot in the door — literally or figuratively — and getting the prospective client to make a very small and harmless-looking commitment initially (e.g., a commitment to approving the format of a series of books). Once that is made, the commitment is increased gradually (e.g., to taking the first volume of the series on approval, then to agreeing to have a few volumes in the home to see how the set looks, and so on up to the original aim: paying for 26 volumes). The technique is based on small increments of commitment at each stage so that the client really feels that each step is a logical and hardly noticeable progression from the last step, until lo and behold, the client owns a fine, extremely expensive encyclopedia.

Would you erect a large and unsightly billboard in your garden, even if it was for a good cause and encouraged careful driving? Not likely. In fact, only 16 percent of residents in Palo Alto, California, agreed when asked directly (Freedman & Fraser, 1976). Of those who were first asked to put a small sticker on road safety in a window of their home, however, 55 percent subsequently agreed to put up the large sign, too. Comparable results are found by several other researchers and De Jong's (1979) review of them concludes that the technique is effective as long as the initial request is small and when no compelling reasons, such as financial inducements, are offered for doing it.

One explanation is that the foot in the door works because the initial compliance allows the persons to feel good about themselves. Kraut (1973) finds that if people are 'labelled' positively when they give to one charity they give more to a second one also. The method of labelling is simple: 'You are really a generous person. I wish more people were as charitable as you'. For such an effect to work, however, the labelled action must be seen by the actor as resulting from 'internal' factors — those under the actor's own control — otherwise there is no credit for having acted that way. External causal factors — those not under the person's own control — often cause people to do things, so the positive label would probably not work if the actor felt that the actions were brought about by other than their personal free choice (Dillard et al., 1984).

Intelligent, generous, and discerning readers like you who have made a thoughtful choice to buy this book will obviously find many ways of using this method in predicaments with strangers and friends. The technique is useful only if we have control over the circumstances or can choose the precise timing of the requests, however. Also, a useful relationship can be established even by some small expression of commitment to help and it can then be exploited. For instance, Cook (1977) notes that some seducers first attempt to get a partner to do a small favour for them before they make any explicit sexual 'move', and they take willingness as an encouraging sign. Then, they increase the scale of the requests and begin to steer to sexual themes.

'Door in the face'

Will persons who refuse a big demand be more likely to agree to a small one (the so-called door-in-the-face method)? In the original study of this possibility (Cialdini et al., 1975), subjects are first asked to serve as voluntary counsellors at a county juvenile detention centre for two years. Almost everyone turned this 'opportunity' down. When they were asked to agree to a much smaller request — that is, to chaperone some juveniles on a trip to the zoo — many did so.

The method seems to work if the initial request is almost ridiculously large, so that the person does not even entertain it as reasonable, and so does not feel negative about himself or herself when turning it down. It also works when the second request is made by the same person who makes the first one — possibly because we would feel bad about ourselves if we turn the same person down twice in a row. It makes us feel mean or unhelpful. The method is also more successful if the second, smaller request is related to the first, such as filling out a small insurance-company survey after declining to fill out a much longer one (Mowen & Cialdini, 1980).

'Low ball'

The low-ball technique (Cialdini et al., 1978) consists of raising the cost of doing something, once the target (client) agrees to do it in ignorance of the true full costs. For instance, if you consent to show up for an experiment you will be more likely to agree to come before dawn if I hold off on information about the time until after you agreed in principle to participate. This technique differs from the foot in the door only insofar as it involves initial commitment to the *same* behaviour that is ultimately requested, whilst foot in the door involves initial commitment to a different smaller request. It is useful in some circumstances (e.g., selling a car) and even more useful for prospective customers to be aware of. It really depends on there being little or no personal relationship between the persons. It loses its effectiveness once we come to realize that someone might use it quite constantly. It is an extremely offensive and exploitative approach, also, and will lose more friends than it will persuade. Save it for selling cars.

Reflections

There is one odd implication in the material reviewed so far. It mostly assumes that persuasiveness 'resides' in the external characteristics of the persuader (e.g., we are persuasive because we dress well or look good); in the internal psychological structure of the target (e.g., people generally change their attitudes in the direction of consistency); or in the broad relationship of parts of the message to other messages that have been recently sent and received (e.g., persuasion follows rejection of other persuasion attempts). The effects are largely assumed to be absolute. The strategies presumably work irrespective of personal circumstances or the situation or the relationship between participants.

Also, it assumes that our only goal is to persuade the other person, but in most predicaments we actually have multiple goals (Clark & Delia, 1979). For instance, we want to ensure no smoking in No Smoking areas, but we do not want to feel bad about it; we want to stop someone pushing ahead of us in line, but we do not want to look as if we are overreacting or officious; we want to get friends to do us a favour, but we certainly do not want to leave them feeling exploited. What is needed, then, is to recognize these multiple goals and explains the ways in which goals might affect the shape of requests that we make.

Was it something I said?

Let us assume that we all have a range of persuasive strategies to choose from in any set of circumstances (Marwell & Schmitt, 1967; Miller & Parks, 1982). In that case, persuasion comes from the style of the communicator's message rather than the psychological characteristics of the target. This approach acknowledges that choices of message might depend on context, circumstances, or the relationship between us and the other person: we choose different methods in different encounters, with different people, or on different occasions with the same person. It sees persuasion as a 'homeless' concept growing from social relations or interactions.

Request strategies

Marwell & Schmitt generated a list of sixteen different strategies (Table 5.1) some of which are reward oriented (i.e., based on positive encouragements) whilst others are punishment oriented (i.e., based on negative features). Thus some strategies stress what the target will gain by complying, whilst others stress the pains that will be avoided by it. Miller & Parks (1982) further categorized them into those with communicator onus (e.g., 'Do this for me') and those with target or recipient onus (e.g., 'Do yourself a favour') — see Figure 5.2. So we can decide to emphasize either what *we* can do or what will happen to the *target* and either the rewarding or the punitive consequences.

The most commonly used strategy is liking, with altruism being a high choice also (see Table 5.1). On the whole, people seem to try to avoid punishing strategies when possible and to

TABLE 5.1: Marwell and Schmitt's typology of 16 compliance-gaining strategies

1. Promise	(If you comply, I will reward you.) You offer to release community property if your relational partner will agree to dissolution.
2. Threat	(If you do not comply, I will punish you.) You threaten to take all community property if your relational partner will not agree to dissolution.
3. Positive expertise	(If you comply, you will be rewarded because of 'the nature of things'.) You tell your relational partner that it will be a lot easier on both of you if he/she agrees to the dissolution.
4. Negative expertise	(If you do not comply, you will be punished because of 'the nature of things'.) You tell your relational partner that if he/she does not agree to the dissolution, it will be an extremely difficult emotional experience for both of you.
5. Pre-giving	(Actor rewards target before requesting compliance.) You finance a vacation for your relational partner to visit friends before telling him/her you wish to dissolve the relationship.
6. Aversive stimulation	(Actor continuously punishes target making cessation contingent on compliance.) You refuse to communicate with your relational partner until he/she agrees to discuss the possibility of dissolution.
7. Debt	(You owe me compliance because of past favours.) You point out to your relational partner that you have sacrificed to put him/her through college and that he/she owes it to you to let you live your life as you desire.
8. Liking	(Actor is friendly and helpful to get target in a 'good frame of mind' so that he/she will comply with the request.) You try to be as friendly and pleasant as possible with your relational partner before bringing up the fact that you want to dissolve the relationship.
9. Moral appeal	(A moral person would comply.) You tell your relational partner that a moral person would let someone out of a relationship in which he/she no longer wished to participate.
10. Positive self-feeling	(You will feel better about yourself if you comply.) You tell your relational partner that he/she will feel better about him/herself if he/she lets you go.
11. Negative self-feeling	(You will feel worse about yourself if you do not comply.) You tell your relational partner that denying you your freedom will make him/her feel like a terrible person.
12. Positive alter-casting	(A person with 'good' qualities would comply.) You tell your relational partner that because he/she is a mature, intelligent person, he/she will want you to do what is best for you.

13. Negative alter-casting	(Only a person with 'bad' qualities would not comply.) You tell your relational partner that only someone who is cruel and childish would keep another in a relationship which the other desired to leave.
14. Altruism	(I need your compliance very badly, so do it for me.) You tell your relational partner that he/she must free you from the relationship to preserve your sanity.
15. Positive esteem	(People you value will think highly of you if you comply.) You tell your relational partner that his/her friends and relatives will think highly of him/her for letting you go.
16. Negative esteem	(People you value will think worse of you if you do not comply.) You tell your relational partner that his/her friends and relatives will be ashamed of him/her if he/she tries to prevent you from leaving.

Source: Marwell & Schmitt (1967), 357–8. Reproduced by permission.

prefer reward-based ones (de Turck, 1985). We can see from Table 1 that the strategy I deduce from Heider's balance theory comes out as number 8 (liking) in the Marwell & Schmitt typology: it is essentially a preparatory strategy that gets the target/recipient in the right frame of mind for a persuasive

FIGURE 5.2: Four-category typology of compliance-gaining message strategies

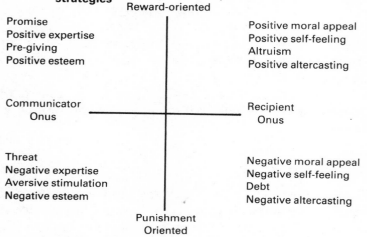

Source: Miller & Parks (1982) Fig 2, p151 in Duck (1982) *Personal Relationships 4: Dissolving Personal Relationships* Academic Press: London. Reproduced by permission.

communication that follows. The one from Festinger's dissonance theory seems to come out as number 15 (positive esteem) and is more direct.

Several attempts to reduce the typology to a more economical size have failed, but Hunter & Boster (1978) reckon that the strongest influence on the choice of strategy is whether the communicator perceives the goal to be to the benefit of the recipient or of the communicator. When the target/recipient is the beneficiary (e.g., when 'Don't drink too much' is the goal) then any strategy is likely to be used and persuaders will go to greater lengths to persuade the target (Boster & Stiff, 1984). When the communicator is the likely beneficiary (e.g., 'Do me this favour'), then the persuader typically does not exert such efforts, although this impressively altruistic model of human nature has been found not to work on every occasion (Clark, 1979).

Other work suggests that the list of strategies is not actually exhaustive (Burgoon et al., 1980) and that subjects can recognize others that are not in the list. For example, Wiseman & Schenk-Hamlin (1981) develop a typology in which two new strategies are 'direct request' (surprisingly absent from the more devious Marwell-Schmitt typology) and 'explanation' (when a straightforward, nonmanipulative set of reasons for making the request is given). At the same time, some other strategies in the list appear to overlap conceptually. For example, positive altercasting ('A person with good qualities would comply') achieves a similar result to that achieved by positive esteem ('People will think highly of you if you comply').

Forms of a request

What are the factors that particularly influence the form of a request? Two influences are variously called 'dominance and intimacy' (Cody et al., 1983), or 'status and familiarity' (Tracy et al., 1984). These define the amount of liking that exists between the two actors (or the degree to which they know one another) and their relative status (cf. chapter 2 on the form of language as a result of the status and solidarity variables described by Brown, 1965). When we know, like, and have power over someone, we choose strategies not used with strangers. The third factor that influences choice of message type is, rather naturally and predictably, the size of the request or the amount of inconvenience or imposition that will result to the target of the request. The larger the request or favour is, the more the requester takes account of felicity conditions and face wants (Tracy et al., 1984).

'Felicity conditions' refer to two elements of messages: the speaker makes clear why the request is being made and hence establishes that there are legitimate needs for making it: the speaker inquires about the hearer's willingness to perform the requested act (in other words, the person establishes that he or she is making a request rather than giving an order or asking for fulfilment of an obligation).

'Face wants' refer to the concern that the speaker has for presenting a positive image of self and partner (Tracy et al., 1984). There are three elements to this:

1 Messages vary in the degree to which they acknowledge the hearer's desire to be liked and appreciated ('I really appreciate your help on this; you're very kind').

2 Messages vary in relation to the negative face wants of the hearer (i.e., the person's desires for autonomy, freedom of action and freedom from imposition). Speakers acknowledge this need by showing reluctance to impose on the hearer or by showing uncertainty in their request ('I hate to ask you this, but . . . . Would it be at all possible for you to?').

3 Messages vary in the attention they give to the speaker's own positive face (e.g., when we ask to borrow money we might make it clear that we have saved some already, but not enough). Note that attention to face wants directly relates to something that we have found here to be vital — making the other person feel good about himself or herself — and that felicity conditions do so less directly but still could help do so.

Strategy selection

What strategies do we see ourselves having available to us and why do we make particular selections? Certain 'types' of person may habitually choose certain types of strategy. For instance, powerful people may regularly choose punitive strategies, explicitly or implicitly, and people who want to be seen as powerful may think that those strategies are the ones to use. Men and women may also choose typically different strategies; women are found to prefer to start with reward-based strategies, but their reaction to reluctance or noncompliance depends on the type and strength of the relationship between the two parties and the consequences for that (deTurck, 1985).

When persuading acquaintances (as distinct from friends), we do choose persuasive strategies that do not 'give us a bad time' if things go wrong (Miller, 1982). Our first thought is 'What are the consequences for me if I do not succeed here or things go wrong?' On the other hand, when attempting to persuade friends, we avoid strategies that the target cannot defend against without feeling obliged by friendship to do something for us that he or she would really much prefer not to (Miller, 1982). We ask 'What are the consequences for the friend and for our relationship if things go wrong?' The relationship between us and the target influences the strategies that we choose.

Everyday Influences on the Influence Process

One prominent influence on our behaviour in predicaments is the way that we feel about ourselves and our way of handling the situation. We all like to feel satisfied not only with the outcome of an attempt at persuasion but with the way that we dealt with the situation. If we are deciding about ways to tackle a predicament or to get another person to do as we want, then our relationship with him or her may affect this assessment of our satisfaction. Just think, if our neighbours turn their stereo up too loud, we *can* get the police, but it is not necessarily the best way from a social or personal point of view. Even if the other person is a stranger to us then our satisfaction with the outcome may depend not only on getting what we want but on doing it in a way that reflects well on our self-image and social presentation. In negotiations, for instance, it often helps to enter with a claim for slightly more than we actually want so that we have something to give away as a concession and with which to create a favourable image of our reasonableness as negotiators.

An important everyday fact, then, is the significance of the persuasion attempt in the here and now of the person's social life: persuasion has consequences for me now here. We often have to make persuasive attempts knowing that we must continue in the situation afterwards. If we try to get a neighbour to turn down the stereo, we may be making our future life less comfortable since the neighbour may become ill-disposed towards other requests, may become 'difficult', or the like. Little persuasive attempts can, nevertheless, have large personal consequences. We would be making a big mistake if we regarded everyday compliance-gaining and persuasion as neatly packaged, done at a distance from insistently helpful friends and friendly advisers; or, if we saw 'compliance-doing' as a pure act of 'information processing' that is relatively rapid and based only on sensible principles.

A second point is that compliance-gaining in everyday life might take up a lot of time. It is not usually a simple, once-for-all event. The target is likely to resist us or challenge us, which will require us to take another shot. Furthermore, some compliance takes times to plan. Attempts to seduce a partner or have an essay grade changed can be thought about or planned in advance, can be modified, and can be thought about later, too, if they fail the first time.

For this reason, we do not try just one persuasive method, see if it works, and then go back to doing whatever we were doing. More often than not, we persist, if the request matters to us. Not only do we persist in a particular encounter but we may persist over a longer timespan, say several encounters. Thus selection of strategies is, I think, a developmental procedure rather than an isolated, one-off choice. Often, we take time to think out alternative strategies and plan ahead. We may even be able to set up circumstances in a way that assists us (e.g., by getting the other person into a good mood first, before we try to influence him or her).

It is in the unpredictable, spontaneous real-life circumstances, where such control or preparation is lacking, that persons are thrown back on general persuasive principles rather than personal knowledge. This is partly because events like queue-jumping 'just happen' and partly because the other actors in the events cut across our intentions and make their own independent attempts to have things go *their* way, too. Each person can react in an almost infinite number of ways to any behaviour, ploy, or words of the other actor. When relationships or preorganized conditions do not exist, the persuader is thrown back on personal resources, such as strategic style or communicative skills.

By contrast, when we are familiar with a target for our compliance-gaining efforts, our knowledge helps us to plan and gives us some awareness of likely consequences. For this reason, in everyday influence, we do not need to be motivated (persuaded) in the usual ways to accept or yield to what we have been told, as we do in advertising and propaganda. In these two cases, for instance, people are depicted as needing to be motivated by fear (Janis & Feshbach, 1953) or by evidence that their behaviour does not match their stated opinions (Festinger, 1957) or by yielding a small, uncontentious point before being given the main issue (Freedman & Fraser, 1976; Cialdini et al., 1975).

When we look at the routine side of real life, though, we see that the 'motivation' is present and implicit in the situation or the role relationship between participants. When we have to get a parent to lend us the car, persuade someone to lend us a valuable book, or obtain an extension of a deadline for an assignment, there are inbuilt relational forces that affect not only the target of the persuasion but also the person attempting to achieve the outcome. For one thing, both parties have a view of themselves and their relationship — and probably wish to preserve it. Sometimes, we would rather give up on an argument than risk losing a friendship. For this reason, we shall most probably be unwilling to act in a way that threatens it, and they may make this fact a key element in their persuasion attempt. If we make a request that we recognize is too demanding, we accompany it by some relational preservative like an appeal to the person's good nature, an offer to restore the balance one day, a reminder of a past occasion when the positions were reversed, or a reference to our overwhelming need and the role requirements of friendship. In other circumstances, when the relationship is more formal, such as between teacher and pupil, such relational references will refer to the demands of the *role* and the participants are unlikely to persuade by use of implied personal friendship.

Once we recognize that most persuasions occur in a context of living relationships, real social lives, and our long-term goals or projects, not just our short-term persuasive objectives, then we see that we need to look carefully into the impact of such contexts on our attempts to gain compliance.

Summary

We have looked at two real-life examples where one person chose to try to stop another person from doing something he wanted to do. I described, and tried to apply, a number of techniques that have been studied by social psychologists and communication scientists for many years. In real life, the relationship between the persuader and the target is vital, and there are a number of ways in which the social and relationship context for real-life decision-making could affect the ways in which we decide to attempt to persuade someone else. However small many of our persuasions are in real life, many of them can be drawn out and anxiety-provoking in ways not true of 'big' attitude change about, say, nuclear power. Our decision-making and persuasion in the context of our everyday life-concerns involve us in thinking about the consequences for our relationships with our partners, friends, and colleagues as well as in assessing the merits or demerits of two sides of an argument or of two alternatives that lie open to us.

Further reading

Petty, R.E. & Cacioppo, J.T. (1981) *Attitudes and Persuasion: Classic and Contemporary Approaches*. W.C. Brown: Dubuque, IA.

Reardon, C. (1981) *Persuasion: Theory and Context*. Sage: Beverly Hills, CA.

Wheeler, L., Deci, E.L., Reis, H. & Zuckerman, M. (1978) *Interpersonal Influence (2nd edn.)*. Allyn & Bacon: Boston.

Zanna, M.P., Higgins, E.T. & Herman, C.P. (1983) *Consistency in Social Behavior*. Erlbaum: Hillsdale, NJ.

CHAPTER 6

Staying Healthy . . . with a Little Help from Our Friends?

There is one aspect to everyday life that seems, on the face of it, to have little to do with relationships, namely health. When one looks more closely, however, as research has recently begun to do, then health is shown to be significantly affected by our personal and social relationships. Not only do relationships influence our beliefs about what it is healthy to do and what not, but the numbers of friends that we have — and even our relationship with our doctor — influence our health status. If we have more friends, and we like our physician, then the chances are that we shall stay healthier.

BOX 6.1 Points to think about

How far is susceptibility to illness influenced by social psychological factors, personality factors, or behavioural style? Can we believe ourselves to death?

What psychological experiences make people decide that they are ill or ill enough to seek medical advice from friends or from professionals? How do psychological variables influence our judgements of our illness and our likely recovery rate?

How far does the relationship between doctor and patient influence the patient's recovery? Should we try harder to like the physician and take fewer pills?

Can we preserve our health by altering our patterns of relationship with other people? Could our friendships keep us alive whilst loneliness kills?

In sickness and in health

Take a good look — or even just a quick look — at the advertising around you, and you will see how much human effort is devoted to prolonging life, trying to stay young, and keeping healthy. Where fifteenth-century alchemists wasted their lives looking for chemical potions and elixirs to prolong life, we do the same thing in a different attitudinal framework: we eat fibre, jog, take yoga, use dye to cover grey hair and skin creams to 'banish' wrinkles. The results are similar, but the attitudes and beliefs are different. Nowadays, we believe that many diseases are curable by science rather than by witchcraft.

Most of us will die because of unhealthy lifestyles which interpersonal persuasion may help people to change (Rogers, 1983). The main causes of death nowadays are not the old unhygienic infestations like cholera and typhoid but heart disease, cancer, and liver disease, which are probably related to our own personal choices about diet, smoking, and alcohol. Other causes in our society are also results of the way we choose to live: dangerous driving, crime, obesity, lack of proper exercise, stress, dangerous sports, and loneliness. We may think that we feel better when we are in love or surrounded by friends; we may become discouraged when we feel lonely; but there could be more to it than feelings. Do social influences actually affect our *physical* well-being and medical status? Some researchers claim that loneliness kills, that divorcing creates physical illness, and that some interpersonal styles of behaviour (e.g., personality, coping style, and self-esteem) can make us more prone to heart failure (Lynch, 1977).

Reporting Sick

The social side of illness

We may think we go to the doctor because we are ill, but it is more complex. Reporting of illness is not based on absolutes: for example, we are not just either sick or well and we can often be somewhere in between. The health-illness continuum is a continuum, not a dichotomy of absolute health versus absolute illness (Shuval, 1981). Why do we move along the health-illness continuum, and why, when, and how do we decide we are ill enough to need help?

We do not report sick just when we *have* germs, viruses, and physical trauma; it depends also on how we *feel* about them. Recovery from illness is more than just a physical matter, since medical intervention focussing only on germs and the like does not always cure people as fast as it should. There is the 'hope factor' and the 'will to live'. Also, reporting sick is partly due to our way of life or personal beliefs and these are also influenced, in their turn, by the beliefs that exist in the surrounding culture.

The decision that one is sick will depend on psychological factors based on the perception of symptoms and what they mean. Some people report sensations and symptoms which are caused by psychological sources, but lead to physical symptoms (Skelton & Pennebaker, 1982). Extreme examples are hysterical 'glove anaesthesia' (when the patient reports loss of sensation in the hand) or various forms of panic attack which lead to asthmatic shortness of breath. Some symptoms are not reported and seem not to occur in some cultures; for instance, Mead (1950) reports that women in the Arapesh tribe show no signs of morning sickness during pregnancy. Finally, wounded soldiers' reports of pain are often unrelated to the extent of their wounds. In the heat of battle, it seems that perception of pain can be depressed (Beecher, 1959).

Clearly, there are individual, cultural, and circumstantial influences on the perception of pain and the reporting of symptoms. These raise the possibility that illness can have social functions as well as medical ones — which is not saying that it has only social functions or always has social functions. Equally, illness can result from social events or experiences — which, again, is not saying that it *always* does. We need to look, then, at the social consequences of becoming ill or defining oneself as sick.

What do the symptoms mean?

Some symptoms in themselves mean little, and we have to decide for ourselves whether they indicate illness — and, if so, whether it is appropriate to consult a doctor. Loss of appetite, for instance, can mean nothing significant at all or it may be sign of illness. It is, in any case, a general symptom of many different kinds of ailment so we can decide that it tells us something or that it does not depending on our psychological attitudes to life. A hypochondriac may decide that loss of appetite means a serious illness and ought to be checked out; other persons may not notice or be influenced by their loss of appetite (they might even be glad — if they are trying to lose weight).

Since many pains are ambiguous, transitory, or due to any one of many possible root causes, they have to be interpreted. Pain initiates a search for causes (Jones, 1982), and people will pin the explanation on any cause that seems both plausible and salient, even if it is actually incorrect. If a recent event seems likely to have caused the symptoms (e.g., headaches following banging one's head) then we are likely to attribute the effect to that cause even if, for example, the real cause is a spontaneous brain tumour.

By contrast, our psychological state can actually contribute to the occurrence of certain symptoms (Mechanic, 1980). For instance, an extremely anxious person might develop ulcers or headaches. Indirectly, also, anxiety may cause us to change our habits: negative attitudes may make us careless or prepared to act in a self-destructive manner, for instance, by drinking excessively, eating irregularly, and driving dangerously (Kelley & Rolker-Dolinsky, 1986). Furthermore, a person can develop symptoms as a result of changes in daily routines or habits, and these can in turn come from psychological changes going on inside. For instance, if we become extremely anxious about life, we may start drinking or smoking and so develop liver or lung ailments.

Psychological variables can also affect health by increasing arousal or raising the level of body monitoring (i.e., by increasing our attention to physical symptoms). Various psychological states increase arousal and can create false 'symptoms', such as sleeplessness or headaches or tension that are really the by-products of increased arousal — a purely psychological change — although we usually fail to see it that way (Mechanic, 1980). We usually feel physiologically aroused, notice that we are sleeping less, have headaches, and the like, then we think that there must be a cause for it: we must be ill.

'Being ill' can itself become closely tied up with our view of ourselves, since it excuses us from poor performance: 'What can you expect? I'm sick'. Also, it may become structured into our daily routines rather like the routines of the heroin addicts' families mentioned in chapter 4. Someone may be easier to deal with when they are 'ill', so the family is happy for them to stay defined that way, or encourages them to see themselves as 'ill'. At least, if they are in bed they are doing no harm.

The point in all this is that psychological factors intertwine with physical factors when it comes to reporting of illness. Even illnesses which are reported fairly often could nevertheless indicate that in the person doing the reporting there is a psychological change taking place rather than a physical problem. We conclude, then, that there is a close relationship between psychological state and the meaning of symptoms to the person who decides to report sick.

Deciding to report sick

There is more to becoming ill than merely feeling a twinge of pain in the stomach. We decide we are sick when we feel that our physical state deserves attention, when we are willing to accept the consequences of being confirmed sick, and when we believe that treatment would be more useful and effective than no treatment. These are psychological factors that link up with our views of ourselves, with our attitudes to pain, physicians, and sickness, and with our general beliefs about illness. If we believe that illness is a punishment for sin then we may be less likely to admit to illness than if we think it is a reward for doing good or if we assume it is caused by an invasion of viruses over which we have no legitimate control.

Equally, there is more to reporting sick than our beliefs about our illness: we have to trust the physician and the treatment. This trust will depend on our beliefs about physicians, the way we are handled in the consultation, whether the physician's breath smells of alcohol, and our own personal model of illness. People nowadays accept antibiotics whereas in previous times they may have believed in the efficacy of boiled newts' tongues, crocodile dung, and the sweat of pregnant women — treatments which were more often effective than we would suppose (DiMatteo & Friedman, 1982).

Neither the decision to report sick nor the confidence in the effectiveness of treatment is based on absolute factors. An individual's personal beliefs and those of friends or cultures at large will also give meaning to pain and illness. Each society takes its own view of why and how people get sick — and what they should do to put it right. Which of the following explains why we get sick? God is punishing us for some sinfulness; our body contains too much blood and needs leeching; a demon has crept into our body; we caught a virus; we failed to make a sacrifice to the health god; we ate the wrong diet; we have bad attitudes towards our comrades; we did not get a regular health checkup; we do not exercise enough; we smoke; a witch stuck a pin into a model of our body; we are lonely; we have just moved house, lost our job, become divorced, and run into debt; an enemy gave us the Evil Eye; it was something we ate last night; we should have washed our hands.

Obviously, such beliefs affect what we do to be cured, whether we blame ourselves for our illness, and how our friends and relatives react to our predicament. For instance, if I regard illness as a punishment for sin then I shall remain silent about the pains in my chest so that my family does not suspect me of being evil. If, on the other hand, I believe the pains are caused by a witch then I shall call a priest to pray with me — and my friends will not think me odd; if I think the pains are 'a heart attack' I shall call an ambulance, which will probably race to the scene while other car drivers get out of its way and accept that the ambulance is justified in making itself heard.

Over and above such background cultural factors, there are

seven individual factors that influence psychological attitudes towards reporting of illness (Mechanic, 1974).

1 Number and persistence of symptoms.

2 Individual abilities to recognize and discriminate symptoms.

3 Individual judgements of their seriousness.

4 The extent of social or physical disability resulting.

5 Cultural or personal attitudes to stoicism and endurance of pain.

6 Amount of medical information available to the person.

7 Availability of help set against perceived costs, whether social or financial.

Whilst these are all individual judgemental influences, they all relate to one crucial point: an individual's (un)willingness to accept the sick role.

The sick role: social consequences of illness

Being ill is a social as well as a purely physical condition and makes the individual enter the 'sick role'. To do this, a person must be legitimated by an accepted authority, such as a physician, or in the case of a child, by a parent (Parsons, 1951). Secondly, the illness must normally be beyond the person's responsibility to control (e.g., someone who is drunk is not 'sick' whereas someone showing similar symptoms as a result of concussion *is* 'sick'). Thirdly, whilst the sick role legitimately excuses us from certain regular obligations like work, it brings others. A person is obliged to 'get well soon' or to act out the role in a socially acceptable way by, for example, 'bearing pain with cheerfulness and fortitude', being uncomplaining when in pain, and appearing to be brave in the face of death. People who do this satisfactorily have it mentioned in their obituaries, whilst those who fail to do so do not have their reactions described at all. You will never see an obituary that says 'When he was told that he was dying he just broke down and cried like a real wimp'.

Illness has three further aspects to it (DiMatteo & Friedman, 1982), all with social psychological overtones: destructive, liberative, and occupational.

First, illness is usually *destructive*: it causes physical deterio-
ration, pains, disability, and discomfort. This can cause
anguish to loved ones, who see a father, mother, child, or friend
deteriorating before their eyes. Insofar as the patient is aware of
these feelings or reactions, then psychological pain, including
feelings of guilt, can also afflict the patient. Equally, the patient
has feelings about the destructive side of illness and is called on
to cope not only with the pain itself but with its social
management (e.g., not 'letting it show' to visitors). Some
people regard acceptance of illness as a personal failure; most
people with a terminal illness become angry ('why me?') and
depressed, often trying to bargain with death ('just a few more
months'), by, for instance, agreeing to leave their body for
scientific research (Kastenbaum, 1982). Such reactions have
social psychological consequences beyond the physical ones:
they affect our views of ourselves, they interfere with relationships with other people, they afflict and poison social recreational activities.

A further social psychological consequence of the destructive
side of illness is the direct effect on status and general 'social
credit'. Many illnesses cause disfigurement or socially unacceptable sights, sounds, and smells. These social stigmata
must be endured by the patient along with the pain (Jones et al.,
1984). Some illnesses disrupt social behaviour and cause inept
actions like involuntary trembling, unexpected extensions of
limbs, lolling of the head and tongue, dribbling, or disturbed
eye movements. These, too, are stigma that make it difficult for
outsiders to interact with the patient in normal social ways and
thus add to the burdens that the patient must endure (Lyons,
1984).

Some medication treats the illness but causes side-effects
with nasty social consequences like drowsiness or inability to
concentrate (e.g., some antipsychotic drugs cause stiffness in
the limbs and occasional uncontrollable dribbling). Alternatively, some treatments restrict patients' social calendars or
require them to withdraw from social contact to carry out
medical procedures (e.g., going to lie down for dialysis on a
kidney machine or going to a private room for regular insulin

injections for diabetes mellitus).

These aspects of illness make extra demands on the patient over and above the need to cope with physical discomfort. These extra demands are social ones that afflict the person's ability to carry out and enjoy normal social relationships.

Second, illness can also serve a *liberative* social function. It frees people from dull routine, legitimates their noncompletion of assignments, and releases them from exams, duties, tasks, and obligations (Parsons, 1951). Social, intellectual, and task-related failures can be excused by reference to their sickness ('I wasn't concentrating: I have a headache'). These are social effects in some sense in that the excuses are not damaging to their social *persona*: they are 'off the hook', it is not their fault, they should not blame themselves, they do not lose their 'social credit' — blame the illness, the person is out of sorts and not responsible for himself or herself.

Third, illness can become *occupational* or can take over a person's life like a full-time job. DiMatteo & Friedman (1982) report the case of a person in the nineteenth century who used to check into hospitals with 'symptoms' all dressed up with great tales of military escapades, wounds, and so on. On closer examination, he was found to have no scars and no sickness, he just liked being treated as a patient.

Sick role and failure

In the light of such points, maybe illness is a mechanism for coping with failure (Shuval et al., 1973). Since illness gives us an appropriate, legitimate, and accepted excuse to tell our friends why we are unable to perform roles, fulfil tasks, or take on responsibility, some people might become ill or report or 'play up' an illness when they come up against evaluation, or when they are afraid of it. In brief, illness helps people to avoid evaluative situations, particularly ones which are important to them. Snyder & Smith (1982) suggest that illness operates as a 'self-handicapping strategy', as they call it, and so people exaggerate reports of illness (and may actually *feel* more ill) when they are faced with an esteem-threatening event. This is also known more dramatically as 'academic wooden leg'. ('What can you expect from someone with a wooden leg?'; it's borrowed from Berne, 1964, *Games People Play*). Such people might feel they have developed some serious illness just before class tests, for instance, if it really matters to them to get a high grade, and they are worried that they are not going to make it. One 'way out' of the problem is to claim an illness which is absolutely debilitating and gives the perfect excuse not to sit the exam or be tested. How could we possibly do well in that exam if we have glandular fever and laryngitis?

Ultimately, the idea of self-handicapping goes back to Adler's explanation that people would report symptoms as self-protecting devices: what they protect is self-esteem. The symptoms provide reasons for failure that are an alternative to self-blame. We do not have to blame ourselves because we cannot do something; we can blame the illness, it's the illness's fault that we cannot perform well in the exam, rather than because of our own incompetence. By developing these self-handicapping strategies (or rather, these pre-emptive self-serving attributions), people could avoid evaluations altogether, but a second point is that if we are ill then we get a lot of attention from people and that bolsters our self-esteem. If we are feeling particularly down-at-heel, then the apparent illness will probably provoke people to become sympathetic and that picks up our self-esteem also. For instance, I know of a case where a girl developed paralysis of the leg that was so convincing that her leg was going to be amputated; but, referral to a psychiatrist led to her admission to an adolescent unit, instead. At this time, her leg was useless and her muscles had atrophied from lack of use. She had had two operations — to no avail. After several months of therapy, she began to walk again. During psychotherapy, it emerged that she had very low self-esteem and felt that she had never been any good at anything. If her leg had been amputated as she had wished, then that would have given her a lifelong excuse for being unable to do certain things.

None of this is to say that people never get ill in the physical sense or that symptoms are nothing but self-protective strategies, but there are some cases where self-protection could be one of the major social roles of illness. If this is so, then manipulation of health and illness must take this into account to some extent. It is futile a physician trying to cure people of particular illnesses, if the real problem is some lack of self-esteem or personal problem with relationships, for instance. A caring physician would take as much account of those kinds of background psychological and interpersonal factors as of the actual symptoms themselves and treat those.

Patient and Physician

Visiting the physician: why and when?

When we decide that we are sick, what influences whether and when we go to the doctor? We go to the doctor when we feel that our physical state is serious enough to interfere with our life and so deserves attention (Zola, 1972). We thus have a considerable amount of personal leeway surrounding the decision whether our physical state does interfere enough to deserve attention. It also depends on what is going on in our life at the time that could become disrupted. If we were going to be married tomorrow, then we may well decide to postpone a visit to the physician to get on with everything else. If we have nothing much planned, then we may need less of 'an illness' to make us feel that we should see a doctor.

A second factor that influences the decision is a person's friendship status (Reis, 1984). People with supportive, closely knit networks of friends, go to the doctor at an earlier point in the illness, presumably because they have been told by their friends that they do not look too well, and it's about time they did something and took professional advice (Hays & DiMatteo, 1984). On the other hand, people with no groups of friends or with only small social networks, go to the doctor more often when there is nothing wrong with them — either because they have no access to preliminary lay advice that would tell them there is no real problem or because they are hoping to meet other people to talk to in the doctor's waiting room (Duck, 1983).

A third reason why people will decide that they are ill enough to go and see the doctor is that they do not feel hostile towards or afraid of doctors (Hays & DiMatteo, 1984). Some people are hostile towards doctors and do not believe that they do any good, or they may fear the waiting room as a source of vicarious infection — as if there were a risk that you go in with a cold and come out with cancer. People who are hostile towards or afraid of doctors are much less likely to go along and report that they are ill, because they dislike going in to see doctors — they dislike the doctors as people.

Lastly, people go to the doctors if they do not regard illness as a personal defeat or if it hurts enough so that they accept their inability to cope (Zola, 1972). Some people dislike classing themselves in the sick role. If they fall ill, they regard themselves as having failed in some way or as just seeking attention they do not deserve or as being soft and needing support when they should be less dependent on other people.

When it hurts too much

What determines a person's timing of the decision that the pain is significant enough for help to be sought? DiMatteo & Friedman (1982) note that more deaths from myocardial infarctions (heart attacks) occur at times when it is socially inconvenient to interpret one's chest pains as a sign of heart problems rather than indigestion or strained muscles. That is, at weekends, when doctors are off duty, patients do not wish to call them out on a possible fool's errand — but by the time the patient acknowledges the true seriousness of his or her condition, it may be too late.

Other social psychological influences affect the decision to seek help at a particular time (Zola, 1972):

1 Some interpersonal crisis calls attention to the symptoms and makes the person dwell on them. For instance, a person may suddenly become aware of feeling faint during an

argument or may experience difficulty breathing during a quarrel.

2 Some interference occurs to valued (social) activity. For instance, the person may not be able to join in a walking jaunt with friends because of breathlessness.

3 Symptoms are sanctioned by outsiders, who, for example, may remark that the person looks ill. If friends say that the person *looks* ill when the person *feels* ill also then that proves that it must show and is not just his or her imagination.

4 Symptoms are perceived as threatening. For instance, when the pain becomes so severe that the person cannot move around properly.

5 Symptoms are perceived as similar to those suffered by other people of the patient's acquaintance. 'My uncle had just that sort of minor pain in the morning but by six o'clock that night he was dead'.

One might also expect that a strong social influence on such timing is provided by the social desirability of the illness and its treatment. We can readily admit to some diseases, but not others. People are more likely to hope that embarrassing symptoms will just clear up themselves, so that the sufferers will not have to go to a crowded drugstore and ask an attractive young assistant for some personally embarrassing medication, like haemorrhoid ointment or louse powder.

Doctor-patient Relationships

Do we get better just because we like our doctor? Willingness to report sick is affected by confidence in and liking for the physician and so, more surprisingly, is recovery (Hays & DiMatteo, 1984). The doctor-patient relationship is one of the factors which affects psychological state, which in turn affects interpretation of symptoms, and whether we maintain the prescribed medication.

Faith in the physician has *some* curative effect. In the past, doctors frequently bled, purged, sweated, or fumigated patients, attached leeches to them, and gave them all manner of strange concoctions, poultices, and elixirs. It is less a miracle that anyone survived, than it is that doctors were allowed to continue to practise (which seems to have been what they were doing in more than one sense). Yet people had faith in these cures and frequently recovered, though one cannot be entirely sure that the threat of further treatment was not what brought it about.

Types of physician-patient relationships

In the 1980s, researchers have begun to understand a little more clearly the means by which physician-patient relationships can contribute to healing. Patients respond not only to their medical treatment but to their social treatment — the ways in which they are treated as human beings — and this speeds recovery. Nowadays, doctors get instruction on ways of relating to patients (Pendleton & Hasler, 1983). Bedside manner can influence the outcome of treatment: the more the patient feels more like an individual and is treated as a person, rather than just as a collection of symptoms, the sooner he or she recovers. Obviously, when treated personally we feel less humiliated by the degrading aspects of treatment (e.g., being stripped and prodded, having to cough, spit, and excrete or produce personal specimens in the presence of observers, and the like).

Being respected as a person can make us feel more important and want to recover, because we are being attended by someone who cares — which affects our desire to recover. It also, incidentally, makes the doctor feel better personally (because he or she feels more skilful, more personable, more important), feel more positive about the job, and more satisfied with doing it (Hays & DiMatteo, 1984). So, one hidden consequence of this relational factor is that it makes doctors do a better job because they begin to feel better about what they are doing.

There are three kinds of possible relationship between a physician and a patient (Szasz & Hollander, 1956):

1 *Activity-passivity*, when an active physician treats a passive and accepting patient.

This is clearly a desirable model when, for instance, the

patient is comatose, but in other settings it implies an authority structure that would be uncomfortable for most people since we regard our bodies as something in which we, too, have a 'voting' interest.

2 *Guidance-cooperation*, when an expert physician offers advice that a willing patient is expected to follow.

This is entirely suitable when advice on, say, acute infections is offered by the doctor and the patient follows it and takes the advice. In other circumstances, however, it implies that the patient somehow has a duty to the doctor rather than vice versa.

3 *Mutual participation*, when physician and patient are mutually interdependent and where 'power' is more evenly distributed.

The mutual-participation model is somewhat rare, even though patients prefer it and claim that they benefit from relationships where they are treated more personally and 'equally'. Physicians with a.'personal' approach to patients are liked more, trusted more, and have their advice followed more consistently by patients (Geersten et al., 1973). Since the patients in the study were suffering from arthritis, a crippling and extremely painful disease of the joints, the results are powerful. We would commonly expect that such people would be less affected by the physicians' styles and more influenced by the effectiveness of treatment. However, these two variables clearly interrelate: the social psychological and communicative elements matter, too.

A patient's perception of the doctor's social and medical skills affects confidence also. For instance, Parker (1960) shows that authoritarian medical students were disliked and disparaged, whilst authoritarian consultants — who are supposed to be expert and are indulged when they act masterfully — were both liked and trusted.

Unfortunately, where respect for a consultant's skills degenerates into fear, there are some serious effects on health. Jarvinäan (1955), working with people in coronary intensive care units, found that the most likely time for patients to have spontaneous relapses or a fatal heart attack was ten minutes before the doctors were due on their rounds to come and visit

their patients. Evidently, stress was a cause of this, and the
patients felt so belittled (in the — 1955 — prebedside manner
days) by the way they were treated by these eminent surgeons
with all their students looking on, and poking them around,
that they just decided they would take the quick way out.

What can be done to improve the physician-patient relationship? If you cast your mind back to the materials on nonverbal
and verbal interaction in chapter 2, you should get some ideas.
For instance, we could devote special care to the physician's
nonverbal style in the initial consultation when patients' expectations are set and when initial diagnosis is made. We could also
look at the patients' nonmedical needs and the ways in which
the physician could be helped to anticipate and deal with them.

**BOX 6.2 An exercise on physician-patient relation-
ships**

*Think back over the materials you have encountered in the
book thus far. What measures could we take of the quality of
the physician-patient relationship?*

*What aspects of the physician's — and, if it comes to that, of
the patient's — behaviour should we, as social psychologists,
expect to be relevant to the relationship?*

*Write a brief list of the components that you would expect to
be most suitable for attention.*

*Think for a moment about the recommendations you would
make if you were appointed to initiate a programme of training
for medical students to improve their rapport with patients.*

The text gives you some answers.

Communication

The central problem in physician-patient relationships is
communication. To make a diagnosis, the physician needs to
obtain all the relevant information, but has a much clearer idea

of what would be relevant than the patient does. The skill is to obtain the details bearing in mind that the patient may be medically unsophisticated and unaware of whether some piece of information is relevant to a diagnosis. If you are breathless, does it matter that you also have swollen ankles, for instance? A doctor would know that these together indicate heart disease and circulatory problems, but the patient may not.

Traditionally, then, the physician takes control of the interactions and asks questions that will lead to the most helpful information. We have seen (chapter 2) that the system of communication has large verbal and nonverbal components. Both, therefore, are involved in physician-patient communication. We have also seen that *encoding* (conveying what you feel) and *decoding* (working out what the other person feels) are important. Let us now look at these in the particular medical context that concerns us here.

Encoding

One special difficulty for physicians is that they are particularly bright people selected and trained for several years in a highly specialized and technical system of description about a common and familiar object: the human body, in its various manifestations. The patient, on the other hand, is concerned about a personal complaint and its cure, but is not necessarily intellectually curious about the why, the how, and the wherefore. The patient comes to a consultation wanting, and perhaps needing, reassurance, and 'information' (indeed a major part of the physician's role is to explain the meaning of illness and to encourage appropriate preventive and curative measures which the patient must follow properly to do any good). Most of us know little or nothing about what our liver does, have no idea why we have a spleen, and could not say where our pancreas is. Sometimes we know we do not know, sometimes we think we do but are wrong, sometimes we have an idea that is partly right.

Most often patients are anxious enough to want reassurance but cannot understand what is said to them to provide it.

Patients persistently request detailed explanations of what was happening to them, yet they do so unsystematically, tending to be passive and general (Boreham & Gibson, 1978). They ask for 'information' but are unclear about the areas of concern: what do they really want to know? In any case, patients mostly fail to comprehend what is said to them even when the 'information' is provided. Part of the problem is that medicine is so complex that most of us have very simple models of illness. We just are not aware of the mechanisms through which we could catch typhoid or do not have the faintest idea how gastroenteritis develops.

A further problem is that patients need to receive descriptions in common language whereas physicians tend to use 'medspeak' (Christy, 1979) and talk in jargon even when talking to patients who are relatively unsophisticated in medical knowledge. A doctor who knows the details of biochemistry must find it difficult to talk in terms of everyday examples that the rest of us can understand: doctors are taught to doctor not to teach. Words taken for granted by doctors will go 'over the heads' of most people: we may know what 'a diagnosis' is, but few know what 'a prognosis' means and can only ask 'How long have I got?'

Since medspeak is technical jargon, it is a high form of code (see chapter 2) with many specialized terms, complex structure, and formality. It instantly freezes out informality and leaves little room for the friendly banter that may relax the patient enough to talk in detail about the symptoms. Patients are aware of very few central rules in the doctor-patient relationship, but two which stand out are: make sure that you are clean; and speak the truth (Argyle & Henderson, 1984). Since both emphasize the extreme power difference in the relationship, they, too, are likely to stand in the way of a friendly encounter — if that is what the patient truly desires.

The risks are that such rules and complex talk will alienate the patient and that they will increase the risk of misunderstanding. In tragic confirmation of this Boyd et al. (1974) found that more than 60 percent of patients misunderstood their physician's instructions about the method of taking their medication, even when they were interviewed soon after leaving the consultation. (I have always wanted to know if Boyd et al. ever did a follow-up, and, if so, how many subjects survived to take part in it?)

What kind of talk do patients really like?

The best way that the physician can improve things is to provide the low code social form of discourse that the patient would like: the informal chatty style of language that we normally use to friends. Patients would rather have reassuring communication than emotionally neutral communications or humorous ones (Linn & DiMatteo, 1983). The second component is that the patient expects more general issues to be covered than simply those that relate directly to the illness. For instance, patients are more satisfied when psychosocial consequences of the ailment are specifically mentioned and addressed (Lau et al., 1982). In particular, how will it affect relationships with the family or the ability to socialize? It also seems likely to me that a preferred style would be one that emphasizes personal recollection of the patient's human individuality rather than simply the patient's medical history. Whether he had secretly written it onto my medical notes I do not know, but the doctor I best remember from my teenage years always ended each consultation with a question about my progress in my Classical Greek class at school. Whilst I forget why I went to see him, I remember this personal treatment and felt more confident about his medical skills than I do with my present local doctor who forgets my name (a name like Duck?). It may be that their skills were equivalent but I, as a patient, find myself not *believing* that they could be.

Decoding

Patients have a story to tell and often want to tell it in their own words. Therefore, the other side to the verbal interaction in a physician–patient interaction is decoding. Whilst a physician may need to ask some prompting 'closed questions' which produce 'yes/no' answers, 'Hearing the patient's true message is the . . . [essential feature] of a great physician' (Pickering, 1978, p. 554). (Interestingly, the original quotation has the Latin words '*sine qua non*', where I put 'essential feature', and this tells us something about physicians — even when they are only thinking about patients.) Attentive listening to what a person *means* rather than what a person *says* is an essential part of decoding messages (see chapter 2), so it is not a surprise to find that patients prefer physicians who have an attentive listening style (Stone, 1979). Such attention can help the physician to learn more about the patient's psychological state (e.g., whether the person seems anxious, upset, depressed, obsessive, tense). Also, it is likely to reveal the patient's psychosocial characteristics (e.g., value system, beliefs, norms, behavioural preferences, and lifestyle) without needing to ask intrusive questions about it. Such information may help the physician to work out whether the patient will take the tablets or whether the other family members will help. The physician may get family members to help the patient keep to a difficult regimen.

Whilst the verbal part of interaction is significant, we know that the nonverbal component is more so — 4.3 times more powerful, according to Argyle et al. (1970), and in chapter 2. Predictably (from chapter 2), both nonverbal encoding and nonverbal decoding will exert strenuous influence on the patient and physician. The whole range of nonverbal cues has effects on the physician's perception of the patient and vice versa, as BOX 6.3 shows.

Naturally, patients are particularly sensitive to the effect that their condition has on other people, too. It is, therefore, crucial that the physician does not 'leak', through nonverbal channels, any sense of disgust, anxiety, or lack of optimism (Friedman, 1982). Interestingly, Milmoe et al. (1967) show that a physician's effectiveness in referring alcoholics for further treatment is negatively correlated with the amount of anger present in the voice whilst talking about alcoholism. Physicians who 'leaked' their distaste for alcoholism by seeming angry with the patient had the effect of discouraging patients from taking further treatment.

BOX 6.3 Nonverbal cues and success in physician-patient relationships

Physicians who adopt a closed-arm position are interpreted as cold, rejecting and inaccessible, whilst moderately open positions convey acceptance (Smith-Hanen, 1977).

Physicians and counsellors who establish eye contact during a pleasant, accepting interaction make patients feel more positive about the encounter (La Crosse, 1975).

Affiliative nonverbal behaviours, such as smiles, nods, and a 20-degree forward lean, increase the patient's perceptions of a physician's warmth, interest, concern — and attractiveness (La Crosse, 1975).

Touch can have reassuring effects on patients, making them feel more relaxed, more comforted, more supported, and more cared-for (Montagu, 1978).

Touch can exert a general enhancing effect on the perceived competence and effectiveness of health professionals (Blondis & Jackson, 1977).

Contact (e.g., in taking a patient's pulse) can influence patients' heart rate and cardiac rhythm, as well as reduce the frequency of ectopic beats — i.e., those that occur irregularly or out-of-place (Lynch et al., 1974).

On the other hand, patients frequently leak their true state of anxiety about an ailment through body posture, voice tone, or (ir)regularity of speech and can also indicate fear or (dis)trust of physicians by the manner in which they regulate distance in the interaction (Hays & DiMatteo, 1984). A physician who attends carefully to the nonverbal cues which accompany the verbal messages will gain extra information about the patient's state of health and also about the patient's beliefs about that state, all of which may be useful in diagnosis.

The art of medicine

Doctor-patient communication is an extremely powerful influence on patients' satisfaction, so it is unsurprising that a number of programmes are started with the intention of training medical students in the 'art' of medicine. Usually, these consist of training in nonverbal or verbal communication skills (Engler et al., 1981; Fine & Therrien, 1977; Poole & Sanson-Fisher, 1979). Typically, they show that the student's interviewing, empathy, and general handling of patients improve. Results are not all positive (Farsad et al., 1978) and may not have long-lasting effects even when they are positive. We also do not really know whether such training leads to better physicians or to more satisfied patients (which may or may not be the same thing). Nevertheless, it would be unusual for a social psychologist to conclude that the outlook for such work is not promising, and I will not so conclude. If improvements in communication continue, then it seems likely that such training benefits both the patients (who feel happier with their treatment) and the physicians (who feel happier with patients' responses and with their own performance as experts). The main questions are whether there is long-term maintenance of the skills and whether we can increase the proportions of physicians who can sustain them.

Social Networks and Health

Can our friendships and social networks keep us alive? A 'social network' is the group of persons with whom a person is involved (usually friends); 'social support' refers to the help that they provide or are felt to provide. There are major questions here of whether and how the existence of a large social support network can 'buffer' people against stress, affect our vulnerability to illness, and increase our chances of recovery (Gottlieb, 1981; 1985). What matters most, the number or quality of supports (Cobb & Jones, 1984)? What happens when the network is disrupted? Is loss of relationships stressful and/or life-threatening and if so, how so (Reis, 1984)?

To suggest that our health might be influenced by our membership of a group and by the practices that are common in that group is not a new idea. One early example of research on epidemiology is based precisely on this idea. The British researcher Snow (1854) shows that cholera was developed by villagers sharing one particular well more frequently than by others using a different source of water. He also shows that Scots who put water in their whisky were more likely to contract some diseases than was a group of people who drank whisky neat or who boiled their water to make tea instead.

The identification of such demographic or lifestyle features which correlate with given diseases remains one of the primary steps that researchers take. By such means, for instance, it is established that disadvantaged children tend to be born to young mothers who have not used antenatal services and are more likely to be smokers (DHSS, 1976).

By an extension of this logic, some researchers have tried to identify specific features of a person's own particular personal groups of friends and family or lifestyle that may relate to the diseases that he or she suffers. In their classic study, Brown & Harris (1978) show that the presence of a close, confiding relationship with a husband or boyfriend significantly reduced the risk of women developing depression after a major loss or disappointment. Brown & Harris argue that long-term feelings of self-worth or self-esteem are especially significant, that these are provided by important close relationships, and that, to a major extent, these feelings could stave off psychiatric disorder in a crisis. One problem here is that the existence of strong close relationships with a small number of friends might be concealed in studies that check on the numbers of friends we have (Hobfoll, 1984). If I do a study that seems to show that people are better off with large numbers of friends, I may miss the point that large numbers are made up of sets of small numbers. So, intimate relationships with a small number of persons are what really counts (O'Connor & Brown, 1984). What may be important is that a minimum level of close relationships is maintained, that is, within a large group of friends is at least one subset of one or two very close relationships with one or two special friends.

So, in broad terms, those are the ideas that drive research on social support: rephrased, it is 'can close relationships prevent illness, promote recovery from illness, and help people to cope with stress?' People tend to suffer stress and illness when their relationships become disturbed (BOX 6.4). Also, the presence

---

BOX 6.4 Health consequences of relational disruption

Widowed men have a higher mortality, rate of mental disorder, and tendency to suicide than have widowed women or married persons (Berardo, 1970).

Widows have a higher rate of health complaints during the year following bereavement than do a group of matched control subjects (Maddison & Viola, 1968).

Lonely people are more likely to suffer from depression, to have general medical complaints, and to attempt suicide (Lynch, 1977).

Men who are in the process of separation or divorce are much more likely to suffer from stress-related illness (Bloom et al., 1978).

Dissatisfied marital partners are more likely to suffer depression (Weiss & Aved, 1978).

Taken generally, several sets of results indicate that persons in disturbed relationships have higher incidences of: low self-esteem; depression; headaches; tonsillitis; tuberculosis; coronaries; sleep disorders; alcoholism; drug dependence; cancer; and admissions to mental hospitals (Bloom et al., 1978; Duck, 1983; Duck & Gilmour, 1981c).

There is a markedly increased risk of separated men being the victim of a homicidal assault (Bloom et al., 1978).

Several sorts of physical symptoms follow closely on a sense of failure in relationships (Schmale, 1958).

of strong, close relationships preserves people from the worst effects of stress (BOX 6.5).

Obviously, there are two separate ideas here — both widely accepted. One tells us that disruption to relationships leads to ill-health, the other, that presence of good relationships leads to well-being. We have to be careful about these two thoughts,

---

BOX 6.5 Social support and (the moderation of) stress or illness

Persons who are not socially isolated had much reduced incidence (i.e., about half the risk) of mortality, in a 9-year follow-up study in Alameda County (Berkman & Syme, 1979).

Positive self-concept and good social support have a combined effect in preventing a state of depression and of anxiety during an acute crisis (Hobfoll & Walfisch, 1984).

Social support is negatively related to the incidence of psychiatric symptoms, and absence of social support is a better predictor of disorders than is incidence of stressful events (Lin et al., 1979; Silberfeld, 1978).

Support from coworkers tends to buffer the stress of the job (La Rocco et al., 1980).

Women who have a close relationship with their husband are less likely to suffer postpartum depression (Paykel et al., 1980).

Those persons who have a high quality of family relationships tend to report fewer general psychiatric symptoms (Dean et al., 1981) and also fewer neurotic symptoms, such as depression and anxiety (Barrera, 1981).

By contrast, Hobfoll & London (1985) show that close networks can increase stress for Israeli women in time of severe pressure such as the mobilization of their husbands for war, since the networks served to transmit rumours and news of disasters.

though, since they are not making quite the same point. If a researcher carried out a study showing that disrupted relationships 'cause' illness, that does not prove that good relations 'cause' health; it may be that good relations do nothing — they are just taken for granted. On the other hand, good ones could promote good health whilst bad ones could cause stress — because they bring rejection and also the need to restructure our life to find alternative partners and establish new routines. Disrupted relationships thus expose one hidden benefit of being in a stable partnership, namely, a division of labour in coping with life's problems: the dissolution of a relationship (chapters 3 and 4) requires the person to take on extra responsibility for the labours of life. An important consequence of relational loss, then, is loss of help with physical chores, as well as loss of emotional support.

What is social support?

When we talk of social support provided by friends and kin, do we mean physical support (e.g., help with car maintenance) or emotional support (e.g., advice about a particularly troublesome problem)? Which matters most, help with routine, help in times of crisis, reassurance of worth, or some generalized support?

There are three important sorts of social support that are essential but are not related to physical provision of support. These are:

1 *Emotional support* i.e., provision of information that one is loved and cared for.

This could be achieved by direct statements to that effect or could be indicated indirectly by, e.g., buying flowers, arranging to spend time together, remembering birthdays, taking an interest in the other's welfare, and promoting that person's best interests.

2 *Esteem support* i.e., provision of information that one is valued and esteemed.

This could be achieved by direct statements to that effect or could be indicated indirectly by, e.g., requests for advice, by treating the person's opinion as important, by allowing oneself to be guided by that person.

3 *Network support* i.e., provision of information that one belongs to a network of mutual obligations).

Support can be measured by looking at three elements (Cobb & Jones, 1984): the supportive behaviour that people actually provide; the properties of the network (i.e., whether it is close and cohesive or spread out); or, the way that a person feels about it (the subjective sense of social support). What would be helpful to know is how people actually get their friends to give them support (Gottlieb, 1985) and how support varies in quality and type as the relationship develops.

Obviously, these distinctions must be recognized, and I sense that our field of research is making progress because it is now in a position to recognize such significant points. However, there are two other points that need to be acknowledged: one made by Hobfoll and one by Gottlieb. They show the way in which this research field will grow during the time when you readers may be the ones developing the research for yourself. Hobfoll's (1985) point is that we must see support in context — or, in Hobfoll's terminology, we must look at the 'ecological congruence' of support and how it matches up to what is needed. A given resource or piece of support is not necessarily appropriate merely because researchers label it as a resource. What may be supportive for a woman in labour may not work in bereavement or unemployment. The resources, then, are only truly supportive relative to the needs of the person in question — they must be ecologically congruent with his or her needs and requirements. Clearly, then, the work we need in future will identify the needs-in-context before it tells us about the support-in-context.

Gottlieb makes a different but equally important point. Essentially, Gottlieb's (1985) point is to indicate the significance of rephrasing the question about social support. He suggests that we need to ask 'Is social support a property of a person or a property of personal relationships?' In other words, is the important aspect of social support the way I feel about it or what I actually get from my network?

As people get to know one another so they feel more supported, but they are probably actually getting more help and support, too. As a relationship develops, so the partners get more from the relationship, and the course of the relationship's development is going to be affected by the amount of support (both felt support and actual support) obtained at various stressful times. For Gottlieb (1985), the key issue is the way in which particular episodes of socially supportive action create in the person the sense of being socially supported. What are the dynamics, what happens, what do people do when they support one another, and how is it recognized and acknowledged by the recipient? Clearly, argues Gottlieb (1985), the actual wresting of supportive behaviour from the environment is more important than just the sense of support. Coping depends on both the manifestation of support and on the belief that others would provide it if asked, not just on one aspect alone.

These are issues for future research rather than matters that can be answered here, but they seem to be significant gaps in our understanding of what actually counts as support. These issues are interesting in their own right (and you might like to think up, or even write out, a list of the behaviours that you find supportive; there may be individual differences in this). However, they are also a useful link with personality variables that are associated with heart disease. One key component of the relevant syndrome is a sense of being isolated from supportive social interaction, coupled with a feeling of inability to extract support from others in the social environment (Hobfoll & Leiberman, in press).

Stress, personality, and heart disease

Stress affects everyone in life and is often caused by worry about everyday life occurrences. However, some specific events, particularly, go with stress and disease. One of the most serious of all is death of a spouse (Holmes & Rahe, 1967), and there are now 'life events scales' which assess and assign scores to these and other events. The scores are determined by allotted points. You get a certain number of points for the death of a relative

(63), for moving house (20), for going to college (20), for changing jobs (36), and so on. (You even score 12 if it is Christmas, but since quarrels and even murders increase in the family at that time, maybe it's not surprising, Duck, 1983). As your score increases — particularly if it does so sharply — there is a much greater risk of you suffering stress and/or severe illness. Usually, these are stress-related illnesses or problems, but all sorts of illness (e.g., hypertension and diabetes) start happening when life-event scores build up (Wyler et al., 1971).

What is the explanatory link between life events and stress? Two aspects of life events are quite significant to the individual, so which of them matters most? Many life events are undesirable (e.g., being fired, death of a relative) but they also have a second element, which is change, just the fact that something has altered, such as, we have moved to a different home or adopted a new work routine or entered a new partnership.

What matters most, then, the undesirability of the event or the fact of the change? Rather surprisingly, Dohrenwend (1973) finds that change per se is the stressor and not undesirability. It is not just the negative aspect of the change that is important, it is the fact that it is a change at all, particularly if the change requires major psychological readjustment or major reformulation of identity — such as is involved in becoming a widow. Obviously, these occurrences affect self-image as well as the routines of life. If we move to a new place, meet many new people and have to begin 'getting acquainted' again, or if we lose a relative who was very close to us or was part of our identity structure, we now have to rethink ourselves, as it were. Such changes to self-image require major psychological readjustment towards social restructuring and that is what we find most difficult to cope with.

Two psychological reactions are relevant here. First is a person's belief in self-efficacy (Bandura, 1977) — that is, a learned capacity and belief in our own control over the environment and our ability to deal with and cope with events. If we believe we can handle the problem, we shall not be overwhelmed by it. A person's beliefs in this regard could be area-specific: I may have great confidence in my self-efficacy as a lecturer but less in my ability to cope with insurance sellers for instance. Whilst a lecture class of 2500 students may hold no terrors for me, the prospect of a brief meeting to discuss life assurance could frighten me to death.

Second, a general psychological reaction to stress is observed by Selye (1956) in the 'general adaptation syndrome'. According to this model, there are three stages to reactions to stress (which Selye regarded as a physical reaction to a noxious or unpleasant stimulus):

1 *Alarm reaction* 'a generalized call to arms of the defensive forces in the organism'.

2 *Resistance (sustained)* a kind of emergency reaction in which the body sustains alertness to danger and preparedness to deal with it.

3 *Exhaustion* the defences become depleted through being 'stretched' for so long.

Later work (see Innes, 1981) indicates that these patterns are dangerous over a prolonged period since they simultaneously aggravate the body's inflammatory reaction to nasty stimuli whilst reducing resistance to them. In other words, risk is increased at exactly the same time as ability to cope is reduced.

Despite the previous findings, there is little agreement about the nature of stress. DiMatteo & Friedman (1982) define it as 'the state of an organism when reacting to new circumstances' (Note: 'state', 'reacting', 'new', 'circumstances'), whilst Selye (1956) defines it as the 'physical reaction to noxious stimuli' (note 'physical', 'noxious', 'stimuli'). From the foregoing, it may be clear that the more recent definition of DiMatteo & Friedman takes account of the Dohrenwend findings that change per se rather than noxiousness can be stressful. The essential point seems to be that any unexpected and massive readjustment of life patterns causes stress at a psychological level, although noxious stimuli have an effect also, particularly at a physiological level. The real question for social psychologists concerns the means by which life events cause enough stress to cause illness, and there are three models proposed (DiMatteo & Friedman, 1982):

1 Life events call upon a person's coping style which is found deficient and leads to unhealthy or odd behaviour that causes a social reaction from others ('What's the matter with her? She's behaving strangely') that leads to a definition of illness ('She must be sick') and acceptance of the sick role. There is no organic disease here. What happens is that disturbed behaviour (drowsiness, hostility, weeping) leads people to assume that the person must be ill.

2 Life events call upon a person's coping style which leads them to unhealthy styles of behaviour (alcohol abuse, nervous smoking, self-mutilation, fast driving) and these lead to organic disease (cirrhosis, lung cancer, heart disease) which then leads directly to illness and the sick role. In this case, there is an organic disease that results but it results indirectly rather than directly from the need to cope. Those who cope by drinking or smoking lead themselves to the illnesses caused by those particular actions rather than to simple illnesses resulting 'directly from' stress.

3 Life events overpower a person's coping style and cause physiological stress (high blood pressure) that leads to organic trauma (stroke, heart attack). In this case, there is a direct link between the life events and the illness, mediated by physiological reactions, such as shock.

These interesting proposals make it clear that there can be several kinds of stress, of reactions to stress and of mediating agents, the most important of which is coping style and personality. Physiological, social and environmental stress can all be distinguished, and we should recognize that a person's social behaviour and social status can expose them to these risks to different degrees. However, personality and social behaviour, on the one hand, and personality and social status, on the other, are not entirely isolated. We assume that people whose personality is a competitive, aggressive, striving one will achieve higher status. Perhaps, they are also exposing themselves to risk of stress and illness.

Type A pattern

There are few obvious directly pathogenic behaviours, but over a period of years now research has begun to show an association between one particular style of behaviour and heart disease. The association is complex and imperfectly understood, yet it exists; it is the association between the so-called Type A personality and coronary heart disease (CHD). As I introduce some of the evidence, think what you would expect Type A to consist of and the effects that it might have.

We understand that emotional behaviour is linked to heart activity and are familiar with sensations of the heart beating faster when we are excited or tense. However, it was only in the nineteenth century that it was accepted that high pressure activity was related to high blood pressure and heart disease. Some theories relate heart disease to repressed aggression — that is, they claim that heart disease can come from strong feelings of aggression that are not expressed, because of the person's style of personality (DiMatteo & Friedman, 1982).

Jenkins (1971; 1976; 1977) notes that life events often are associated with heart disease, but that many of the methodologically sound studies produce negative results. It suggests, then, that some pattern of behaviour or some difference in coping style in subjects could account for the variety of results. Some differences could be related, for instance, to the different paths taken from stress to reaction via poor coping, poor adaptation, lack of concern over self, or self-destructive behaviour of which suicide is merely an extreme form. Jenkins (1976) notes that certain forms of behaviour or experience usually precede *angina pectoris* (a chronic long-term disease of the heart characterized by sporadic paroxysms or surges of intense pain) but not myocardial infarction (sudden, one-off heart attacks). These are likely to be anxiety, depression, neuroticism, and interpersonal problems. On the other hand, obsessional tendencies and overcontrol of emotions relate more closely to myocardial infarctions. (One has to be somewhat careful here in that patients' accounts of their behaviour *before* illness are likely to be gathered only *after* the illness has begun, so their reports may be clouded by their own particular models to explain illness.) Thus, a Type A-CHD relationship was proposed.

Type A is characterized by achievement-striving, hostility, competitiveness, aggressiveness, and a strong sense of time urgency (Jenkins, 1971). Type A persons are oppressed by a constant sense of external constraints on their behaviour; a feeling that they must do things for demanding others; a personal struggle to do more and more, in less and less time. They are hasty, impatient, impulsive, hyperalert, very tense/ intense, and committed to professional life to the exclusion of other parts of life where achievement is less measurable, such as family, friendships, and social activity. Yet even here Type A can turn relaxing social occasions into high pressure competition; there is no such thing as a gentle recreational game of tennis with a Type A. Furthermore, the Type A pattern includes a tendency to obsessionality and a strong overcontrolling of emotions, such that they suppress anger (or, at least, the signs of its slow building up) and then suddenly explode — much to everyone else's surprise, but not to theirs.

That is a striking and noticeable set of styles: note that so far I have described mostly the feelings or beliefs that Type A pattern has, along with some particular styles of relating to or attitudes about other people. There are, however, some behaviours that help to identify such persons also, and help to classify them.

Classification into Type A or Type B (i.e., those who are not Type A) is usually based mainly on self reports or interviews, and usually retrospectively. However, some tests work independently of this and some are based on the Type A tendency to misjudge the lapse of time. When asked to judge the elapse of sixty seconds, a Type A will usually mark a minute to have passed in fifty seconds or so. A fuller test is provided by the Jenkins Activity Survey which characterizes the patients according to three factors: H (Hard driving competitiveness), J (Job involvement), S (Speed and impatience). All the same, these factors do not themselves individually predict CHD in any clear way, and it is unclear how they combine to have their effects (Innes, 1981).

Type A persons can also be identified by the speed, volume, or tenseness of their utterances or body movements. They walk and eat rapidly, hurry other persons along impatiently in conversation, speak with strong emphasis (often swearing a lot), frequently clench hands and teeth, try to do two things at once, experience great time pressure, and usually work at maximum capacity even on trivial tasks. We are not exactly a bundle of laughs.

Discussion

Type A pattern is, as I have noted, associated with coronary heart disease. Whilst some physiological peculiarities are noted in Type A subjects responding to stress or to challenge (Carver & Humphries, 1982), it is not entirely clear whether there are inborn physical differences between A and B types or whether they are a psychological result of the Type A tendency to react strongly to challenge — which is what produces the physiological effects.

Given the general patterns of Type A behaviour, we can see quite readily that Type A will lead persons to carry out behaviours which expose a person to risk: overwork, upward social mobility, frequent change of circumstances brought about by increased responsibilities or job promotions, interpersonal stress, and self-destructiveness. These are not strictly a part of the Type A pattern, but they are consequences of it that in themselves are risky. Equally, and conversely, high job involvement does not, of itself, predict CHD and in any case Type A persons are precisely those who are most likely to see themselves as capable of taking an overload and to have a reasonably strong view of their self-efficacy. So on this particular factor, there are likely to be plus and minus points combined.

Type A pattern is a general style, but is one with certain components which may be more important than others. Is it the total pattern that increases the risks of CHD or is it one (or more) of the component elements only? One impressive feature that explains or, at least, underpins many other aspects of the behaviour is a marked wish to retain control of the environment (Carver & Humphries, 1982). In several studies conducted by Glass and coworkers, it is clear that Type A subjects exhibit strong reactions to threats to their control of the environment. They may not be inherently more aggressive, but could simply react to threats to their own mastery of the situation in a more pronounced way. In other words, it is their response to the 'situation as they see it' that causes the difference between Types A and B, rather than some in-built physical difference.

These different reactions to threat are intriguing. For instance, in response to relatively small threats, the Type A subject redoubles efforts to regain mastery of the situation; in response to more serious and uncontrollable threats, Type A subjects typically lapse into extreme helplessness and hopelessness, becoming unduly negative about themselves and extremely pessimistic about the future (and their future performance). Glass (1977) further finds, in a retrospective study, that those Type A subjects who suffer CHD report an unusually high number of uncontrollable events in their lives during the year prior to their hospitalization. This feature of the Type A pattern thus begins to look like an extremely significant one. Particularly, patients who do have CHD and are identified as Type A often report the 'Sisyphus reaction' just before the onset of the disease. Sisyphus was one of the inhabitants of Hades in Greek mythology, condemned to spend his time rolling a stone up a hill, only to have it fall again to the bottom whenever he reached the top. Hence the Sisyphus reaction is characterized by a sense that what you are doing has become repetitive, pointless, and unrewarding.

The hostility component of Type A is also highly predictive of physiological change under stress (Dembrowski et al., 1977). Clearly, hostility is a frequent reaction, in all subjects, to threatened loss of control. Kelly's (1955) personality theory essentially defines hostility as reactions to loss of control and the attempt to deny that it has actually occurred (see also Kelly, 1969). Kelly's proposal is particularly relevant to interpersonal conflict, and it is here again that we see a key factor in the Type A pattern. Dembrowski & MacDougall (1978) show a particularly interesting feature of Type A, namely, that such persons often have markedly small networks of friends and prefer to work on their own. We can go further and suppose that Type A persons are uncomfortable in groups, feel particularly insecure in relationships, devalue social contact, deliberately rather than adventitiously keep smaller networks of friends, and perhaps feel threatened by intimacy. Type A persons are also significantly more self-referent than others (Scherwitz et al., 1978). They use the words 'I', 'me', 'mine' frequently and are chronically self-aware (which leads to high feelings of the need to meet challenges as personal ones).

This evidence give us a key to the Type A-job involvement dilemma (Innes, 1981). Job involvement means not only task-involvement (which Type A persons should handle rather well) but involvement in the social relationships of work (which Type A persons handle rather badly). Many, indeed most, jobs require people to interact socially and, as status increases, to take responsibility for subordinates and their performance. Imagine the Type A in this setting, particularly when faced with colleagues who are less motivated and less competent. Since team performance will be the criterion on which a Type A team leader will be judged, any less perfect contributions by underlings will detract from team performance and hence from Type A's sense of achievement. Equally, the sense of control that seems to be a major need of Type A is lost when tasks are delegated to subordinates who, almost by definition, are less competent (or else are potentially threatening challenges). This presumably leads both to stress (through lost achievement) and to social overload, in that the Type A is then faced with a set of circumstances that is threatening, namely, facing up to someone else in a relationship, where skilful social handling may be needed.

When one distinguishes job (task) involvement and job (social) involvement, it appears that the type of involvement most dangerous to a Type A is the social involvement — a relationship factor again.

One final point, Type A–Type B is frequently treated as a dichotomy when it may not be so clear cut as that. Quite probably, there are degrees of saturation with Type A patterns, some being Super A and some being marginal. Also, since the personality profiles of CHD patients are more complex than the simple Type A–B distinction suggests, we can expect to find more complex relationships between personality and CHD than have yet been proposed.

Kobasa (1982) argues that we should expect marked individual differences of approach to stress: for some people it is intolerable whilst others would regard it as a challenge providing a desirable opportunity for personal growth. There are three key elements here: *commitment* (the ability to believe in the truth, importance and interest value of what we are doing); *control* (the tendency to believe that we can influence the course of events); and *challenge* (based on the idea that change, not stability, is the normative mode of life and can be seen as an opportunity or an incentive). Stress is not inevitably negative, and many people seek it out as a thrilling and challenging stimulant. Using such arguments, Kobasa (1982) contends that there is a Hardy Personality type that feeds on stress, as Frankenstein's monster fed on electricity. If the Type A classification happens to include Hardy Personalities, too, then no wonder the Type A–CHD relationship is not perfect.

These points are particularly significant because one remaining mystery about Type A concerns its personal origins. We do not know if the pattern is learned or based on some physiological undergroundings. However, one line of research that may be developed in future concerns the possible influence of parental style with children and its possible precipitation of Type A style (Innes, 1981). If parents act impatiently and generate a sense of extreme demand and expectation, then the child is likely to internalize these styles and so develop Type A. However, until we know more about the physiology associated with Type A and its components, we cannot rule out the possibility that the pattern is a physical rather than an interpersonal creation.

Death, on the other hand, is usually thought of as a physical event. Let us look at how it can be both physical and interpersonal.

Death, Dying, and Bereavement

In the last four centuries not only have the most frequent causes of death changed in relative proportions but so have there been alterations in our attitudes to death and the social psychological reactions to it.

Cultural beliefs about death

One of the earliest markers of social evolution of mankind is the change in attitudes to the dead. When a culture begins to bury the dead in ritualistic ways (e.g., with food and weapons), it marks the beginning of a change in beliefs about the nature of death and beyond. If we believe that people should be buried with weapons, food, and slaves, that they should be ceremonially dressed, embalmed, and lying outstretched, then it is because we believe that the weapons, food, and slaves will be needed after death, that the dead person will need to be ceremonially identifiable and, therefore, needs badges of rank on the body, that the person will 'need' his or her body in an undeteriorated state after death, and that death is only like sleeping.

Any treatment of the dead in such careful ways also presumes a set of beliefs about what happens after death, and also some thoughts about the nature of death itself (e.g., that it is similar to a journey from here to somewhere else, whose nature can be described, such as a Happy Hunting Ground or Paradise or Hades which involves crossing several rivers, such as the rivers of hate and forgetting). Early concepts of death usually regarded it as a journey to another place rather similar to the life experienced before death. The dead person, therefore, needed to have food buried with him or her so that the journey could be made safely.

It was quite a bit later that people began to believe that obtaining the full benefits of the after-life depended on what we had done on earth. The Egyptians were early believers in the idea that our heart and soul would be weighed to judge our earthly life and we would get eternal after-life only if we had been good. It was not actually until relatively late (i.e., Christian times) that the notion of transfiguration (rather than simple continuance of previous bodily forms, ranks and activities) entered into the system of beliefs.

In the fourteenth century, the dead were represented, if at all, in two forms, one as in life, one as in death: on top of the tomb was a representation of them lying at length, in full living dress; beneath this was a representation of their naked, rotting body. In those times, the body of the person was buried not in a coffin but in a winding sheet, and the person was referred to as still a member of the living community (e.g., the burial service said 'we commit *your* body to the ground'). Later the dead were represented at a transitory stage, kneeling in prayer in full dress half way between life and death. At roughly the same time, coffins were introduced, and the person was regarded as gone from the earthly community (therefore, 'we commit *his/her* body to the ground' was introduced to the burial service). Later still, the dead were represented only in the living form and statues now show them standing or sitting, in full living dress, doing something that typified them when alive (e.g., delivering a speech, riding a horse).

In the early days, sudden death was greatly feared, since it deprived the person of time to prepare for it by prayer and religious sacraments. It was also true that most people saw death fairly often not only because of diseases, war, and famine but because public executions and public torture were well-tried methods of social control and, let's face it, entertainment. Naturally, all these fears and experiences, as well as the beliefs in the surrounding culture, affected people's perceptions about their own death and those that they witnessed around them.

What now characterizes our attitudes to death? One general difference is perhaps that natural death is expected by most people, although we also hope for it to be swift. A fear nowadays is that rampant technology could keep us alive as a vegetable somewhere between death and semiconsciousness (Kastenbaum, 1982). Edgar Allen Poe's and the Victorians' writings about being buried alive caused fears within their readers;

common anxieties, nowadays, emerge from the same problem dressed up in concern over technical definitions of brain death and the use of life-support machines to sustain those who are incapable of independent life.

Along with such changes in central concerns come reduced tolerance for minor pains (the 'headache pill' society), a considerable amount of medical game-playing (since patients fear that doctors no longer tell the truth), and such pronouncements as 'the patient's bill of rights'. Death has become a social psychological, attitudinal experience as well as a physical event.

How do people cope, in a social psychological sense, with impending death? There are essentially three foci for their concern:

1 The pain, discomfort, disability, and social stigma of a terminal illness (cf. above);

2 The reactions and emotions of others, particularly of close others or life partners;

3 The person's own reactions.

Kübler-Ross (1969) proposed that there were five stages of psychological adjustment to death:

1 Denial (it's a mistaken diagnosis)

2 Anger (why me?)

This can lead to envy of those still fit, resentment against them, and even to surprising verbal attacks on helpers, nurses, and friends.

3 Bargaining (dealing with Fate for more time)

Terminal patients often leave their body to medical science as part of an implicit bargain with Death for more time, and with medical staff for better care that may help them stay alive longer.

4 Depression, sadness, and crying

5 Acceptance

This is often characterized by silence, withdrawal, and a marked detachment from other people.

Some criticize this neat system on the grounds that the terminally ill more probably oscillate between the stages, rather than move steadily to each next one. Others note that some patients show all the stages at once or that the stages occur and re-occur.

Whether these criticisms are valid, it makes sense to attend to the psychological dimension to dying and to concern ourselves with the psychological treatment of such patients as well as with their medical treatment.

The timing of death

There is some evidence that the timing of dying is influenced by psychological factors, such as whether the person gives up and whether significant dates are approaching. For instance, Jewish populations show a marked 'death dip' (a significant decrease in death rate) during the time prior to their solemn holy day Yom Kippur — the Day of Atonement (Phillips, 1970; 1972). Others show that birthdays and anniversaries exert effects on death of widowed spouses (Bornstein & Clayton, 1972), who tend to die on days close to dates that had significance in the marriage. A personal observation is the number of people who die just after they have completed a major task or survived some major stress. When I point this out to friends and colleagues, the usual explanation is that people energize themselves to stay the course through the stress and so exhaust themselves. I call this the 'foot off the gas pedal theory of death'. However, cars do not stop just because you stop pressing the accelerator; they stop when you press the brake. It makes me wonder if there is not some overreaction by a close-down mechanism which would have been just right if the stress still remained, but overacts once the stress has lessened (the 'foot on the brake pedal theory').

Reactions to the death of a close partner have begun to interest social psychologists working on relationships recently. 'Death of a spouse' carries the highest risk on the life events scales, and bereavement brings with it a considerable need for large-scale readjustments to the routines of life. Adults responding to bereavement typically show stress and health problems over an extended period of time (Greenblatt, 1978). They also show a sequence of reactions comparable to but not identical with the responses of patients to their terminal diagnosis: first, *exhaustion and hollowness*, characterized by a sense of emptiness, stress, and overwhelming responsibility;

second, a *preoccupation with the image of the deceased*, even extending to hallucinations or imagining that the person is still alive, has been seen in the street, and the like; third, *guilt* or a sense of things unsaid, feelings gone unexpressed, time together unspent; fourth, *hostility to others* or the 'leave me alone' reaction; fifth, *changes to daily activity*. The fifth reaction can be healthy or unhealthy depending on the nature and extent of the change, of course. Greenblatt's (1978) point, however, is that the psychological reaction to grief is a process that extends over time and is essential to the bereaved person, who naturally enough needs to reconstruct his or her life and identity. In many ways, the reactions of the grieving spouse mark out readjustments and changes to identity as the person comes to grips with the new demands upon them that stem from loss of partner and makes decisions about the parts, mannerisms, styles, or traits of the lost person they wish to retain in their active life, perhaps by imitation.

Conclusions and summary

We began by thinking about eternal youth and ended on death. Throughout, however, we have seen some important and mounting evidence that social factors and relationships influence or are present in many aspects of health, illness, and recovery. Some factors are quite obvious, some are not, but they run the whole range from attitudinal influences derived from the surrounding community to personal beliefs derived from interpersonal experiences and even influences coming from the network of other people to which we belong and the friendships that we have. Further, social psychologists and communication scientists contribute positively to preventive medicine and attempts to persuade us all to lead more healthy lives (Rogers, 1983). Whilst it is clearly not yet time for us to cry 'This person is sick. Send for the relationships expert', a number of major features of health and illness are relational in nature and will obviously receive deeper exploration in future.

Further reading

DiMatteo, M.R. & Friedman, H.S. (1982) *Social Psychology and Medicine*. Oelgeschlager: New York.

Friedman, H.S. & DiMatteo, M.R. (1982) *Interpersonal Issues in Health Care*. Academic Press: New York.

Hays, R. & DiMatteo, M.R. (1984) 'Towards a more therapeutic physician-patient relationship'. In S.W. Duck (ed.) *Personal Relationships 5: Repairing Personal Relationships*. Academic Press: London.

Pendleton, D. & Hasler, J. (1983) *Doctor-Patient Communication*. Academic Press: London.

Reis, H.T. (1984) 'Social interaction and well-being'. In S.W. Duck (ed.) *Personal Relationships 5: Repairing Personal Relationships*. Academic Press: London & New York.

Afterword

This book grew out of my conviction that the relationships in our lives are of major concern to us but, more than that, they are major organizers of our social experience. It is, therefore, primarily a book showing how relationships affect our daily lives, our social behaviour, and our personal experiences with other people. However, a second intention was to show the ways in which close personal relationships affect the social behaviour that people can be made to show in the 'vacuum' of the laboratory. Personal relationships can modify general rules of behaviour. However I may pressure people to buy soap powder, that is not how I influence a friend to take up my astrology classes. Whatever my general attitude to smoking, the way I handle a friend's lighting up in my house will differ from the methods that are appropriate for a stanger or for my boss or for the friend of one of my guests. There is a great power and social significance of the phrase 'Oh well, seeing as it's you'.

These were my main reasons for spending time trying to show the need for adding work on relationships to the materials already available in social psychological texts. Another was to generate some thoughts for future research.

In writing the book, I have become aware of several promising issues that remain to be explored. How do everyday concerns, hopes, anxieties, and plans about relationships affect other daily social behaviour? Why is there no work on the effects of disliking or disappointment or remorse or regret on behaviour in interactions? Why do our models of behaviour so often assume that we always know what we are doing, where we are going in relationships, and how our lives will develop when all around and within us we see instances of confusion and indecision? Despite their frequency in social life, there is no social psychology of flirtation, of forgiving, of regret, of remorse, of disappointment, of polite refusals, or of the content of ordinary conversations in different types of relationships and relationship circumstances. Journal articles traditionally report that data from suspicious subjects are discarded, but, except on unexplored intuitive grounds, we do not actually know whether suspicion affects social behaviour, and, if so, how exactly it does so. How exactly do two people behave when they distrust one another, when they are enemies, or when they are 'falling out'? What precise differences are there in their interaction as compared to the interactions of friends? What variables differentiate the interactions of strangers from those of friends?

I hope that in presenting relationships as the organizing theme for this book I have stimulated present readers — from whom the future researchers in this field may ultimately come — to undertake to fill these gaps.

Appendix:
To Help You and Your Instructor

Library and Research Skills

It can be frustrating to find that someone else has taken the only remaining copy in the library of the book or article that was the basis of a class assignment, but with a little extra knowledge about some library techniques — and a bit of practice — you can get around the problem. The same techniques can help you to follow-up on any topics in this book that you particularly want to pursue, and, as I mention earlier in the book, my students are all taught these methods to allow them to expand their abilities to 'read around' a favourite topic. It is to your advantage to have these skills available to you, so I want to round off by presenting them here and then building them into the exercises that will help you to apply the topics in the book to your life.

Many volumes in your library are there to help you to do your own research if you are particularly interested in a topic. The most useful are: *Current Contents*, *Psychological Abstracts*, and *Social Science Citation Index (SSCI)*.

Current Contents

Current Contents is published in sections and simply prints the contents pages of journals recently published. There are seven sections, and the one you need is for the social and behavioural sciences. By turning to the psychology or communication sections, you can see the titles of papers that you may be interested in for research. It also lists authors' addresses so that

you can contact them and ask for a reprint of their article.
Useful for: showing you what has happened most recently.
Disadvantage: gives you only the title — and titles can often be
misleading.

Psychological Abstracts

Psychological Abstracts deals with specific years or half-years
and prints and catalogues the abstracts/summaries which
appear at the start of most journal articles. It also lists the source
(i.e., the journal that published it), the title, and authors' affiliations. It comes in two parts: index and catalogue. The index
lists subjects and authors, and gives a code number for the
relevant abstract; the catalogue lists the abstracts by code
number. You start with the index to find the abstracts you need,
then go to the appropriate catalogue section to find the
abstracts. If they are of interest to you, you can find the original
article in the journal where it was published.
Useful for: the list of keywords enables you to track down, say,
all the articles on 'friendship in children' or 'prejudice' or 'self-
esteem'. It is excellent for broadly encompassing a particular
topic, and, because it prints the abstracts in full it enables you
quickly to find pertinent details of papers and so make a list of
those that you should read in full.
Disadvantages: it is produced semiannually in volumes relating
to a particular (half) year and so is not as up to date as *Current
Contents*. It lists only those items published in a given year,
without cross reference.

(Social) Science Citation Index (SSCI)

SSCI is published in annual volumes, although sections
covering parts of the current year are available separately. It
gives: a list of keywords (permuterm subject index), a list of
papers and authors consulted that year (source index), and a list
of citations made to particular authors (citation index). (Always
ensure that you are using the correct section.) The citation
index is extremely useful. Suppose I want to find all the papers

in 1983 that referred to S.E. Asch's study on conformity: I would look up Asch, S.E. in the citation index and there would be the list. This is useful because you can, for instance, trace the way in which a piece of classic work has been used in more recent work or criticized by subsequent researchers. Another advantage is that if someone has taken the very article that you wanted to read out of the library, then you can find others on the same topic that cite the article on loan. This is useful for essays and seminar classes because the more recent article may give you some good ideas about how to evaluate or criticize the set article.

Useful for: coming up to date on classic work; doing a broad review of related research; finding out the different lines that have been developed from one particular starting point; finding alternative reading sources.

Disadvantages: somewhat difficult to learn to use, but the effort really is worth it — and not only in psychology but for all your subjects of study.

Exercises

As a part of your learning of the subject and as a test of your growing abilities, you might like to try the following exercises — or your instructor may assign them to you. Some questions are intended to encourage you to experience the materials and some are meant to stimulate you to use your growing knowledge to apply to practical issues — but they can make useful topics for small group discussion in class or with friends (instead of, or in addition to, the preceding purposes). All should help to illustrate the principles described in the book as they operate in real life — *your* real life.

Practising your library skills

Think of a topic that interests you and find out all you can about it using the preceding methods. Allow two hours to do this, and pick one particular year, say, 1983, for *Psychological Abstracts* and *SSCI* but carry through up to date with *Current Contents*.

Chapter 1: Emotions

1 Pair up with another member of the class (or with an interested friend) for a couple of hours or so and keep a diary of your emotions and his or her emotions. As an alternative or an addition, take it in turns to say 'If Peter calls, tell him I'm out' in a tone that conveys different emotions (without telling each other what you are intending to convey). Each of you should keep a list of the emotions that are 'sent' and 'received' on each occasion and then compare notes to see if the 'decoder' received the message intended by the 'encoder' each time. At the end of the time, check your two lists and discuss the extent to which they match up: do you display your emotions effectively? Does your partner? What are the problems in doing this exercise?

2 Find extra reading for chapter 1. Start with a book by Buss (1980) and find some people who have cited it recently. If you use the 1983 volumes of *SSCI* you should find eighteen citations, of which Schlenker (1982) is one that you could profitably consult.

Chapter 2: Verbal and nonverbal language

1 At the start of chapter 2, I ask how we should teach the deaf to communicate. Using the library skills outlined, find out if there is any research showing that the deaf stammer and whether they convey anxiety in the same ways that 'hearing speakers' do.

2 Also at the start of chapter 2, I suggest that language is related to identity. We saw some ways in which it can convey attitudes about self (e.g., confidence, power, status); so it is related to our self-concept, and we select language codes to suit our social purposes on particular occasions. Using your library skills, find out if there are any books relating language acquisition in young children to the learning of identity. Do we learn who we are only when we start to speak? Is our view of ourself

dependent on our ability to communicate? If so, what does this mean for the deaf and how might the development of a deaf child be impaired by this?

3 Sit next to someone who is reading a newspaper and begin to read it; *or* Find a room or bus that is less than a quarter full and sit in the seat next to someone there whom you do not know; *or* Hold a conversation with a friend whilst standing at the 'wrong' distance.

Record your experiences for class discussion, especially noting the proxemic behaviour, the consequences of the encounter, and your own personal feelings during the 'breaking of the rules'.

Chapter 3: Long-term relationships

Think about the following four items and construct three arguments for and three arguments against the statement:

We have completely free choice over the friendships that we make.

Friendships should be arranged for us by our parents.

Friendships should be arranged for us by a national computer containing data on our personalities.

Friendships should be arranged randomly according to, say, birthdates, hair colour or IQ level. (Think up your own system for doing this.)

As well as trying this in class discussion, you could try talking to your friends about it.

Chapter 4: The family

1 Look back at the exercise for chapter 3. Repeat each step here, substituting the word 'marriage' for the word 'friendships'. Are cultures that arrange marriages really doing anything substantially different from what happens in cultures where love is the ostensible basis of the relationship?

2 Do you think that it would reduce or increase the divorce rate if marriages were fixed up by:

Parents for their children,

Mutual friends,
Computers,
Chance

3 Give three reasons for and three reasons against teaching 'relationships' in school. Should teachers be trained to identify unpopular children? What difficulties might there be with this notion? What did the unpopular children at your school do?

Chapter 5: Persuasion

1 Spend one day keeping a list of all the examples of persuasion or influence which you witness. At the end of the day, look at the list and work out what methods were used. Is there any relationship, do you think, between the strategy and
The person's goals
The positivity/negativity of the request
The power differences between the persons involved
The closeness or distance of the relationship between the
persons

2 Persuade your instructor that you have prepared a good answer to the preceding exercise.

Chapter 6: Medicine

1 Find the latest review of work on the relationship between Type A personality and CHD. If you were asked by a national government to advise on health education, what three proposals would you recommend them to adopt with Type A personalities? (One piece of advice that I have seen is that they should be made to stop wearing a watch. Another is that they should be encouraged to make appointments with people and then deliberately fail to turn up.)

2 If an insurance company asked you for advice on social risk factors for their life assurance policies, what topics would you suggest they ask questions about on their proposal forms?

3 Look through the article by Bloom et al. (1978) on the consequences of separation and divorce (use library skills to find it if you don't know the reference or haven't thought of

checking this book's Reference Section!). When is the 'separating man' at greatest risk and at what point are women most vulnerable? How would you suggest we monitor such risks and how could counsellors, friends, or volunteer 'crisis' organizations help?

General

Look out for the ways in which the relationship between two persons affects the ways that they behave towards one another. How does it influence their spatial relationships, their verbal relationships, their nonverbal behaviour, their persuasive efforts, and their topics of conversation? Can you tell the relationship between two people from any of these forms of behaviour and if so, which? How do you know you are right?

References

Adorno, T.W., Frenkel-Brunswick, E., Levinson, D. & Sanford, N. (1950) *The Authoritarian Personality*. Harper & Row: New York.

Anderson, S.A. (1985) 'Parental and marital role stress during the school entry transition'. *Journal of Social and Personal Relationships* (2), 59–80.

Argyle, M. (1964) *Psychology and Social Problems*. Methuen: London.

Argyle, M. (1967) *The Psychology of Interpersonal Behaviour*. Penguin Books: Harmondsworth, UK.

Argyle, M. (1969) *Social Interaction*. Methuen: London.

Argyle, M. (1975) *Bodily Communication*. Methuen: London.

Argyle, M. (1983) *The Psychology of Interpersonal Behaviour (4th Edn)*. Penguin Books: Harmondsworth, UK.

Argyle, M., Alkema, F. & Gilmour, R. (1972) 'The communication of friendly and hostile attitudes by verbal and nonverbal signals'. *European Journal of Social Psychology* (1), 385–402.

Argyle, M., Collett, P. & Clark, D. (1984) 'Long Term Relationships'. Report to Social Science Research Council, UK.

Argyle, M. & Cook, M. (1976) *Gaze and Mutual Gaze*. Cambridge University Press: Cambridge, UK.

Argyle, M. & Dean, J. (1965) 'Eye contact, distance and affiliation'. *Sociometry* (28), 289–304.

Argyle, M., Furnham, A. & Graham, J.A. (1981) *Social Situations*. Cambridge University Press: Cambridge, UK.

Argyle, M. & Henderson, M. (1984) 'The rules of friendship'. *Journal of Social and Personal Relationships* (1), 209–35.

Argyle, M., Lalljee, M. & Cook, M. (1968) 'The effects of visibility on interaction in a dyad'. *Human Relations* (21), 3–17.

Argyle, M. & McHenry, R. (1971) 'Do spectacles really affect judgements of intelligence?' *British Journal of Social and Clinical Psychology* (10), 27–9.

Argyle, M., Salter, V., Nicholson, H., Williams, M. & Burgess, P. (1970) 'The communication of inferior and superior attitudes by verbal and non-verbal signals'. *British Journal of Social and Clinical Psychology* (9), 222–31.

Aronson, E. & Golden, B.W. (1962) 'The effect of relevant and irrelevant aspects of communicator credibility on attitude change'. *Journal of Personality* (30), 135–46.

Asher, S.R. (1984) 'Children's goals and social relationships'. Paper to Second International Conference on Personal Relationships, Madison, WI, July.

Asher, S.R. & Gottman, J.M. (1981) *The Development of Children's Friendships*. Cambridge University Press: Cambridge, UK.

Asher, S.R. & Wheeler, V.A. (in press) 'Children's loneliness: a comparison of rejected and neglected peer status'. *Journal of Consulting and Clinical Psychology*.

Athanasiou, R. & Sarkin, R. (1974) 'Premarital sexual behavior and postmarital adjustment'. *Archives of Sexual Behavior* (3), 207–25.

Bandura, A. (1977) *Social Learning Theory*. Prentice Hall: Englewood Cliffs, NJ.

Barrera, J., Jr. (1981) 'Social support in the adjustment of pregnant adolescents: assessment issues'. In B.H. Gottlieb (ed.) *Social Networks and Social Support*. Sage: Beverly Hills, CA.

Baumrind, D. (1972) 'Socialization and instrumental competence in young children'. In W.W. Hartup (ed.) *The Young Child: Reviews of Research, Vol. 2*. National Association for the Education of Young Children: Washington, DC.

Baxter, L.A. (1979) 'Self-disclosure as a relationship disengagement strategy'. *Human Communication Research* (5), 215–22.

Baxter, L.A. (1984) 'Trajectories of relationship disengagement'. *Journal of Social and Personal Relationships* (1), 29–48.

Baxter, L.A. & Wilmot, W.W. (1984) 'Secret Tests: Social strategies for acquiring information about the state of the relationship'. *Human Communication Research* (11), 171–202.

Baxter, L.A. & Wilmot, W.W. (1985) 'Taboo topics in close relationships'. *Journal of Social and Personal Relationships* (2), 253–69.

Beattie, G.W. (1981) 'A further investigation of the cognitive interference hypothesis of gaze patterns in interaction'. *British Journal of Social Psychology* (20), 243–8.

Beck, A.T. (1976) *Cognitive Therapy and the Emotional Disorders*. International Universities Press: Garden City, New York.

Beecher, H.K. (1959) *Measurement of Subjective Responses: Quantitative Effects of Drugs*. Oxford University Press: New York.

Bell, R.A. & Daly, J.A. (1984) 'Affinity-seeking: its nature and correlates'. Paper presented to International Communication Association, San Francisco, May.

Bentler, P.M. & Newcomb, M.D. (1978) 'Longitudinal study of marital success and failure'. *Journal of Consulting and Clinical Psychology* (46), 1053–70.

Berardo, F.M. (1970) 'Survivorship and social isolation: the case of the aged widower'. *Family Coordinator* (19), 11–25.

Berger, C.R. & Bradac, J. (1982) *Language and Social Knowledge*. Arnold: London.

Berkman, L.F. & Syme, S.L. (1979) 'Social networks, host resistance and mortality: a nine-year follow-up of Alameda County residents'. *American Journal of Epidemiology* (109), 186–204.

Bernard, J. (1972) *The Future of Marriage*. World: New York.

Berne, E. (1964) *Games People Play*. Penguin Books: Harmondsworth, UK.

Berscheid, E. (1966) 'Opinion-change and communicator-communicatee similarity and dissimilarity'. *Journal of Personality and Social Psychology* (4), 670–80.

Berscheid, E. (1983) 'Emotion'. In H.H. Kelley et al. (eds.) *Close Relationships*. Freeman: San Francisco.

Berscheid, E. & Walster, E. (1974) 'Physical attractiveness'. In L. Berkowitz (ed.) *Advances in Experimental Social Psychology, Vol. 7*. Academic Press: New York.

Bierce, A. (1985) *The Devil's Dictionary*. Fosdyke: New Cranton, PA.

Bierman, K.L. & Furman, W. (1982) 'The effects of social skills training and peer involvement on the social adjustment of pre-adolescents'. *Child Development* (53), 27–41.

Birchler, G.R. (1972) 'Differential patterns of instrumental affiliative behavior as a function of degree of marital distress and level of intimacy'. PhD dissertation, University of Oregon.

Blondis, M.N. & Jackson, B.E. (1977) *Nonverbal Communication with Patients*. Wiley: New York.

Bloom, B., Asher, S.J., & White, S.W. (1978) 'Marital disruption as a stressor: A review and analysis'. *Psychological Bulletin*, (85), 867–94.

Bochner, A.P. (1976) 'Conceptual frontiers in the study of communication in families: an introduction to the literature'. *Human Communication Research* (2), 381–97.

Bochner, A.P. (1983) 'Functions of communication in interpersonal bonding'. In C. Arnold & J.W. Bowers (eds.) *Handbook of Rhetoric and Communication*. Allyn & Bacon: Boston, MA.

Boissevain, J. (1974) *Friends of Friends: Networks, Manipulators, and Coalitions*. Basil Blackwell: Oxford, UK.

Boreham, P. & Gibson, D. (1978) 'The informative process in private medical consultations: a preliminary investigation'. *Social Science and Medicine* (12), 409–16.

Bornstein, P.E. & Clayton, P.J. (1972) 'The anniversary reaction'. *Diseases of the Nervous System* (33), 470–2.

Boster, F.J. & Stiff, J.B. (1984) 'Compliance-gaining message selection behaviour'. *Human Communication Research* (10), 539–56.

Bourhis, R.Y. & Giles, H. (1977) 'The language of intergroup distinctiveness'. In H. Giles (ed.) *Language, Ethnicity and Intergroup Relations*. Academic Press: London.

Bowlby, J. (1951) *Maternal Care and Mental Health*. WHO: Geneva.

Boyd, J.R., Covington, T.R., Stanaszek, W.F. & Coussons, R.T. (1974) 'Drug-defaulting II: Analysis of noncompliance patterns'. *American Journal of Hospital Pharmacy* (31), 485–91.

Bradburn, N. (1969) *The Structure of Psychological Well-Being*. Aldine: Chicago.

Brehm, J.W. (1966) *A Theory of Psychological Reactance*. Academic Press: New York.

Brehm, S. & Brehm, J.W. (1981) *Psychological Reactance: A Theory of Freedom and Control*. Academic Press: New York.

Brown, G.W. (1984) 'Social support and psychiatric disorder'. Paper to Second International Conference on Personal Relationships, Madison, WI, July.

Brown, G.W. & Harris, T. (1978) *The Social Origins of Depression*. Tavistock: London.

Brown, R. (1965) *Social Psychology*. Free Press: New York.

Bugental, D.E., Kaswan, J.E. & Love, L.R. (1970) 'Perception of contradictory meanings conveyed by verbal and nonverbal channels'. *Journal of Personality and Social Psychology* (16), 647–55.

Burgess, R.L. (1981) 'Relationships in marriage and the family'. In S.W. Duck & R. Gilmour (eds.) *Personal Relationships 1: Studying Personal Relationships*. Academic Press: London & New York.

Burgoon, M., Dillard, J.P. & Doran, N.E. (1980) 'Situational determinants of message strategy selection: an exploratory analysis'. Unpublished manuscript, Michigan State University, East Lansing.

Burgoon, M. & Koper, R.J. (1984) 'Nonverbal and relational communication associated with reticence'. *Human Communication Research* (10), 601–27.

Burns, G.L. & Farina, A. (1984) 'Social competence and adjustment'. *Journal of Social and Personal Relationships* (1), 99–114.

Buss, A.H. (1980) *Self-Consciousness and Social Anxiety*. Freeman: San Francisco.

Buunk, A. (1980) 'Sexually open marriages: ground rules for countering potential threats to marriage'. *Alternative Life Styles* (3), 312–28.

Buunk, A. & Bringle, R. (1986) 'Jealousy'. In D. Perlman & S.W. Duck (eds.) *Intimate Relationships*. Sage: Beverly Hills.

Byrne, D. (1961) 'Interpersonal attraction and attitude similarity'. *Journal of Abnormal and Social Psychology* (62), 713–15.

Byrne, D. (1971) *The Attraction Paradigm*. Academic Press: New York.

Byrne, D., Ervin, C.R. & Lamberth, J. (1970) 'Continuity between the experimental study of attraction and real-life computer dating'. *Journal of Personality and Social Psychology* (16), 157–65.

Byrne, D. & Lamberth, J. (1971) 'Cognitive and reinforcement theory as complementary approaches to the study of attraction'. In B.I. Murstein (ed.) *Theories of Attraction and Love*. Springer: New York.

Byrne, D. & Nelson, D. (1965) 'Attraction as a linear function of proportion of positive reinforcements'. *Journal of Personality and Social Psychology* (1), 659–63.

Byrne, D., Nelson, D. & Reeves, K. (1966) 'The effects of consensual validation and invalidation on attraction as a function of verifiability'. *Journal of Experimental Social Psychology* (2), 98–107.

Cannon, W.B. (1929) 'The James-Lange theory of emotions: a critical examination and an alternative theory'. *American Journal of Psychology* (39), 106–24.

Cappella, J.N. (1984) 'The relevance of the microstructure of interaction to relationship change'. *Journal of Social and Personal Relationships* (1), 239–64.

Carr, S.E. & Dabbs, J.M., Jr. (1974) 'The effects of lighting, distance and intimacy of topic on verbal and visual behaviour'. *Sociometry* (37), 592–600.

Carver, C.S. & Humphries, C. (1982) 'The social psychology of the Type A coronary prone behaviour pattern'. In G.S. Sanders & J. Suls (eds.) *Social Psychology of Health and Illness*. Erlbaum: Hillsdale, NJ.

Check, J., Perlman, D. & Malamuth, N. (1985) 'Loneliness and aggressive behaviour'. *Journal of Social and Personal Relationships* (2), 243–52.

Cheek, J.M. & Busch, C.M. (1981) 'The influence of shyness on loneliness in a new situation'. *Personality and Social Psychology Bulletin* (7), 572–7.

Cherlin, A.J. (1981) *Marriage, Divorce, Remarriage*. Harvard University Press: Cambridge, MA.

Cheyne, W.M. (1970) 'Stereotyped reactions of speakers with Scottish and English regional accents'. *British Journal of Social and Clinical Psychology* (9), 77–9.

Christopher, F.S. & Cate, R.M. (1985) 'Premarital sexual pathways and relationship development'. *Journal of Social and Personal Relationships* (2), 271–88.

Christy, N.P. (1979) 'English is our second language'. *New England Journal of Medicine* (300), 979–81.

Cialdini, R.B., Cacioppo, J.T., Bassett, R. & Miller, J.A. (1978) 'Lowball procedure for producing compliance: commitment then cost'. *Journal of Personality and Social Psychology* (36), 463–76.

Cialdini, R.B., Vincent, J.E., Lewis, S.K., Catalan, J., Wheeler, D. & Darby, B.L. (1975) 'A reciprocal concessions procedure for inducing compliance: The door-in-the-face technique'. *Journal of Personality and Social Psychology* (21), 206–15.

Clark, R.A. & Delia, J.G. (1979) 'Topoi and rhetorical competence'. *Quarterly Journal of Speech* (65), 187–206.

Clark, R.A. (1979) 'The impact of selection of persuasive strategies on self-interest and desired liking'. *Communication Monographs* (46), 257–73.

Clore, G.L. (1977) 'Reinforcement and affect in attraction'. In S.W. Duck (ed.) *Theory and Practice in Interpersonal Attraction*. Academic Press: London.

Clore, G.L. & Byrne, D. (1974) 'A reinforcement-affect model of attraction'. In T.L. Huston (ed.) *Foundations of Interpersonal Attraction*. Academic Press: New York.

Clore, G.L. & Gormly, J.B. (1974) 'Knowing, feeling and liking: a psychophysiological study of attraction'. *Journal of Research in Personality* (8), 218–30.

Cobb, S. & Jones, J.M. (1984) 'Social support, support groups and marital relationships'. In S.W. Duck (ed.) *Personal Relationships 5: Repairing Personal Relationships*. Academic Press: London & New York.

Cody, M.J., Woelfel, M.L. & Jordan, W.J. (1983) 'Dimensions of compliance-gaining situations'. *Human Communication Research* (9), 99–113.

Cole, C.A. (1976) 'A behavioral analysis of married and living together couples'. Unpublished PhD dissertation, University of Houston, TX.

Cook, M. (1968) 'Studies of orientation and proximity'. Unpublished manuscript. Oxford University, UK.

Cook, M. (1971) *Interpersonal Perception*. Penguin Books: Harmondsworth, UK.

Cook, M. (1977) 'Social Skills and Attraction'. In S.W. Duck (ed.) *Theory and Practice in Interpersonal Attraction*. Academic Press: London & New York.

Cooper, D. (1970) *The Death of the Family*. Vintage: New York.

Coyne, J.C. (1976) 'Depression and the response of others'. *Journal of Abnormal Psychology* (85), 186–93.

Cunningham, J.D. & Antill, J.K. (1981) 'Love in developing romantic relationships'. In S.W. Duck & R. Gilmour (eds.) *Personal Relationships 2: Developing Personal Relationships*. Academic Press: London & New York.

Curran, J.P. (1977) 'Skills training as an approach to the treatment of heterosexual-social anxiety: A review'. *Psychological Bulletin* (84), 140–57.

Cutrona, C.E. (1982) 'Transition to college: Loneliness and the process of social adjustment'. In L.A. Peplau & D. Perlman (eds.) *Loneliness: A Sourcebook of Current Theory, Research and Therapy*. Wiley-Interscience: New York.

Davis, J.D. & Sloan, M. (1974) 'The basis of interviewee matching of interviewer self disclosure'. *British Journal of Social and Clinical Psychology*, (13), 359–67.

Davis, J.D. (1978) 'When boy meets girl: sex roles and the negotiation of intimacy in an acquaintance exercise'. *Journal of Personality and Social Psychology* (36), 684–92.

Davis, K. (1936) 'Jealousy and sexual property'. *Social Forces* (14), 395–405.

Davis, K.E. & Todd, M. (1985) 'Assessing friendship: prototypes, paradigm cases and relationship description'. In S.W. Duck & D. Perlman (eds.) *Understanding Personal Relationships*. Sage: London.

Davitz, J.R. (1964) *The Communication of Emotional Meaning*. McGraw-Hill: New York.

Dean, A., Lin, N. & Ensel, W.M. (1981) 'The epidemiological significance of social support in depression'. In R. Simmons (ed.) *Research in Community and Mental Health*. SAI Press: New York.

DeJong, W. (1979) 'An examination of the self-perception mediation of the foot-in-the-door effect'. *Journal of Personality and Social Psychology* (37), 221–39.

Dembrowski, T.M. & MacDougall, J.M. (1978) 'Stress effects on affiliation preferences among subjects possessing the Type A coronary-prone behavior pattern'. *Journal of Personality and Social Psychology* (36), 23–33.

Dembrowski, T.M., MacDougall, J.M. & Shields, J.M. (1977) 'Physiologic reactions to social challenge in persons evidencing the Type A coronary-prone behavior pattern'. *Journal of Personality and Social Psychology* (35), 23–33.

Department of Health and Social Security (1976) *Smoking and Pregnancy*. HMSO: London.

Dickens, W.J. & Perlman, D. (1981) 'Friendship over the life cycle'. In S.W. Duck & R. Gilmour (eds.) *Personal Relationships 2: Developing Personal Relationships*. Academic Press: London & New York.

Dillard, J.P., Hunter, J.E. & Burgoon, M. (1984) 'Sequential-request persuasive strategies: metaanalysis of foot-in-the-door and door-in-the-face'. *Human Communication Research* (10), 461–88.

DiMatteo, M.R. & Friedman, H.S. (1982) *Social Psychology and Medicine*. Oelgeschlager: Cambridge, MA.

Dindia, K. & Fitzpatrick, M.A. (1985) 'Marital communication: three approaches compared'. In S.W. Duck & D. Perlman (eds.) *Understanding*

Personal Relationships. Sage: London.

Dohrenwend, B.S. (1973) 'Life events as stressors: a methodological inquiry'. *Journal of Health and Social Behavior* (14), 167–75.

Doob, A.N., Carlsmith, J.M., Freedman, J.L., Landaver, T.K. & Tom, S., Jr. (1969) 'Effects of initial selling price on subsequent sales'. *Journal of Personality and Social Psychology* (11), 345–50.

Driscoll, R., Davis, K.E. & Lipetz, M.E. (1972) 'Parental interference and romantic love: the Romeo and Juliet effect'. *Journal of Personality and Social Psychology* (24), 1–10.

Duck, S.W. (1973) *Personal Relationships and Personal Constructs: A Study of Friendship Formation*. Wiley: Chichester, UK.

Duck, S.W. (1975a) 'Attitude similarity and interpersonal attraction: right answers and wrong reasons'. *British Journal of Social and Clinical Psychology* (14), 311–12.

Duck, S.W. (1975b) 'Personality similarity and friendship choices by adolescents'. *European Journal of Social Psychology* (5), 351–65.

Duck, S.W. (1977) *The Study of Acquaintance*. Gower Press: Farnborough, UK.

Duck, S.W. (1980) 'Personal relationships in the 1980s: towards an understanding of complex human sociality'. *Western Journal of Speech Communication* (44), 114–19.

Duck, S.W. (1982a) 'A topography of relationship disengagement and dissolution'. In S.W. Duck (ed.) *Personal Relationships 4: Dissolving Personal Relationships*. Academic Press: London & New York.

Duck, S.W. (1982b) *Personal Relationships 4: Dissolving Personal Relationships*. Academic Press: London & New York.

Duck, S.W. (1983) *Friends, for Life*. Harvester: Brighton, UK.

Duck, S.W. (1984a) 'A perspective on the repair of personal relationships: repair of what, when?'. In S.W. Duck (ed.) *Personal Relationships 5: Repairing Personal Relationships*. Academic Press: London & New York.

Duck, S.W. (1984b) *Personal Relationships 5: Repairing Personal Relationships*. Academic Press: London & New York.

Duck, S.W. & Gilmour, R. (1981a) *Personal Relationships 1: Studying Personal Relationships*. Academic Press: London & New York.

Duck, S.W. & Gilmour, R. (1981b) *Personal Relationships 2: Developing Personal Relationships*. Academic Press: London & New York.

Duck, S.W. & Gilmour, R. (1981c) *Personal Relationships 3: Personal Relationships in Disorder*. Academic Press: London & New York.

Duck, S.W. & Miell, D.E. (1984) 'Towards an understanding of relationship development and breakdown'. In H. Tajfel, C. Fraser & J. Jaspars (eds.) *The Social Dimension: European Perspectives on Social Psychology*. Cambridge University Press: Cambridge, UK.

Duck, S.W., Miell, D.E. & Miell, D.K. (1984) 'Relationship growth and decline'. In H.E. Sypher & J.L. Applegate (eds.) *Communication by Children and Adults*. Sage: Beverly Hills, CA.

Duck, S.W., Miell, D.K. & Gaebler, H.C. (1980) 'Attraction and communication in children's interactions'. In H.C. Foot, A.J. Chapman & J.R. Smith (eds.) *Friendship and Social Relations in Children*. Wiley: Chichester, UK.

Duck, S.W. & Perlman, D. (1985) 'The thousand islands of personal relationships: a prescriptive analysis for future exploration'. In S.W. Duck & D. Perlman (eds.) *Understanding Personal Relationships*. Sage: London.

Duck, S.W. & Sants, H.K.A. (1983) 'On the origin of the specious: are personal relationships really interpersonal states?' *Journal of Social and Clinical Psychology* (1), 27–41.

Eagly, A.H., Wood, W. & Chaiken, S. (1978) 'Causal inferences about communications and their effect on opinion change'. *Journal of Personality and Social Psychology* (36), 424–35.

Edelmann, R.J. (1985) 'Social embarrassment: an analysis of the process'. *Journal of Social and Personal Relationships* (2), 195–213.

Edelmann, R.J. & Hampson, S.E. (1979) 'Changes in nonverbal behaviour during embarrassment'. *British Journal of Social and Clinical Psychology* (18), 385–90.

Ellis, C. & Weinstein, E. (1986) 'Jealousy and the social psychology of emotional experience'. *Journal of Social and Personal Relationships* (3).

Ellsworth, P.C., Carlsmith, J.M. & Henson, A. (1972) 'The stare as a stimulus to flight in human subjects: A series of field experiments'. *Journal of Personality and Social Psychology* (21), 302–11.

Emler, N. & Fisher, S. (1982) 'Gossip and social participation'. Paper to Annual Conference of Social Psychology Section, British Psychological Society, Oxford, September.

Engler, C.M., Saltzman, G.A., Walker, M.L. & Wolf, F.M. (1981) 'Medical student acquisition and retention of communication and interviewing skills'. *Journal of Medical Education* (56), 572–9.

Erickson, B., Lind, E.A., Johnson, B.C. & O'Barr, W.M. (1978) 'Speech style and impression formation in a court setting. The effect of "powerful" and "powerless" speech'. *Journal of Experimental Social Psychology* (14), 266–79.

Exline, R.V. (1971) 'Visual interaction: the glances of power and preference'. In J.K. Cole (ed.) *Nebraska Symposium on Motivation (Vol. 19)*. University of Nebraska Press: Lincoln.

Exline, R.V. & Winters, L.C. (1965) 'Affective relations and mutual gaze in dyads'. In S. Tomkins & C. Izard (eds.) *Affect, Cognition and Personality*. Springer: New York.

Exline, R.V. & Yellin, A. (1969) 'Eye contact as a sign between man and monkeys'. Symposium on Nonverbal Communication, 19th International Congress of Psychology, London.

Farsad, P., Galliguez, P., Chamberlain, R. & Roghmann, K.J. (1978) 'Teaching interviewing skills to pediatric house officers'. *Pediatrics* (61), 384–8.

Feldman, P. & Orford, J. (1980) *Psychological Problems: The Social Context*. Wiley: Chichester, UK.

Ferreira, A.J. & Winter, W.D. (1968) 'Information exchange and silence in normal and abnormal families'. *Family Process* (7), 251–76.

Festinger, L. (1954) 'A theory of social comparison processes'. *Human Relations* (7), 117–40.

Festinger, L. (1957) *A Theory of Cognitive Dissonance*. Stanford University Press: Stanford, CA.

Festinger, L. & Carlsmith, J.M. (1959) 'Cognitive consequences of forced compliance'. *Journal of Abnormal and Social Psychology* (58), 203–10.

Filsinger, E.E. & Lewis, R.A. (1981) *Assessing Marriage: New Behavioral Approaches*. Sage: Beverly Hills, CA.

Fine, V.K. & Therrien, M.E. (1977) 'Empathy in the doctor-patient relationship: skill training for medical students'. *Journal of Medical Education* (52), 752–7.

Fishbein, M. & Ajzen, I. (1972) 'Attitudes and opinions'. *Annual Review of Psychology* (23), 487–544.

Fisher, B.A. (1970) 'Decision emergence: phases in group decision-making'. *Speech Monographs* (37), 53–66.

Fitzpatrick, M.A. (1977) 'A typological approach to communication in relationships'. In B. Ruben (ed.) *Communication Yearbook I*. Transaction Press: New Jersey.

Fitzpatrick, M.A. & Badzinski, D. (1985) 'All in the family'. In G.R. Miller & M.L. Knapp (eds.) *Handbook of Interpersonal Communication*. Sage: Beverly Hills, CA.

Fransella, F. (1968) 'Self-concepts and the stutterer'. *British Journal of Psychiatry* (114), 1531–5.

Fransella, F. (1972) *Personal Change and Reconstruction*. Academic Press: London.

Fraser, C. & Scherer, K. (1982) *Advances in the Social Psychology of Language*. Cambridge University Press: Cambridge, UK.

Freedman, J.L. & Fraser, S.C. (1976) 'Compliance without pressure: The foot-in-the-door technique'. *Journal of Personality and Social Psychology* (4), 195–202.

Frenkel, O.J. & Doob, A.N. (1976) 'Post-decision dissonance at the polling-booth'. *Canadian Journal of Behavioral Science* (8), 347–50.

Friedman, H.S. (1982) 'Nonverbal communication in medical interaction'. In H.S. Friedman & M.R. DiMatteo (eds.) *Interpersonal Issues in Health Care*. Academic Press: New York.

Friedman, H.S. & DiMatteo, M.R. (1982) *Interpersonal Issues in Health Care*. Academic Press: New York.

Furman, W. (1984) 'Enhancing children's peer relations and friendships'. In S.W. Duck (ed.) *Personal Relationships 5: Repairing Personal Relationships*. Academic Press: London & New York.

Furman, W., Rahe, D.F. & Hartup, W.W. (1979) 'Rehabilitation of socially-withdrawn preschool children through mixed age and same age socialisation'. *Child Development* (50), 915–22.

Furstenberg, F.F. (1979) 'Premarital pregnancy and marital instability'. In G. Levinger & O.C. Moles (eds.) *Divorce and Separation*. Basic Books: New York.

Gallup, C. (1980) 'A study to determine the effectiveness of a social skills training program in reducing the perceived loneliness of social isolation'. *Dissertation Abstracts* (41), 3424.

Garrard, G.G. & Kyriacou, C. (1985) 'Social sensitivity among young children'. *Journal of Social and Personal Relationships* (2), 123–36.

Geersten, H.R., Gray, R.M. & Ward, J.R. (1973) 'Patient non-compliance within the context of seeking medical care for arthritis'. *Journal of Chronic Diseases* (26), 689–98.

Gelles, R.J. (1974) *The Violent Home: A Study of Physical Aggression Between Husbands and Wives*. Sage: Beverly Hills, CA.

Giles, H. (1977) 'Social psychology and applied linguistics: towards an integrative approach'. *ITL: Review of Applied Linguistics* (33), 27–42.

Giles, H. (1978) 'Linguistic differentiation in ethnic groups'. In H. Tajfel (ed.) *Differentiation Between Social Groups*. Academic Press: London.

Giles, H. & Powesland, P.F. (1975) *Speech Style and Social Evaluation*. Academic Press: London.

Giles, H., Taylor, D.M. & Bourhis, R.Y. (1973) 'Towards a theory of interpersonal accommodation through language use'. *Language in Society* (2), 177–92.

Glass, D. (1977) *Behavior Patterns, Stress and Coronary Disease*. Erlbaum: Hillsdale, NJ.

Goffman, E. (1959) *The Presentation of Self in Everyday Life*. Penguin Books: Harmondsworth, UK.

Gore, S. (1978) 'The effect of social support in moderating the health consequences of unemployment'. *Journal of Health and Social Behavior* (19), 157–65.

Gormly, J.B. & Gormly, A.V. (1981) 'See you later, alligator: Goodbyes and farewells'. *Language in Society* (17), 221–3.

Gottlieb, B.H. (1981) *Social Networks and Social Support*. Sage: Beverly Hills, CA.

Gottlieb, B.H. (1983) 'Social support as a focus for integrative research in psychology'. *American Psychologist* (38), 278–87.

Gottlieb, B.H. (1985) 'Social support and the study of personal relationships'. *Journal of Social and Personal Relationships* (2), 351–75.

Gottman, J. (1979) *Empirical Investigations of Marriage*. Academic Press: New York.

Gottman, J.M. (1982) 'Temporal form in personal relationships'. Paper presented to the First International Conference on Personal Relationships, Madison, WI, July.

Gottman, J., Markman, H. & Notarius, C. (1977) 'The topography of marital conflict: A sequential analysis of verbal and nonverbal behavior'. *Journal of Marriage and the Family* (39), 461–78.

Greenblatt, M. (1978) 'The grieving spouse'. *American Journal of Psychiatry* (135), 43–47.

Greene, J.O., O'Hair, H.D., Cody, M.J. & Yen, C. (1985) 'Planning and control of behavior during deception'. *Human Communication Research* (11), 335–64.

Gresham, F.M. & Nagle, R.J. (1980) 'Social skills training to children: Responsiveness to modeling and coaching as a function of peer orientation'. *Journal of Consulting and Clinical Psychology* (48), 718–29.

Gross, E. & Stone, G.P. (1964) 'Embarrassment and the analysis of role requirements'. *American Journal of Sociology* (70), 1–15.

Guralnick, M.J. (1976) 'The value of integrating handicapped and non-handicapped pre-school children'. *American Journal of Orthopsychiatry* (42), 236–45.

Hagestad, G.O. & Smyer, M.A. (1982) 'Types of divorce and their consequences'. In S.W. Duck (ed.) *Personal Relationships 4: Dissolving Personal Relationships*. Academic Press: London & New York.

Haley, J. (1964) 'Research on family patterns: an instrument measurement'. *Family Process*, (3), 41–65.

Hall, E.T. (1966) *The Hidden Dimension*. Doubleday/Anchor: New York.

Hamilton, G.V. (1924) Reported in G.V. Hamilton (1948) *A Research in Marriage*. Lear: New York.

Hansson, R.O. & Jones, W.H. (1981) 'Loneliness, cooperation and conformity among American undergraduates'. *Journal of Social Psychology* (115), 103–8.

Harré, R. (1979) *Social Being*. Basil Blackwell: Oxford.

Harvey, J., Weber, A., Yarkin, K. & Stewart, B.E. (1982) 'An attributional approach to relationship breakdown and dissolution'. In S.W. Duck (ed.) *Personal Relationships 4: Dissolving Personal Relationships*. Academic Press: London & New York.

Haslett, B. (1983a) 'Preschoolers' communicative strategies in gaining compliance from peers: a developmental study'. *Quarterly Journal of Speech* (69), 84–100.

Haslett, B. (1983b) 'Communicative functions and strategies in children's conversations'. *Human Communication Research* (9), 114–29.

Hatfield, E. & Traupmann, J. (1981) 'Intimate relationships: A perspective from Equity Theory'. In S.W. Duck & R. Gilmour (eds.) *Personal Relationships 1: Studying Personal Relationships*. Academic Press: London & New York.

Hays, R. & DiMatteo, M.R. (1984) 'Towards a more therapeutic physician-patient relationship'. In S.W. Duck (ed.) *Personal Relationships 5: Repairing Personal Relationships*. Academic Press: London & New York.

Hays, R.B. (1984) 'The development and maintenance of friendship'. *Journal of Social and Personal Relationships* (1), 75–98.

Heider, F. (1944) 'Social perception and phenomenal causality'. *Psychological Review* (51), 358–74.

Heider, F. (1958) *The Psychology of Interpersonal Relations*. Wiley: New York.

Hendrick, C., Hendrick, S., Foote, F. & Slapion-Foote, M. (1984) 'Do men and women love differently?' *Journal of Social and Personal Relationships* (1), 177–96.

Hetherington, E.M. (1979) 'Divorce: A child's perspective'. *American Psychologist* (34), 851–58.

Hetherington, E.M., Cox, M. & Cox, R. (1982) 'Effects of divorce on parents and children'. In M. Lamb (ed.) *Nontraditional Families*. Erlbaum: Hillsdale, NJ.

Hinde, R.A. (1979) *Towards Understanding Relationships*. Academic Press: London & New York.

Hobfoll, S. (1984) 'Limitations of social support in the stress process'. Paper presented at the NATO Advances Study Seminar on Social Support, Bonas, France.

Hobfoll, S. (1985) 'Stress, social support and women: an ecological life span perspective'. In S. Hobfoll (ed.) *Stress, Social Support and Women*. Hemisphere: Washington, DC.

Hobfoll, S.E. & Leiberman, J.R. (in press) 'Personality and social resources in immediate and continued stress resistance among women'. *Journal of Personality and Social Psychology*.

Hobfoll, S.E. & London, P. (1985) 'The relationship of self-concept and social support to emotional distress among women during war'. *Journal of Social and Clinical Psychology*, (3) 231–48.

Hobfoll, S.E. & Walfisch, S. (1984) 'Coping with a threat to life: a longitudinal study of self concept, social support and psychological distress'. *American Journal of Community Psychology* (12), 87–100.

Hochschild, A.R. (1979) 'Emotion work, feeling rules and social structure'. *American Journal of Sociology* (85), 551–75.

Holmes, T.H. & Rahe, R.H. (1967) 'The social readjustment rating scale'. *Journal of Psychosomatic Research* (11), 213–18.

Hopper, R. & Bell, R.A. (1984) 'Broadening the deception construct'. *Quarterly Journal of Speech* (70), 288–302.

Hopper, R., Knapp, M.L. & Scott, L. (1981) 'Couples' personal idioms: exploring intimate talk'. *Journal of Communication* (31), 23–33.

Hovland, C., Janis, I. & Kelley, H.H. (1953) *Communication and Persuasion*. Yale University Press: New Haven, CT.

Howells, K. (1981) 'Social relationships in violent offenders'. In S.W. Duck & R. Gilmour (eds.) *Personal Relationships 3: Personal Relationships in Disorder*. Academic Press: London & New York.

Huesmann, L.R. & Levinger, G. (1976) 'Incremental Exchange Theory'. In L. Berkowitz & E.H. Walster (eds.) *Advances in Experimental Social Psychology*. Academic Press: New York.

Hunter, J.E. & Boster, F.J. (1978) 'Situational differences in the selection of compliance-gaining messages'. Unpublished paper, Department of Communication, Arizona State University, Tempe.

Huston, T.L., Surra, C., Fitzgerald, N. & Cate, R. (1981) 'From courtship to marriage: Mate selection as an interpersonal process'. In S.W. Duck & R. Gilmour (eds.) *Personal Relationships 2: Developing Personal Relationships*. Academic Press: London & New York.

Hyde, J.S. (1984) 'Children's understanding of sexist language'. *Developmental Psychology* (20), 697–706.

Innes, J.M. (1980) 'Fashions in Social Psychology'. In R. Gilmour & S.W. Duck (eds.) *The Development of Social Psychology*. Academic Press: London & New York.

Innes, J.M. (1981) 'Social psychological approaches to the study of the induction and alleviation of stress: Influences of health and illness'. In G. Stephenson & J. Davis (eds.) *Progress in Applied Social Psychology*. Wiley: Chichester, UK.

Jacob, T. (1984) *Family Interaction and Psychopathology*. Plenum: New York.

Janis, I.L. & Feshbach, S. (1953) 'Effects of fear-arousing communications'. *Journal of Abnormal and Social Psychology* (48), 78–92.

Jarvinäan, K.A.J. (1955) 'Can ward rounds be a danger to patients with myocardial infarction?'. *British Medical Journal* (1), 318–20.

Jellison, J. (1984) 'Social aspects of emotion'. Paper to International Conference on The Self, Cardiff, July.

Jenkins, C.D. (1971) 'Psychological and social precursors of coronary disease'. *New England Journal of Medicine* (284), 244–55, 307–16.

Jenkins, C.D. (1976) 'Recent evidence supporting psychological and social risk factors for coronary heart disease'. *New England Journal of Medicine* (294), 1033–8.

Jenkins, C.D. (1977) 'Epidemiological studies of the psychosomatic aspects of coronary heart disease'. *Advances in Psychosomatic Medicine* (9), 1–19.

Johnson, F.N. (1984) *The Psychopharmacology of Lithium*. Macmillan: London.

Johnson, M.P. (1982) 'Social and cognitive features of dissolving commitment to relationships'. In S.W. Duck (ed.) *Personal Relationships 4: Dissolving Personal Relationships*. Academic Press: London & New York.

Jones, R.A. (1982) 'Expectations and illness'. In H.S. Friedman & M.R. DiMatteo (eds.) *Interpersonal Issues in Health Care*. Academic Press: London & New York.

Jones, W.H., Cavert, C.W., Snider, R.L. & Bruce, T. (1985) 'Relational stress: an analysis of situations and events associated with loneliness'. In S.W. Duck & D. Perlman (eds.) *Understanding Personal Relationships*. Sage: London.

Jones, W.H., Freemon, J.E. & Goswick, R.A. (1981) 'The persistence of loneliness: Self and other determinants'. *Journal of Personality* (49), 27–48.

Jones, W.H., Hansson, R.O. & Cutrona, C. (1984) 'Helping the lonely: Issues of intervention with young and older adults'. In S.W. Duck (ed.) *Personal Relationships 5: Repairing Personal Relationships*. Academic Press: London & New York.

Jones, W.H., Hobbs, S.A. & Hockenbury, D. (1982) 'Loneliness and social skill deficits'. *Journal of Personality and Social Psychology* (42), 682–9.

Kane, J. (1971) 'Body buffer zones in Glaswegian prisoners'. Unpublished MA Thesis, Glasgow University, Scotland.

Kastenbaum, R. (1982) 'Dying is healthy and death a bureaucrat: our fantasy machine is alive and well'. In H.S. Friedman & M.R. DiMatteo (eds.) *Interpersonal Issues in Health Care*. Academic Press: New York.

Kelley, H.H. (1983) 'Love and commitment'. In H.H. Kelley et al. (eds.) *Close Relationships*. Freeman: San Francisco.

Kelley, K. & Rolker-Dolinsky, B. (1986) 'The psychosexology of female initiation and dominance'. In D. Perlman & S.W. Duck (eds.) *Intimate Relationships*. Sage: Beverly Hills, CA.

Kelly, C., Huston, T.L. & Cate, R.M. (1985) 'Premarital relationship correlates of the erosion of satisfaction in marriage'. *Journal of Social and Personal Relationships* (2), 167–78.

Kelly, G.A. (1955) *The Psychology of Personal Constructs*. Norton: New York.

Kelly, G.A. (1969) *Clinical Psychology and Personality* (ed. B. Maher). Wiley: New York.

Kelly, L. (1982) 'A rose by any other name is still a rose: a comparative analysis of reticence, communication apprehension, unwillingness to communicate and shyness'. *Human Communication Research* (8), 99–113.

Kelly, L. (1984) 'Social skills training as a mode of treatment for social communication problems'. In J. Daly & J.C. McCroskey (eds.) *Avoiding Communication: Shyness, Reticence and Communication Apprehension*. Sage: Beverly Hills, CA.

Kelvin, P. (1977) 'Predictability, power and vulnerability in interpersonal attraction'. In S.W. Duck (ed.) *Theory and Practice in Interpersonal Attraction*. Academic Press: London & New York.

Kemper, T.D. & Bologh, R.W. (1981) 'What do you get when you fall in love? Some health status effects'. *Sociology of Health and Illness* (3), 72–88.

Kendon, A. (1967) 'Some functions of gaze direction in social interaction'. *Acta Psychologica* (26), 22–63.

Kendon, A. & Ferber, A. (1973) 'A description of some human greetings'. In R.P. Michael & J.H. Crook (eds.) *Comparative Ecology and Behavior of Primates*. Academic Press: New York.

Kephart, W.M. (1967) 'Some correlates of romantic love'. *Journal of Marriage and the Family* (29), 470–4.

Kerckhoff, A.C. (1974) 'The social context of interpersonal attraction'. In T.L. Huston (ed.) *Foundations of Interpersonal Attraction*. Academic Press: New York.

Kerckhoff, A.C. & Davis, K.E. (1962) 'Value consensus and need complementarity in mate selection'. *American Sociological Review* (27), 295–303.

Klinger, E. (1977) *Meaning and Void: Inner Experience and the Incentives in People's Lives*. University of Minnesota Press: Minneapolis.

Knapp, M.L. & Comadena, M.E. (1979) 'Telling it like it isn't: a review of theory and research on deceptive communication'. *Human Communication Research* (5), 270–85.

Knox, R.E. & Inkster, J.A. (1968) 'Postdecision dissonance at post time'. *Journal of Personality and Social Psychology* (8), 319–23.

Kobasa, S.C. (1982) 'The Hardy Personality: toward a social psychology of stress and health'. In G.S. Sanders & J. Suls (eds.) *Social Psychology of Health and Illness*. Erlbaum: Hillsdale, NJ.

Kraut, R.E. (1973) 'Effects of social labelling on giving to charity'. *Journal of Experimental Social Psychology* (9), 551–62.

Kressel, K., Jaffee, N., Tuckman, B., Watson, C. & Deutsch, M. (1980) 'A typology of divorcing couples: implications for mediation and the divorce process'. *Family Process* (9), 101–16.

Kübler-Ross, E. (1969) *On Death and Dying*. Macmillan: New York.

Ladd, G. (1981) 'Effectiveness of a social learning method for enhancing children's social interaction and peer acceptance'. *Child Development* (52), 171–8.

Lakoff, R. (1973) 'Language and women's place'. *Language in Society* (2), 45–79.

Lakoff, R. (1975) *Language and Women's Place*. Harper & Row: New York.

Langer, E. (1978) 'Rethinking the role of thought in social interaction'. In J. Harvey, W. Ickes & R.F. Kidd (eds.) *New Directions in Attribution Research, Vol 2*. Erlbaum: Hillsdale, NJ.

Larson, F., Csikszentmihalyi, M. & Graef, R. (1982) 'Time alone in daily experience'. In L.A. Peplau & D. Perlman (eds.) *Loneliness: A Sourcebook of Current Theory, Research and Therapy*. Wiley-Interscience: New York.

Lau, R.R., Williams, S., Williams, L.C., Ware, J.E. & Brook, R.H. (1982) 'Psychosocial problems in chronically ill children: physician concern, parent satisfaction and the validity of medical diagnosis'. *Journal of Community Health* (7), 250–61.

LaCrosse, M.B. (1975) 'Nonverbal behaviour and perceived counsellor attractiveness and persuasiveness'. *Journal of Counselling Psychology* (22), 563–6.

La Gaipa, J.J. (1981) 'Children's friendships'. In S.W. Duck & R. Gilmour (eds.) *Personal Relationships 2: Developing Personal Relationships.* Academic Press: London & New York.

La Gaipa, J.J. (1982) 'Rules and rituals in disengaging from relationships'. In S.W. Duck (ed.) *Personal Relationships 4: Dissolving Personal Relationships.* Academic Press: London & New York.

La Greca, A.M. & Santogrossi, D.A. (1980) 'Social skill training with elementary school students: a behavioral group approach'. *Journal of Consulting and Clinical Psychology* (48), 220–7.

LaRocco, J.M., House, J.S. & French, J.R.P., Jr. (1980) 'Social support, occupational stress and health'. *Journal of Health and Social Behavior* (21), 202–18.

Lea, M. & Duck, S.W. (1982) 'A model for the role of similarity of values in friendship development'. *British Journal of Social Psychology* (21), 301–10.

Leary, M.R. (1983) *Understanding Social Anxiety.* Sage: Beverly Hills, CA.

Leary, M.R. & Dobbins, S.E. (1983) 'Social anxiety, sexual behavior, and contraceptive use'. *Journal of Personality and Social Psychology* (47) 775–94.

Lee, J.A. (1973) *The Colors of Love: An Exploration of the Ways of Loving.* New Press: Ontario.

Lee, L. (1984) 'Sequences in separation: a framework for investigating endings of the personal (romantic) relationship'. *Journal of Social and Personal Relationships* (1), 49–74.

Lewis, R.A. & McAvoy, P. (1984) 'Improving the quality of relationships: therapeutic interventions with opiate-abusing couples'. In S.W. Duck (ed.) *Personal Relationships 5: Repairing Personal Relationships.* Academic Press: London & New York.

Libet, J.M. & Lewisohn, P.M. (1973) 'Concept of social skill with special reference to the behavior of depressed persons'. *Journal of Consulting and Clinical Psychology* (40), 304–12.

Lin, N., Simeone, R.L., Ensel, W.M. & Kuo, W. (1979) 'Social support, stressful life events and illness: a model and an empirical test'. *Journal of Health and Social Behavior* (20), 108–19.

Linn, L.S. & DiMatteo, M.R. (1983) 'Humor and other communication: preferences in physician-patient encounters'. *Medical Care* (21), 1223–31.

Lips, H.M. & Morrison, A. (1986) 'Changes in the sense of family among couples having their first child'. *Journal of Social and Personal Relationships*, (3).

Lloyd, S.A. & Cate, R.M. (1985) 'The developmental course of conflict in dissolution of premarital relationships'. *Journal of Social and Personal Relationships* (2), 179–94.

Lynch, J.J. (1977) *The Broken Heart: Medical Consequences of Loneliness.*

Basic Books: New York.

Lynch, J.J., Thomas, S.A., Mills, M.E., Malinow, K. & Katcher, A.H. (1974) 'The effects of human contact on cardiac arrythmia in coronary care patients'. *Journal of Nervous and Mental Diseases* (158), 88–99.

Lyons, R. (1984) 'Friendship in the disabled'. Paper to Second International Conference on Personal Relationships, Madison, WI, July.

Macklin, E.D. & Rubin, R.H. (1983) *Contemporary Families and Alternative Lifestyles*. Sage: Beverly Hills, CA.

Maddison, D. & Viola, A. (1968) 'The health of widows in the year after bereavement'. *Journal of Psychosomatic Research* (12), 297–306.

Malinowski, B. (1929) *The Sexual Life of Savages*. Harcourt Brace: New York.

Mandler, G. (1975) *Mind and Emotion*. Wiley: New York.

Mangham, I.L. (1981) 'Relationships at work: A matter of tension and tolerance'. In S.W. Duck & R. Gilmour (eds.) *Personal Relationships 1: Studying Personal Relationships*. Academic Press: London & New York.

Manning, M. & Herrman, J. (1981) 'The relationships of problem children in nursery schools'. In S.W. Duck & R. Gilmour (eds.) *Personal Relationships 3: Personal Relationships in Disorder*. Academic Press: London & New York.

Markman, H.J. (1979) 'The application of a behavioral model of marriage in predicting relationship satisfaction of couples planning marriage'. *Journal of Consulting and Clinical Psychology* (46), 743–9.

Markman, H.J. (1981) 'The prediction of marital distress: a five year follow-up'. *Journal of Consulting and Clinical Psychology* (49), 760–2.

Markman, H.J., Floyd, F. & Dickson-Markman, F. (1982) 'Towards a model for the prediction and primary prevention of marital and family distress and dissolution'. In S.W. Duck (ed.) *Personal Relationships 4: Dissolving Personal Relationships*. Academic Press: London & New York.

Marwell, G. & Schmitt, D.R. (1967) 'Dimensions of compliance-gaining behavior: An empirical analysis'. *Sociometry* (30), 350–64.

Matarazzo, J.D. (1979) 'A good friend: one of mankind's most effective and inexpensive psychotherapists'. *Journal of Clinical Psychology* (35), 231–2.

Maxwell, G.M. (1985) 'Behavior of lovers: measuring the closeness of relationships'. *Journal of Social and Personal Relationships* (2), 215–38.

Mazur, R. (1977) 'Beyond jealousy and possessiveness'. In G. Clanton & L. Smith (eds.) *Jealousy*. Prentice Hall: Englewood Cliffs, NJ.

McAdams, D.P. & Losoff, M. (1984) 'Friendship motivation in fourth and sixth graders: a thematic analysis'. *Journal of Social and Personal Relationships* (1), 11–27.

McCall, G.J. (1982) 'Becoming unrelated: The management of bond dissolution'. In S.W. Duck (ed.) *Personal Relationships 4: Dissolving Personal Relationships*. Academic Press: London & New York.

McCarthy, B. (1983) 'Social cognition and personal relationships'. Paper to Lancaster University Relationships Research Group, November.

McGinnis, J. (1970) *The Selling of the President, 1968*. Pocket Books: New York.

McMillan, J.A., Clifton, A.K., McGrath, C. & Gale, W.S. (1977) 'Women's language: uncertainty or interpersonal sensitivity and emotionality?' *Sex*

Roles (3), 545–59.

McPartland, T.S. & Hornstra, R.K. (1964) 'The depressive datum'. *Comprehensive Psychiatry* (5), 253–61.

Mead, M. (1950) *Sex and Temperament in Three Primitive Societies*. Mentor: New York.

Mechanic, D. (1974) *Politics, Medicine and Social Science*. Wiley: New York.

Mechanic, D. (1980) 'The experience and reporting of common physical complaints'. *Journal of Health and Social Behavior* (21), 146–55.

Mehrabian, A. (1971) *Silent Messages*. Wadsworth: Belmont, CA.

Menges, R.J. (1969) 'Student-instructor cognitive compatibility in the large lecture class'. *Journal of Personality* (37), 444–59.

Menzel, J. & Katz, D. (1957) 'Social relations and innovation in the medical profession: the epidemiology of a new drug'. In E. Maccoby, (ed.) *Readings in Social Psychology*. Academic Press: New York.

Miell, D.E. (1984) 'Cognitive and communicative strategies in developing relationships'. Unpublished PhD thesis, University of Lancaster, UK.

Miell, D.E. & Duck, S.W. (1985) 'Strategies in developing close relationships'. In V. Derlega & B. Winstead (eds.) *Friendship: A Sourcebook of Theory, Research and Application*. Springer-Verlag: New York.

Milardo, R., Johnson, M.P. & Huston, T.L. (1983) 'Developing close relationships: changing patterns of interaction between pair members and social networks'. *Journal of Personality and Social Psychology* (44), 964–76.

Milardo, R.M. (1982) 'Friendship networks in developing relationships: converging and diverging social environments'. *Social Psychology Quarterly* (45), 162–72.

Miller, G.R. & Parks, M.R. (1982) 'Communication in dissolving relationships'. In S.W. Duck (ed.) *Personal Relationships 4: Dissolving Personal Relationships*. Academic Press: London & New York.

Miller, M.D. (1982) 'Friendship, power and the language of compliance gaining'. *Journal of Language and Social Behavior* (1), 111–22.

Milmoe, S., Rosenthal, R., Blane, H.T., Chafetz, M.L. & Wolf, I. (1967) 'The doctor's voice: postdictors of successful referral of alcoholic patients'. *Journal of Abnormal Psychology* (72), 78–84.

Minuchin, S., Rosman, B.L. & Baker, L. (1978) *Psychosomatic Families: Anorexia Nervosa in Context*. Harvard University Press: Cambridge, MA.

Montagu, A. (1978) *Touching*. Harper & Row: New York.

Montgomery, B.M. (1981a) 'Verbal immediacy as a behavioral indicator of open communication'. *Communication Quarterly* (30), 28–34.

Montgomery, B.M. (1981b) 'The form and function of quality communication in marriage'. *Family Relations* (30), 21–30.

Montgomery, B.M. (1984) 'Behavioral characteristics predicting self and peer perceptions of open communication'. *Communication Quarterly* (32), 233–42.

Morris, D. (1971) *Intimate Behaviour*. Cape: London.

Morton, T.L., Alexander, I. & Altman, I. (1976) 'Communication and relationship definition'. In G.R. Miller (ed.) *Explorations in Interpersonal Communication*. Sage: Beverly Hills, CA.

Mott, F.L. & Moore, S.F. (1979) 'The causes of marital disruption among young American women: An inter-disciplinary perspective'. *Journal of*

Marriage and the Family (41), 335–65.

Mowen, J.C. & Cialdini, R.B. (1980) 'On implementing the door-in-the-face compliance technique in a business context'. *Journal of Marketing Research* (17), 253–8.

Murstein, B.I. & Glaudin, V. (1968) 'The use of the MMPI in the determination of marital maladjustment'. *Journal or Marriage and the Family* (30), 651–5.

Newcomb, M.D. & Bentler, P.M. (1981) 'Marital breakdown'. In S.W. Duck & R. Gilmour (eds.) *Personal Relationships 3: Personal Relationships in Disorder.* Academic Press: London & New York.

Newcomb, T.M. (1971) 'Dyadic balance as a source of clues about interpersonal attraction'. In B.I. Murstein (ed.) *Theories of Attraction and Love.* Springer: New York.

Nisbett, R.E. & Wilson, T. De C. (1977) 'Telling more than we can know: verbal reports on mental processes'. *Psychological Review* (84), 231–59.

Noller, P. (1982) 'Channel consistency and inconsistency in the communication of married couples'. *Journal of Personality and Social Psychology* (43), 732–41.

Norton, R. (1978) 'Foundations of a communicator style construct'. *Human Communication Research* (4), 99–112.

O'Connor, P. & Brown, G.W. (1984) 'Supportive relationships: fact or fancy?'. *Journal of Social and Personal Relationships* (2), 159–76.

Oden, S. & Asher, S.R. (1977) 'Coaching children in social skills for friendship making'. *Child Development* (48), 495–506.

Orford, J. (1976) 'A study of the personalities of excessive drinkers and their wives, using the approaches of Leary and Eysenck'. *Journal of Consulting and Clinical Psychology* (44), 534–45.

Orford, J. (1980) 'The domestic context'. In M.P. Feldman & J. Orford (eds.) *Psychological Problems: The Social Context.* Wiley: Chichester, UK.

Orford, J., Oppenheimer, E., Egert, S., Hensman, C. & Guthrie, S. (1976) 'The cohesiveness of alcoholism-complicated marriages and its influence on treatment outcome'. *British Journal of Psychiatry* (128), 318–49.

Orford, J. & O'Reilly, P. (1981) 'Disorders in the family'. In S.W. Duck & R. Gilmour (eds.) *Personal Relationships 3: Personal Relationships in Disorder.* Academic Press: London & New York.

Parker, S. (1960) 'The attitudes of medical students towards their patients: an exploratory study'. *Journal of Medical Education* (35), 849–55.

Parks, M.R. & Adelman, M. (1983) 'Communication networks and the development of romantic relationships: an expansion of uncertainty reduction theory'. *Human Communication Research* (10), 55–80.

Parsons, T. (1951) *The Social System.* Free Press: Glencoe, IL.

Paykel, E.S., Emms, E.M., Fletcher, J. & Rassaby, E.S. (1980) 'Life events and social support in puerperal depression'. *British Journal of Psychiatry* (136), 339–46.

Pendleton, D. & Hasler, J. (1983) *Doctor-Patient Communication.* Academic Press: London.

Peplau, L.A., Miceli, M. & Morasch, B. (1982) 'Loneliness and self-evaluation' In L.A. Peplau & D. Perlman (eds.) *Loneliness: A Sourcebook of Current Theory, Research and Therapy.* Wiley-Interscience: New York.

Peplau, L.A. & Perlman, D. (eds.) (1982) *Loneliness: A Sourcebook of Current Theory, Research and Therapy*. Wiley-Interscience: New York.

Perlman, D. & Peplau, L.A. (1981) 'Loneliness'. In S.W. Duck & R. Gilmour (eds.) *Personal Relationships 3: Personal Relationships in Disorder*. Academic Press: London & New York.

Perlman, D. & Serbin, R. (1984) 'A sports report: the effects of racquet matches on loneliness'. Paper to Second International Conference on Personal Relationships. Madison, WI. July.

Perlman, D., Gerson, A.C. & Spinner, B. (1978) 'Loneliness among senior citizens: An empirical report'. *Essence* (2), 239–48.

Petty, R.E. & Cacioppo, J.T. (1981) *Attitudes and Persuasion: Classic and Contemporary Approaches*. W.C. Brown: Dubuque, IA.

Phillips, D.P. (1970) 'Dying as a form of social behavior'. PhD dissertation, Ann Arbor, MI.

Phillips, D.P. (1972) 'Deathday and birthday: an unexpected connection'. In J.M. Tanur (ed.) *Statistics: A Guide to the Unknown*. Holden Day: San Francisco.

Pickering, G. (1978) 'Medicine on the brink: The dilemma of a learned profession'. *Perspectives in Biology and Medicine*, Summer.

Pike, G. & Sillars, A. (1985) 'Reciprocity of marital communication'. *Journal of Social and Personal Relationships* (2), 303–24.

Pilkonis, P.A. (1977) 'The behavioral consequences of shyness'. *Journal of Personality* (45), 596–611.

Planalp, S. & Honeycutt, J.M. (1984) 'When uncertainty increases in relationships'. Paper presented to International Communication Association, San Francisco, May.

Poole, A.D. & Sanson-Fisher, R.W. (1979) 'Understanding the patient: a neglected aspect of medical education'. *Social Science and Medicine* (13A), 37–43.

Putallaz, M. & Gottman, J.M. (1981) 'Social skills and group acceptance'. In S.R. Asher & J.M. Gottman (eds.) *The Development of Children's Friendship*. Cambridge University Press: Cambridge.

Rackham, N. & Morgan, T. (1977) *Behavior Analysis and Training*. McGraw-Hill: New York.

Raush, H.L., Barry, W.A., Hertel, R.K. & Swain, M.A. (1974) *Communication, Conflict and Marriage*. Jossey-Bass: San Francisco.

Reis, H.T. (1984) 'Social interaction and well-being'. In S.W. Duck (ed.) *Personal Relationships 5: Repairing Personal Relationships*. Academic Press: London & New York.

Reis, H.T. (1986) 'Gender effects in social participation: intimacy, loneliness and the conduct of social interaction'. In R. Gilmour & S.W. Duck (eds.) *The Emerging Field of Personal Relationships*. Erlbaum: Hillsdale, NJ.

Reis, H.T., Nezlek, J. & Wheeler, L. (1980) 'Physical attractiveness and social interaction'. *Journal of Personality and Social Psychology* (38), 604–17.

Reis, H.T., Wheeler, L., Kernis, M.H., Spiegel, N. & Nezlek, J. (1983) 'On specificity in the impact of social participation on physical and psychological health'. Unpublished manuscript, University of Rochester, NY.

Reisman, J. (1981) 'Adult friendships'. In S.W. Duck & R. Gilmour (eds.) *Personal Relationships 2: Developing Personal Relationships*. Academic Press: London & New York.

Renne, K.S. (1970) 'Correlates of dissatisfaction in marriage'. *Journal of Marriage and the Family* (32), 54–67.

Renne, K.S. (1971) 'Health and marital experience in an urban population'. *Journal of Marriage and the Family* (33), 338–50.

Ridley, C.A. & Nelson, R.R. (1984) 'The behavioural effects of training premarital couples in mutual problem solving skills'. *Journal of Social and Personal Relationships* (2), 197–210.

Riskin, J. & Faunce, E.E. (1972) 'An evaluative review of family interaction research'. *Family Process* (11), 365–455.

Rogers, R.W. (1983) 'Preventive health psychology: an interface of social and clinical psychology'. *Journal of Social and Clinical Psychology* (1), 120–7.

Rollins, B.C. & Feldman, H. (1970) 'Marital satisfaction over the lifecycle'. *Journal of Marriage and the Family* (32), 20–8.

Rook, K.S. (1984) 'Interventions for loneliness: a review and analysis'. In L.A. Peplau & S.E. Goldston (eds.) *Preventing the Harmful Consequences of Severe and Persistent Loneliness*. NIMH: Bethseda, Maryland.

Rubenstein, C. & Shaver, P. (1982) 'The experience of loneliness'. In L.A. Peplau & D. Perlman (eds.) *Loneliness: A Current Sourcebook of Theory, Research and Therapy*. Wiley Interscience: New York.

Rubin, R.B. (1977) 'The role of context in information seeking and impression formation'. *Communication Monographs* (44), 81–90.

Rubin, Z. (1973) *Liking and Loving*. Holt, Rinehart & Winston: New York.

Rutter, M. (1972) *Maternal Deprivation Reassessed*. Penguin Books: Harmondsworth, UK.

Sabatelli, R. & Pearce, J. (1986) 'Exploring marital expectations'. *Journal of Social and Personal Relationships* (3).

Sants, H.K.A. (1984) 'Conceptions of friendship, social behaviour and school achievement in six year old children'. *Journal of Social and Personal Relationships* (1), 293–309.

Schachter, S. & Singer, J. (1962) 'Cognitive, social and physiological determinants of emotional states'. *Psychological Review* (69), 379–99.

Scherer, K.R. & Giles, H. (1979) *Social Markers in Speech*. Cambridge University Press: Cambridge, UK.

Scherwitz, L., Berton, K. & Leventhal, H. (1978) 'Type A behavior, self involvement and cardiovascular response'. *Psychosomatic Medicine* (40), 593–609.

Schlenker, B.R. (1984) 'Identities, identifications and relationships'. In V.J. Derlega (ed.) *Communication, Intimacy and Close Relationships*. Academic Press: Orlando.

Schlenker, B.R. & Leary, M.R. (1982) 'Social anxiety and self presentation: a conceptualisation and a model'. *Psychological Bulletin* (92), 641–69.

Schmale, A.H., Jr. (1958) 'The relationship of separation and depression to disease'. *Psychosomatic Medicine* (20), 259–75.

Schofield, M.J. & Kafer, N.F. (1985) 'Children's understanding of friendship issues: development by stage or sequence?'. *Journal of Social and Personal Relationships* (2), 151–66.

Schulz, R. & Barefoot, J. (1974) 'Nonverbal responses and affiliative conflict theory'. *British Journal of Social and Clinical Psychology* (13), 237–43.

Scotton, C.M. & Udry, W. (1977) 'Bilingual strategies — social functions of code switching'. *Linguistics* (193), 5–20.

Seligman, C.R., Tucker, G.R. & Lambert, W. (1972) 'The effects of speech style and other attributes on teachers' attitudes towards pupils'. *Language in Society* (1), 131–4.

Selman, R.L. & Jaquette, D. (1977) 'Stability and oscillation in interpersonal awareness: A clinical-developmental analysis'. In C.B. Keasey (ed.) *Nebraska Symposium on Motivation Vol. 25*. University of Nebraska Press: Lincoln.

Selye, H. (1956) *The Stress of Life*. McGraw-Hill: New York.

Semin, G.R. & Manstead, A.S.R. (1982) 'The social implications of embarrassment displays and restitution behaviour'. *European Journal of Social Psychology* (12), 367–77.

Shanas, E., Townsend, P., Wedderburn, D., Friis, H., Milhoj, P. & Stehouwer, J. (1968) *Old People in Three Industrial Societies*. Atherton: New York.

Shaver, P., Furman, W. & Buhrmester, D. (1985) 'Transition to college: network changes, social skills and loneliness'. In S.W. Duck & D. Perlman (eds.) *Understanding Personal Relationships*. Sage: London.

Shettel-Neuber, J., Bryson, J.B. & Young, L.E. (1978) 'Physical attractiveness of the "other person" and jealousy'. *Personality and Social Psychology Bulletin* (4), 612–15.

Shorr, P. & Moen, J. (1979) 'The single parent and public policy'. *Social Policy* (9), 15–21.

Shorter, E. (1975) *The Making of the Modern Family*. Basic Books: New York.

Shotland, R.L. (1976) 'Spontaneous vigilantism: A bystander response to criminal behavior'. In H.J. Rosenbaum & D.C. Sederberg (eds.) *Vigilante Politics*. University of Pennsylvania Press: Philadelphia.

Shotland, R.L. & Straw, M.K. (1976) 'Bystander response to an assault: when a man attacks a woman'. *Journal of Personality and Social Psychology* (34), 990–9.

Shulz, R. (1976) 'Effects of control and predictability on the physical and psychological well-being of the institutionalized aged'. *Journal of Personality and Social Psychology* (33), 563–73.

Shuval, J.T. (1981) 'The contribution of psychological and social phenomena to an understanding of the aetiology of disease and illness'. *Social Science and Medicine* (15A), 337–42.

Shuval, J.T., Antonovsky, A. & Davies, A.M. (1973) 'Illness: a mechanism for coping with failure'. *Social Science and Medicine* (7), 259–65.

Silberfeld, M. (1978) 'Psychological symptoms and social supports'. *Social Psychiatry* (13), 11–17.

Sillars, A.L., Pike, G.R., Jones, T.S. & Redmon, D. (1983) 'Communication and conflict in marriage'. In R. Bostrom (ed.) *Communication Yearbook 7*. Sage: Beverly Hills, CA.

Siperstein, G.N. & Gale, M.E. (1983) 'Improving peer relationships of rejected children'. Paper to Society for Research in Child Development, Detroit, M1.

Skelton, J.A. & Pennebaker, J.N. (1982) 'The psychology of physical symptoms and sensations'. In G.S. Sanders & J. Suls (eds.) *The Social Psychology of Health and Illness*. Erlbaum: Hillsdale, NJ.

Slater, P.E. (1968) 'Some social consequences of temporary systems'. In W.G. Bennis & P.E. Slater (eds.) *The Temporary Society*. Harper & Row: New York.

Smith-Hanen, S. (1977) 'Effects of nonverbal behaviors on judged level of counsellor warmth and empathy'. *Journal of Counselling Psychology* (24), 87–91.

Snow, J. (1854) 'On the mode of communication of cholera'. Reprinted in *Snow on Cholera* (1936), Commonwealth Fund: New York.

Snyder, C.R. & Smith, T.W. (1982) 'Symptoms as self-handicapping strategies: the virtues of old wine in a new bottle'. Unpub. Manuscript.

Sobol, M.P. & Earn, B.M. (1985) 'What causes mean: an analysis of children's interpretations of the causes of social experience'. *Journal of Social and Personal Relationships* (2), 137–50.

Solano, C., Batten, P.G. & Parish, E.A. (1982) 'Loneliness and patterns of self-disclosure'. *Journal of Personality and Social Psychology* (43), 524–31.

Sommer, R. (1969) *Personal Space: The Behavioral Basis of Design*. Prentice-Hall: Englewood Cliffs, NJ.

Stang, D.J. (1973) 'Effect of interaction rate on ratings of leadership and liking'. *Journal of Personality and Social Psychology* (27), 405–8.

Staples, L. & Robinson, W.P. (1974) 'Address forms used by members of a department store'. *British Journal of Social and Clinical Psychology* (13), 1–11.

Stiff, J.B. & Miller, G.R. (1984) 'Deceptive behaviors and behaviors which are interpreted as deceptive: an interactive approach to the study of deception'. Paper to International Communication Association, San Francisco, May.

Stone, A.C. (1979) 'Patient compliance and the role of the expert'. *Journal of Social Issues* (35), 34–59.

Stotland, E., Zander, A. & Natsoulas, T. (1960) 'Generalisation of interpersonal similarity'. *Journal of Abnormal and Social Psychology* (62), 250–6.

Strain, P.S., Shores, R.E. & Kerr, M.A. (1976) 'An experimental analysis of "spillover" effects on the social interactions of behaviorally handicapped preschool children'. *Journal of Applied Behavior Analysis* (9), 31–40.

Straus, M.A. (1985) 'Family violence'. Paper to HDFR, University of Connecticut, Storrs, April.

Stroebe, W. (1980) 'Process loss in social psychology: failure to exploit?'. In R. Gilmour & S.W. Duck (eds.) *The Development of Social Psychology*. Academic Press: London.

Stroebe, W. & Stroebe, M. (1983) 'Who suffers more? Sex differences in health risk of the widowed'. *Psychological Bulletin* (93), 279–301.

Sunnafrank, M. (1983) 'Attitude similarity and interpersonal attraction in communication processes: in pursuit of an ephemeral influence'. *Communication Monographs* (50), 273–84.

Sunnafrank, M. & Miller, G.R. (1981) 'The role of initial conversations in determining attraction to similar and dissimilar strategies'. *Human Communication Research* (8), 16–25.

Surra, C. (1984) 'Attributions about the decision to wed: variations by style of courtship'. Paper to Second International Conference on Personal Relationships, Madison, WI, July.

Szasz, T.S. & Hollander, M.H. (1956) 'A contribution to the philosophy of medicine: the basic models of the doctor-patient relationships'. *Archives of Internal Medicine* (97), 585–92.

Takens, R.J. (1982) 'Psychotherapist-client relationships and effectiveness of therapy'. Paper to International Conference on Personal Relationships, Madison, WI, July.

Tracy, K., Craig, R.T., Smith, M. & Spisak, F. (1984) 'The discourse of requests: assessment of a compliance-gaining approach'. *Human Communication Research* (10), 513–38.

Trower, P., Bryant, B. & Argyle, M. (1978) *Social Skills and Mental Health*. Methuen: London.

Tunstall, J. (1967) *Old and Alone*. Humanities Press: New York.

de Turck, M.A. (1985) 'A transactional analysis of compliance-gaining behavior: the effects of noncompliance relational contexts and actors' gender'. *Human Communication Research* (12), 54–78.

Walker, H.M. & Hops, H. (1973) 'The use of group and individual reinforcement contingencies in the modification of social withdrawal'. In L.A. Hanerlynck, L.C. Hardy & E.J. Mosh (eds.) *Behavior Change: Methodology, Concept and Practice*. Research Press: Champaign, IL.

Walster, E.H., Aronson, V. & Abrahams, D. (1966) 'On increasing the persuasiveness of a low prestige communicator'. *Journal of Experimental Social Psychology* (2), 325–42.

Walster, E.H. & Walster, G.W. (1978) *A New Look at Love*. Addison-Wesley: Reading, MA.

Watson, O.M. & Graves, T.D. (1966) 'Quantitative research in proxemic behavior'. *American Anthropologist* (68), 971–85.

Watzlawick, P., Beavin, J. & Jackson, D. (1967) *Pragmatics of Human Communication: A Study of Interactional Patterns, Pathologies and Paradoxes*. Norton: New York.

Weber, A. (1983) 'The breakdown of relationships'. Paper presented to conference on Social Interaction and Relationships, Nags Head, North Carolina, May.

Weiss, R.L. & Aved, B.M. (1978) 'Marital satisfaction and depression as predictors of physical health status'. *Journal of Consulting and Clinical Psychology* (46), 1379–84.

Wellman, B. (1985) 'From social support to social network'. In I. Sarason & B. Sarason (eds.) *Social Support: Theory, Research and Applications*. Nijhoff: The Hague.

Wheeler, L. & Nezlek, J. (1977) 'Sex differences in social participation'. *Journal of Personality and Social Psychology* (35), 742–54.

Wheeler, L., Reis, H.T. & Nezlek, J. (1983) 'Loneliness, social interaction and sex roles'. *Journal of Personality and Social Psychology* (45), 943–53.

White, G.L. (1981) 'A model of romantic jealousy'. *Motivation and Emotion* (5), 295–310.

Wilkinson, J. & Canter, S. (1982) *Social Skills Training Manual*. Wiley: Chichester, UK.

Williams, E. (1974) 'An analysis of gaze in schizophrenia'. *British Journal of Social and Clinical Psychology* (13), 1–8.

Wilson, C. & Orford, J. (1978) 'Children of alcoholics: report of a preliminary study and comments on the literature'. *Journal of Studies on Alcohol* (39), 121–42.

Wiseman, R.L. & Schenk-Hamlin, W. (1981) 'A multidimensional scaling validation of an inductively derived set of compliance-gaining strategies'. *Communication Monographs* (48), 251–70.

Wyler, A.R., Masuda, M. & Holmes, T.H. (1971) 'Magnitude of life events and seriousness of illness'. *Psychosomatic Medicine* (33), 115–22.

Yaffe, M. (1981) 'Disordered sexual relationships'. In S.W. Duck & R. Gilmour (eds.) *Personal Relationships 3: Personal Relationships in Disorder*. Academic Press: London & New York.

Young, J.E. (1982) 'Loneliness, depression and cognitive therapy: Theory and application'. In L.A. Peplau & D. Perlman (eds.) *Loneliness: a Current Sourcebook of Theory Research and Therapy*. Wiley-Interscience: New York.

Youniss, J. (1980) *Parents and Peers in Social Development*. University of Chicago Press: Chicago.

Zaidel, S.F. & Mehrabian, A. (1969) 'The ability to communicate and infer positive and negative attitudes facially and vocally'. *Journal of Experimental Research in Personality* (3), 233–41.

Zakahi, W.R. & Duran, R.L. (1982) 'All the lonely people: the relationship among loneliness, communicative competence and communication anxiety'. *Communication Quarterly* (30), 203–9.

Zakahi, W.R. & Duran, R.L. (1985) 'Loneliness, communicative competence and communication apprehension: extension and replication'. *Communication Quarterly* (33), 50–60.

Zola, A.K. (1972) 'Studying the decision to see a doctor'. In Z.J. Lipowski (ed.) *Psychological Aspects of Physical Illness*. Karger: Basel.

Author Index

Adelman, M., 9
Adorno, T.W., 130
Ajzen, I., 171
Anderson, S.A., 145
Antill, J.K., 7
Argyle, M., 37, 39, 41, 42, 43, 46, 47,
    48, 51, 52, 54, 57, 62, 63, 68, 71, 96,
    141, 204, 206
Aronson, E., 161
Asher, S.R., 149, 151, 154
Athanasiou, R., 141
Aved, B.M., 210

Badzinski, D., 124, 130, 133, 134
Bandura, A., 107, 215
Barefoot, J., 43
Barrera, M., Jr., 211
Baumrind, D., 130
Baxter, L.A., 32, 50, 86, 88, 92, 101,
    103, 104
Beattie, G.W., 48
Beck, A.T., 21
Beecher, H.K., 189
Bell, R.A., 69, 85, 86, 87
Bentler, P.M., 141
Berardo, F.M., 210
Berger, C.R., 64, 81
Berkman, L.F., 211
Bernard, J., 127
Berscheid, E., 4, 5, 16, 31, 33, 160
Bierman, K.L., 153
Bigelow, B.J., 147
Birchler, G.R., 124
Blondis, M.N., 207
Bloom, B., 109, 128, 210
Bochner, A.P., 32, 89, 133
Boissevain, J., 93
Bologh, R.W., 10

Boreham, P., 204
Bornstein, P.E., 227
Boster, F.J., 180
Bourhis, R.Y., 67
Bowlby, J., 129
Boyd, J.R., 204
Bradac, J., 64, 81
Bradburn, N., 23
Brehm, J.W., 172
Brehm, S., 172
Bringle, R., 11, 33, 120
Brown, G.W., 136, 209
Brown, R., 59, 61, 181
Bugenthal, D.E., 68
Burgess, R.L., 131, 137
Burgoon, M., 20, 180
Burns, G.L., 96
Busch, C.M., 19, 22
Buss, A.H., 19
Buunk, A., 11, 15, 33, 120
Byrne, D., 75, 76, 77, 78, 80

Cacioppo, J.T., 161, 186
Cannon, W.B., 3
Canter, S., 53
Cappella, J.N., 48, 81, 92
Carlsmith, J.M., 170
Carr, S.J., 43
Carver, C.S., 220, 221
Cate, R.M., 117, 118, 119
Check, J., 25, 109
Cheek, J.M., 19, 22
Cherlin, A.J., 113
Cheyne, W.M., 54
Christopher, F.S., 118, 119
Christy, N.P., 204
Cialdini, R.B., 175, 176, 184
Clark, R.A., 176, 180

Clayton, P.J., 227
Clore, G.L., 42, 77, 80
Cobb, S., 73, 108, 208, 213
Cody, M.J., 180
Cole, C.A., 141
Comadena, M.E., 69
Cook, M., 42, 44, 46, 56, 175
Cooper, D., 114
Coyne, J.C., 108, 136
Cunningham, J.D., 7
Curran, J.P., 53
Cutrona, C.E., 27

Dabbs, J.M., Jr., 43
Daly, J.A., 34, 85, 87, 88
Davis, J.D., 84, 86
Davis, K.E., 15, 83, 96
Davitz, J.R., 10, 40
Dean, A., 211
Dean, J., 43
DeJong, W., 174
Delia, J.G., 176
Dembrowski, T.M., 221
Dickens, W.J., 98, 144
Dillard, J.P., 175
Dindia, K., 124
DiMatteo, M.R., 52, 73, 192, 193,
    195, 197, 198, 199, 200, 205, 207,
    216, 218, 229
Dohrenwend, B.S., 215
Doob, A.N., 170
Driscoll, R., 93
Duck, S.W., 2, 29, 32, 71, 72, 73, 77,
    79, 82, 83, 84, 88, 90, 92, 93, 96,
    101, 105, 106, 108, 110, 111, 123,
    132, 144, 146, 148, 153, 154, 198,
    210, 215
Duran, R.L., 22

Eagly, A.H., 161
Earn, B.M., 150
Edelmann, R.J., 17, 18, 48
Ellis, C., 13, 14
Ellsworth, P.C., 43
Emler, N., 98
Engler, C.M., 208
Erickson, B., 63
Exline, R.V., 46, 48

Farina, A., 96
Farsad, P., 208
Faunce, E.E., 124, 133
Feldman, H., 141
Feldman, P., 135
Ferber, A., 48
Ferreira, A.J., 139
Feshbach, S., 184
Festinger, L., 164, 168, 170, 184
Filsinger, E.E., 154
Fine, V.K., 208
Fishbein, M., 171
Fisher, S., 98
Fitzpatrick, M.A., 124, 125, 130, 133,
    134
Fransella, F., 56
Fraser, C., 56
Fraser, S.C., 174, 184
Freedman, J.L., 174, 184
Frenkel, O.J., 170
Friedman, H.S., 192, 193, 195, 206,
    216, 218, 229
Furman, W., 150, 152, 153
Furstenberg, F.F., 141

Gale, M.E., 152
Gallup, C., 29
Garrard, G.G., 144
Geersten, H.R., 201
Gelles, R.J., 112
Gibson, D., 204
Giles, H., 53, 56, 66, 67, 71
Gilmour, R., 111, 154, 210
Glass, D., 221
Glaudin, V., 141
Goffman, E., 8
Golden, B.W., 161
Gore, S., 135
Gormly, A.V., 77
Gormly, J.B., 77
Gottlieb, B.H., 108, 143, 154, 208,
    213, 214
Gottman, J.M., 124, 139, 145, 154
Graves, T.D., 44
Greenblatt, M., 227, 228
Greene, J.O., 49
Gresham, F.M., 152
Gross, E., 17
Guralnick, M.J., 152

Hagestad, G.O., 104, 121, 140, 141
Haley, J., 111, 139
Hall, E.T., 38
Hamilton, G.V., 127
Hampson, S.E., 48
Hansson, R.O., 28
Harre, R., 89
Harris, T., 136, 209
Harvey, J., 103
Hasler, J., 200, 229
Haslett, B., 65
Hatfield, E., 90
Hays, R., 52, 73, 197, 198, 199, 200, 207, 229
Hays, R.B., 98, 99
Heider, F., 168, 179
Henderson, M., 96, 141, 204
Hendrick, C., 79
Hendrick, S., 79
Herrman, J., 132
Hetherington, E.M., 143
Hinde, R.A., 111
Hobfoll, S.E., 209, 211, 213
Hochschild, A.R., 15
Hollander, M.H., 200
Holmes, T.H., 214
Honeycutt, J.M., 82
Hopper, R., 64, 69
Hops, H., 151
Hornstra, R.K., 135
Hovland, C., 159, 160, 161
Howells, K., 25, 52, 109
Huesmann, L.R., 90
Humphries, C., 220, 221
Hunter, J.E., 180
Huston, T.L., 99, 115, 116, 117
Hyde, J.S., 60

Inkster, J.A., 170
Innes, J.M., 216, 219, 222, 223

Jackson, B.E., 207
Janis, I.L., 184
Jaquette, D., 146, 147
Jarvinäan, K.A.J., 201
Jellison, J., 14
Jenkins, C.D., 218, 219
Johnson, F.N., 136
Jones, J.M., 73, 108, 208, 213

Jones, R.A., 190
Jones, W.H., 25, 26, 28, 29, 53

Kafer, N.F., 149
Kane, J., 44
Kastenbaum, R., 194, 225
Katz, D., 73
Kelley, H.H., 5
Kelley, K., 190
Kelly, C., 117, 118, 126
Kelly, G.A., 221
Kelly, L., 19, 21, 22
Kelvin, P., 123
Kemper, T.D., 10
Kendon, A., 46, 48
Kephart, W.M., 9
Kerckhoff, A.C., 82, 83
Klinger, E., 72
Knapp, M.L., 69
Knox, R.E., 170
Kobasa, S.C., 223
Koper, R.J., 20
Kraut, R.E., 174
Kressel, K., 108
Kubler-Ross, E., 226
Kyriacou, C., 144

Ladd, G., 152
Lakoff, R., 62
Lamberth, J., 77
Larson, R., 23, 24
Lau, R.R., 205
LaCrosse, M.B., 207
LaGaipa, J.J., 103, 134, 147
LaGreca, A.M., 152
LaRocco, J.M., 211
Lea, M., 377
Leary, M.R., 17, 20, 34
Lee, J.A., 57
Lee, L., 101, 103, 104
Lewis, R.A., 109, 138, 154
Lewisohn, P.M., 48, 52
Libet, J.M., 48, 52
Lin, N., 211
Linn, L.S., 205
Lips, H.M., 118, 121
Lloyd, S.A., 117
London, P., 211
Losoff, M., 148

Lynch, J.J., 109, 137, 188, 207, 210
Lyons, R., 194

McAdams, D.P., 148
McAvoy, P., 109, 138
McCall, G.J., 94, 105, 120
McCarthy, B., 92, 93
McCroskey, J.C., 34
MacDougall, J.M., 221
McGinnis, J., 160
Macklin, E.D., 154
McMillan, J.A., 63
McPartland, T.S., 135
Maddison, D., 210
Malinowski, B., 15
Mandler, G., 30, 31
Mangham, I.L., 73
Manning, M., 132
Manstead, A.S.R., 17
Markman, H.J., 118, 127
Marwell, G., 177
Maxwell, G.M., 8
Mazur, R., 12
Mead, M., 189
Mechanic, D., 190, 191, 193
Mehrabian, A., 63, 68
Menges, R.J., 73
Menzel, J., 73
Miell, D.E., 86, 88
Milardo, R.M., 9, 93, 94
Miller, G.R., 47, 49, 78, 110, 177, 178–9
Miller, M.D., 182
Milmoe, S., 206
Minuchin, S., 111, 135
Moen, J., 113
Montagu, A., 207
Montgomery, B.M., 84, 85
Moore, S.F., 141
Morgan, T., 53
Morris, D., 38, 43
Morrison, A., 118, 121
Morton, T.L., 64
Mott, F.L., 141
Mowen, J.C., 175
Murstein, B.I., 141

Nagle, R.J., 152
Nelson, D., 77

Nelson, R.R., 127
Newcomb, M.D., 141
Newcomb, T.M., 168
Nezlek, J., 100
Nisbett, R.E., 92
Noller, P., 124
Norton, R., 85

O'Connor, P., 136, 209
O'Reilly, P., 52, 108, 138
Oden, S., 151
Orford, J., 52, 108, 135, 137, 138

Parker, S., 201
Parks, M.R., 9, 110, 177, 178–9
Parsons, T., 193, 195
Paykel, E.S., 211
Pearce, J., 122
Pendleton, D., 200, 229
Pennebaker, J.N., 189
Peplau, L.A., 23, 24, 34
Perlman, D., 23, 24, 28, 34, 72, 98, 144
Petty, R.E., 161, 186
Phillips, D.P., 227
Pickering, G., 206
Pike, G.R., 126
Pilkinis, P.A., 19
Planalp, S., 82
Poole, A.D., 208
Powesland, P.F., 53, 66, 67
Putallaz, M., 145, 153

Rackham, N., 53
Rahe, R.H., 214
Raush, H.L., 124
Reardon, C., 186
Reis, H.T., 10, 23, 73, 100, 108, 128, 197, 209, 229
Reisman, J., 144
Renne, K.S., 135, 141
Ridley, C.A., 127
Riskin, J., 124, 133
Robinson, W.P., 62
Rogers, R.W., 188, 228
Rolker-Dolinsky, B., 190
Rollins, B.C., 141
Rook, K.S., 28
Rubenstein, C., 25, 26
Rubin, R.B., 124

Rubin, R.H., 154
Rubin, Z., 8, 9, 48
Rutter, M., 129

Sabatelli, R., 122
Sanson-Fisher, R.W., 208
Santogrossi, D.A., 152
Sants, H.K.A., 2, 90, 92, 108, 149
Sarkin, R., 141
Schachter, S., 4
Schenk-Hamlin, W., 180
Scherer, K.R., 56
Scherwitz, L., 222
Schlenker, B.R., 17, 86
Schmale, A.H., Jr., 210
Schmitt, D.R., 177
Schofield, M.J., 149
Schulz, R., 43
Scotton, C.M., 67
Seligman, C.R., 53, 54
Selman, R.L., 146, 147
Selye, H., 217
Semin, G.R., 17
Serbin, R., 24
Shanas, E., 23
Shaver, P., 25, 26, 27
Shettel-Neuber, J., 11
Shorr, P., 113
Shorter, E., 113
Shulz, R., 22, 26
Shuval, J.T., 189, 195
Silberfeld, M., 211
Sillars, A.L., 125, 126
Singer, J., 4
Siperstein, G.N., 152
Skelton, J.A., 189
Slater, P.E., 113, 114
Sloan, M., 84
Smith, T.W., 195
Smith-Hanen, S., 207
Smyer, M.A., 104, 121, 140, 141
Snow, J., 209
Snyder, C.R., 195
Sobol, M.P., 150
Solano, C., 25
Sommer, R., 44
Stang, D.J., 55
Staples, L., 62

Stiff, J.B., 47, 49, 180
Stone, A.C., 206
Stone, G.P., 17
Stotland, E., 165
Strain, P.S., 152
Straus, M.A., 112
Stroebe, M., 109, 128
Stroebe, W., 109, 128, 169
Sunnafrank, M., 78
Surra, C., 117
Syme, S.L., 211
Szasz, T.S., 200

Takens, R.J., 109
Therrien, M.E., 208
Todd, M., 96
Tracy, K., 180, 181
Traupmann, J., 90
Trower, P., 48, 53
Tunstall, J., 23
de Turck, M.A., 179, 182

Udry, W., 67

Viola, A., 210

Walfisch, S., 211
Walker, H.M., 151
Walster, E.H., 4, 5, 9, 161
Walster, G.W., 9
Watson, O.M., 44
Watzlawick, P., 124
Weber, A., 103
Weinstein, E., 13, 14
Weiss, R.L., 210
Wellman, B., x
Wheeler, L., 23, 100, 186
Wheeler, V.A., 149
White, G.L., 11
Wilkinson, J., 53
Williams, E., 52
Wilmot, W.W., 50, 86, 88, 92
Wilson, C., 137
Wilson, T.De C., 92
Winter, W.D., 139
Winters, L.C., 48
Wiseman, R.L., 180
Wyler, A.R., 215

Yaffe, M., 109
Yellin, A., 48
Young, J.E., 29
Youniss, J., 148

Zaidel, S.F., 68
Zakahi, W.R., 22
Zanna, M.P., 186
Zola, A.K., 197, 198

Subject Index

Accent, 53
Accommodation in speech, 67
Accounts, 92ff
Acquaintance, 79ff, 100
Affinity seeking, 87
Agape, 7
Alcoholism, 137
Appearance, 73
Assistant professors, 42
Assumptions of social psychologists, ix
Attention, 159
Attitudes, similarity of, 76ff

Behavioural intentions, 171
Byrne's attraction paradigm, 75ff

Children's friendships, 144ff
Classical Greek, 205
Cognitive therapy, 21, 28
Communication apprehension, 19
Communication skills, 35
Communication style, 123
Communicative competence, 22
Compliance, 156ff
Compliance gaining, 178–9, 183
Conflict, 117ff
Consistency, 168
Conversation, regulation of, 46
Courtship, 114ff
Current contents, 232

Dating, 20, 27
Deafness, 35
Death, 188, 224
Death, timing of, 227
Deception, 69
Decision to wed, 116
Decoding, 37, 205
Depression, 109, 136

Dissolution of relationships, phases
    of, 101ff
Dissonance, 168ff
Divorce, 113, 140
    and children, 143; disorderly, 141ff;
    orderly, 140
Doctor-patient relationships, 199ff
Door in the face, 175

Embarrassment, 16–19
Emotions, 1–34
Encoding, 37, 203
Eros, 5, 7, 8
Extramarital relationships, 11
Eye contact, 43, 46, 48

Facial messages, 68
Families, 112ff, 131, 134, 135ff
Feelings, labels for, 3ff
Felicity conditions, 181
Filtering, 83
First impressions, 73
Flirting, 15
Fluency, 55, 56
Foot in the door, 174
Forms of requests, 180

Gaze, 42, 48
General Adaptation Syndrome, 216
Gossip, 103

Hardy personality, 223
Health, and love, 10
Heart disease, 214
Hostility, 221

Illness, social psychological aspects of,
    193
Independent couples, 125ff

Influence, 182
Interpersonal communication, *see* Shyness
Intimate idioms, 95

James-Lange Theory, 3
Jealousy, 10ff
Jealousy, rules about, 14
Jealousy, types of, 12–13
Julius Caesar, 60

Laboratory research, ix
Language, children's use of, 64
Language codes, 57
Langue, 35
Life events, 217
Loneliness, 23–30
Loneliness, chronic, 27; coping with, 26
Lonely people, behaviour of, 25ff
Love, 4–10
falling in, 10; development of, 7; types of, 5–7
Love and health, 10
Lovers, behaviour of, 8ff
Low ball, 176
Ludus, 5, 7, 13
Lying, 47, 49, 69

Mania, 6, 7
Marital satisfaction, 124
Marital stability, 126
Marriage, 120
typology of, 124
Maternal deprivation, 129

Neglected children, 149ff
Networks, 94, 208ff
Niceness, ix
Nonverbal communication, 37ff, 45
Nonverbal cues, 68, 89
Nonverbal cues, in physician-patient interaction, 206–8

Open communication, 84
Opiate abuse, 109
Outsiders' perspectives, 93

Pain, 190
Parental style, 130ff
Parenthood, transition towards, 121
Parole, 36
Perspectives, 107
Persuasion, 156ff, 173ff
Physicians, visiting, 197
Power, 40, 59
speech style and, 62ff
Powerless speech, 62
Pragma, 6, 7, 8
Proxemics, 38
Psychological Abstracts, 233

Quakers, 61

Rejected children, 149
Relational disruption, 210
Relationships,
accounts of, 92ff; developing, 90ff; language and, 60ff; making sense of, 95f; repair of, 105; rules and skills of, 96; thinking about, 91ff
Reporting sick, 188, 191
Request strategies, 177
Reticence, 19
Retrospections, 108
Routines, ix, 90f, 97, 98
Rules, 2, 94, 96

Satisfaction, 123, 126
Secret tests, 50
Self-disclosure, 84, 86ff
Self-handicapping, 195
Separate couples, 125
Sex, 109, 118ff, 119
Shyness, 19–22
Sick role, 188, 193, 195
Skill, 96, 150
Social anxiety, 17
Social comparison, 164ff
Social emotions, accounts of, 2
Social participation, 100
Social psychology, role of, ix–xi
Social Science Citation Index, 233
Social skills training, 21, 28f, 51, 151
Social support, 211, 212ff
Solidarity, 59

Source credibility, 160–1
Space, 39
Speech, 55ff
Speech errors, 54
Status, 59, 62
Storge, 5, 7
Strangers, attraction to, 79
Stress, 214
Summary Affect Statements, 2
Switching, 66ff
Symbolic decoration, 41
Symptoms, reporting of, 189

Territories, 38
Tie signs, 8
Traditional couples, 124ff
Two Factor Theory, 4
Type A pattern, 218ff

Uncertainty reduction, 82
Unpopularity, 145, 149ff

Vaughan Williams, 158

Wudgemaking, 60